More praise for...

CONSTANTINE'S
Bible

"Dungan has performed a very useful service for canon inquiry by focusing on one of the most neglected areas of the discussion, namely the social-historical context that begins in the emergence of the Greek *polis* ... and the concomitant call for truth, accuracy, and critical thought. ... Dungan provides frequently overlooked primary sources in support of his conclusions and draws our attention to differing ways of looking at some of the more familiar ancient texts from the classics. ..."

—*Lee Martin McDonald*
President and Professor of New Testament Studies,
Acadia Divinity College, Wolfville, Nova Scotia

CONSTANTINE'S *Bible*

POLITICS *and* the *Making of the* NEW TESTAMENT

DAVID L. DUNGAN

scm press

© David L. Dungan 2006

Published in 2006 by SCM Press
9–17 St Alban's Place, London N1 0NX

Published in the United States in 2007 by Fortress Press,
an imprint of Augsburg Fortress,
Box 1209, Minneapolis, MN 55440.

www.scm-canterburypress.co.uk

British Library Cataloguing in Publication data

A catalogue record for this book is available
from the British Library

0 334 04105 8/978 0 334 04105 4

Printed and bound in Great Britain by
William Clowes Ltd, Beccles, Suffolk

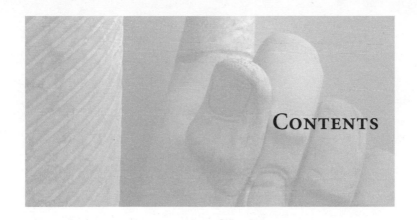

Contents

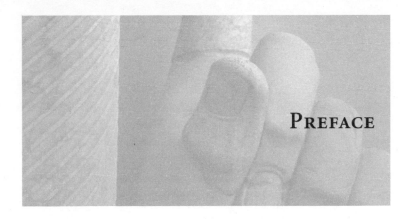

PREFACE

This book has been growing and changing for a long time. It was born and nurtured in a course on "The Making of the New Testament" that I taught for thirty-five years at the University of Tennessee. As every teacher will understand, I regularly learned more from my students than they did from me, not only because they regularly made every major mistake also found in the scholarly literature on the process of Christian canonization of the New Testament, but also because they frequently noticed things in the text that I had completely overlooked. Most importantly, they regularly turned in astonishingly precise, complete, and articulate explications of the making of the New Testament, which I knew were original because they were unlike anything available in print in the library (or, later, on the Internet). For all these reasons, I hereby happily and proudly dedicate this book to my generations of industrious "Eusebius-farers" at the University of Tennessee.

I call them by that name because the core of my course always was an arduous, lengthy, in-depth reading of Eusebius' *Ecclesiastical History*. Adding to the inherent difficulty of the text was the often antiquated language of the translation by C. F. Cruse, which I nevertheless chose not only because at the time it was the only English translation widely available, but because I admired the way Cruse translated key terms consistently throughout the work, making it possible to use the book in scholarly study. Where he stumbled (which was rare), I would provide the students with alternative translations from Kirsopp Lake (Loeb) and/or Arthur Cushman McGiffert (Nicene Fathers). I follow the same procedure in this book.

The first scholarly expression of what I was learning in the course of my teaching came when Prof. Ed Sanders, at that time Professor of Early Christianity at McMaster University, Hamilton, Ontario, invited me to give a report in the McMaster University project on "Self-definition in Judaism and Early Christianity," which ran for three years in the early 1970s. Elements of that report are now embedded in Chapters 1, 2, and 3 of this book. Assisting me in preparing for that report, I received a faculty research stipend from the University of Tennessee to work at Harvard's Andover-Harvard Library during the summer of 1972, where I received welcome assistance from Charles Woodbury in the Circulation Department and Dr. Rita Grossmann, Director of the Library, who extended library privileges to me while I was there.

In 1983, in the course of preparing an essay on the selection of scripture in third- and fourth-century Christianity, I was happy to draw on the important collection of essays edited by my colleague, Miriam Levering, *Rethinking Scripture: Essays from a Comparative Perspective* (Albany: State University of New York Press, 1989). I wish to thank Prof. Levering and Prof. Bruce Metzger for reading a draft of that essay. Its original appearance in print was too long delayed; I am happy to include its insights in Chapters 4 and 5 below.

Through the years, I have benefited from some superb analyses of Eusebius's *Ecclesiastical History* written by my students, including Dent Davis, now Dean and Vice President of Continuing Education at Columbia Seminary, Decatur, Georgia; Wayne Pitard, now professor of Old Testament at University of Illinois, Champagne/Urbana; and Mike Ralston, who went on to study Asian languages (esp. Korean) in 1982. As I have periodically re-read these brilliant papers, they have served to remind me what undergraduates can do if they have sufficient determination, academic skills, and native intelligence. Over a three-year period, I invited a few of my best students to collaborate with me in creating a "Students' Guide to Eusebius" so more students could benefit from a close, in-depth reading of the *Ecclesiastical History*. Stand-out contributions from among the volunteers who took an independent study course to collaborate on different aspects of the project include Matt Shipley, Lindsey Miller, Susan Mihalczo, Jimmy Barker, Mark Maus, Chris Beatty, Paul Robertson, Raul Fernandez, Kim Obiala, Jason Woodle, Elizabeth Hart, Meagan Carter, Bryan Berretta, Brad Bratten, Kate Anderson, Heidi Cummings, Pam McCreary, Ryan Dix, Beth Brewer, and Nick Jacobson.

In 1992, Prof. David Noel Freedman, of the University of California at San Diego, invited me to contribute a volume to the Anchor Bible Reference Library on the history of the investigation of the Synoptic Problem. As I was carrying out preliminary research for this lengthy and forbidding topic, I discovered Origen's brilliant methodological division of the problem into its constituent parts: the *text* of the Gospels, their selection as *scripture* (in contrast to other available Gospels), the question of their original *composition,* and their proper *interpretation.* That volume, *A History of the Synoptic Problem,* appeared in 1999, and I hereby thank once again my good friend Andrew Corbin at Doubleday, but above all Noel Freedman, for more than patience, for their openness and support of my painstaking (not to say torturous) process of germination and writing. I have cited many discussions from that book in Chapter 5.

In the Spring of 2004, Prof. Alberto Ferreiro, a member of the History Department at Seattle Pacific University, invited me to come to his institution to give a series of lectures on recent developments pertaining to the N.T. canon. I spoke about the Enlightenment assault on the Christian canonization process, recent claims made regarding the historical and theological value of the Gospel of Thomas, the popularity of "Q–Thomas Christianity," and Elaine Pagels' claims regarding Thomas and the Gospel of John in her recent book *Beyond Belief: The Secret Gospel of Thomas* (New York: Random House, 2003). To prepare for that lecture series, I benefited greatly from the just published collection of first-rate essays on virtually all aspects of Christian and Jewish scripture and canonization, entitled *The Canon Debate,* edited by Lee Martin McDonald and James A. Sanders (Peabody, Mass.: Hendrickson, 2002). I am happy to take this opportunity to thank Prof. Ferreiro for his warm hospitality, and Prof. Michael Hamilton, chair of the History Department, for a most stimulating and cordial series of meetings with faculty, students, and staff. As a result of those discussions with the History faculty, I gave up the idea of a "Students' Guide to Eusebius" and focused on writing a book for teachers and students of the Christian canonization process.

In the Summer of 2004, I was invited by Rev. Paul Rader, pastor of the First Presbyterian Church of Knoxville, to give a series in their Summer Vacation Bible School on the topic: "How Did We Get Our Bible?" I approached this series with some trepidation, since my audience would not be 18- and 19-year-old undergraduates, but mature, well-educated Christians. I am happy to take this opportunity to express my great enjoyment in speaking to and with that group, and thank them for their probing questions and observations. In many ways, that experience convinced me I might be able to write something useful for a wider audience.

A few months later, I approached Fortress Press with my much revised McMaster report, which had become a 90-page essay with the forbidding title, "The Cultural Background of the Christian Canonization Process." K. C. Hanson, then Acquiring Editor for Fortress, suggested that I recast the article as a small book, focusing on the canonization process itself, that could be used in introductory courses on the New Testament. I presented a draft of this work to a small club of retired faculty here in Knoxville, bearing the name *In Illo Tempore.* This group, consisting of Ralph Norman, (philosophical theology, theology of literature), Stan Lusby (comparative religion), David Linge (philosophical theology, hermeneutics), and Jim Bennett (philosophy and philosophical ethics), gently but persuasively showed me numerous flaws and shortcomings in what I had written. After taking stock of Hanson's suggestion and my colleagues' critique, I went back to the drawing board and rewrote the whole work. I showed the result to K. C. Hanson's successor at

Fortress, Neil Elliott, who made a number of further suggestions on ways to clarify the concluding chapters of this book, and has faithfully seen the book through the whole editing process. I am most grateful to him for his patience, perceptiveness, sense of humor, and skill in working with me on this project.

Over the years, I have drawn repeatedly on the services and staff of the University of Tennessee Hodges Library. They have unfailingly procured interlibrary loan books, made office space available, and dealt gently with overdue books. I wish to thank Joan Riedl, Secretary of the Department of Religious Studies, for checking the spelling and grammar of the entire manuscript; Sarah Graham, student assistant in our department, for meticulously checking the comprehensive list of citations in Appendix A; my friend, Dr. Larry Bushkell, M.D., member of the Cokesbury United Methodist Church, for reading and commenting on the whole manuscript; and especially Jimmy Barker, my former student and currently a graduate student in New Testament at Vanderbilt Divinity School, for carefully reading this draft and making many helpful comments and bibliographical suggestions.

I wish to thank the Catholic Biblical Association for sending me as the 2005–2006 Visiting Professor to the Pontifical Biblical Institute, Gregorian University, Rome, and to express my deepest appreciation and thanks to the superb Rector of that institution, Stephen Pisano, S.J.; the most excellent Dean, Jean-Noël Aletti, S.J.; the always prepared and supportive General Secretary of the Biblicum, Carlo Valentino; the outstanding and friendly Librarian, Jim Dugan, S.J., and Paolo Bizzarri, the Biblicum's webmaster; and the multi-talented Director of the Biblicum's publishing program, Peter Brook, for his many kindnesses and cordial hospitality. Teaching a course there this Spring on the Synoptic Problem, with a component on the Christian scripture selection process, has been an inspiring and broadening experience.

Lastly, I thank my wife Anne and our sons Nathan, James, and Bill, for their support and insightful observations along the way. Given my headstrong nature, I am especially grateful for Anne's calm encouragement to see this project through to publication.

Finally, a note to my readers. I use "Catholic" throughout the book only as a descriptive label and synonym for "orthodox." I do not use these terms because I intend to pass any sort of judgment that the original Christians who used these terms were in fact "catholic" in their views or "orthodox" in their beliefs, but simply because they were the labels they used for themselves. Therefore, "Catholic" (always with a capital C) is a *technical term* that always refers to one of the factions in early Christianity, serving to differentiate it from other factions with labels like Valentinians, Montanists, Marcionites, Ebionites, etc. As I show in Chapter 6, this faction was the one the emperor Constantine favored, as we can see from many edicts in which he bestowed gifts, reparations, and privileges upon them, using this specific Christian term. *I do not use it as a synonym for "Roman Catholic,"* a term that did not even come into existence until much later. I repeat this warning later in the book, but I wish to state it clearly here as well, to avoid all possible misunderstanding.

Pontifical Biblical Institute, Rome
June 2006

Chapter 1

WHAT A "CANON" OF SCRIPTURE IS—AND IS NOT

A true canon of scripture is a rare event.
    Scholars of comparative religions often use the term *canon* to refer to any traditional assemblage of sacred texts. One sees references, for example, to the "Vedic Canon," the "Taoist Canon," the "Canon of the Five Confucian Classics," and so on. But as we shall see, the term *canon* is properly restricted to a much more specific phenomenon that is not the same as the gradual accumulation, over time, of a set of sacred scriptures. However popular and widespread, using the terms *canon* and *scripture* as if they were roughly synonymous involves a comprehensive misunderstanding. When comparative religions scholars use the term *canon* to refer to any collection of scriptures, the result is widespread confusion.

    Similarly, biblical specialists often speak of the "canon of scripture," or "the biblical canon," without realizing how peculiar or unusual that phrase would have sounded when it first appeared. The terms *canon* and *scripture* are not synonymous, although some recent studies of the process by which the Christian scriptures were selected use the terms as if they were. For example, consider this statement: "There are no agreed-upon definitions of canon in contemporary writing. Perhaps what we mean by scripture is covered by a scripture canon, namely, that which is written down and

1

becomes normative for a religious community is *both scripture and canon.*"[1]

A true canon of scripture is actually a rare event in the history of the world's religions. The few actual canons that exist were created in fourth- and fifth-century Mediterranean Christianity, third-century rabbinic Judaism, and seventh-century Islam. To understand the unusual circumstances that caused canons of scripture to appear in just these three religious traditions, we must begin by clarifying from a comparative religions perspective the historical difference between *scripture* and *canon.*

In the comparative study of religions,[2] the term *scripture* refers to a semidurable, semifluid, *slowly evolving* conglomeration of sacred texts (not by any means necessarily all in written form) in use by members of a religious tradition over hundreds or even thousands of years. Such conglomerations of sacred texts exhibit a strikingly unbounded quality, defying clear-cut definition as to which writings belong to the body of sacred scripture or which text is the "official" or "correct" text of a particular writing. As Chinese religions expert Miriam Levering explains: "It is a fallacy . . . to expect scriptures . . . to be neatly bounded. . . . In the rather rare cases where communities saw value in closing the canon, new scriptural or semi-scriptural forms [were immediately] created (e.g., the Talmud) to allow for the ongoing process of insight or revelation."[3]

The vast conglomeration of Hindu sacred texts provides a good example of this semifluid, boundless character. In his study, "Scripture in India," Thomas Coburn writes:

> The traditional Hindu view is that there are 108 Upanishads and, of these, a dozen or so are identified as "early," that is, composed in the half millennium or so after about 700 B.C.E. And yet in the word index of Vedic material that began appearing five decades ago, the Vaidika padānukrama-kosa, no fewer than 206 Upanishads are indexed and some of these have been written occasionally even in modern times and certainly right up to the Middle Ages. The relatively recent origin of these Upanishads, together with the fact that some of them are highly sectarian and that there even exists an "Allah Upanishad"—written in praise of Islam . . . is exceedingly

[disconcerting] for any view that takes only the early Upanishads as normative.[4]

As we shall see, a canon results when someone seeks to impose a strict boundary around a smaller subset of writings or teachings within the larger, slowly evolving "cloud of sacred texts." Any effort to promulgate the new subset with the force of law creates an immediate tension between the new subset and the powerful, living religion surrounding it. The fixed boundary requires strenuous official efforts to enforce it. Efforts to prevent additions or deletions often fail, however, since it is the nature of sacred scripture to grow and change along with the changing religious situation. Moreover, creating this kind of authoritative subset—whether the specific term *canon* is used or not—is never a minor or obscure event.

In terms of the history of Christianity, a canon of scripture, properly so called, did not appear until church officials, acting under the guidance of the highest levels of the Roman government, met together on several specific occasions to create a rigid boundary around the approved texts, forever separating them from the larger "cloud of sacred texts." These actions, which we properly call canonization, were high-profile events and are easily detectible because they have had such a major impact on the whole religious community from that moment onward.

It is possible to say exactly when a canon of scripture was created in Judaism, Christianity, and Islam, but not in any of the other religions of the world. I know of no evidence to suggest, for example, that religious officials ever met for the specific purpose of putting a boundary around anything within the vast conglomeration of Vedic texts mentioned by Coburn. Thus, to refer to all of the Upanishads as "the Vedic canon" results in serious confusion, leading to numerous false assumptions. The Upanishads were never canonized. Similarly, in his discussion, "Taoism: Classic and Canon,"[5] L. Thompson writes that the entire corpus of Taoist texts, called the *Tao Tsang* (meaning "hidden or secret texts on Taoist subjects"), is extremely vast, covering all sorts of materials, some of which are not religious at all:[6] "This 'Bibliotheca Taoica' is a huge assemblage of writings covering all kinds of subjects, ranging in date from as early as the fourth or third century B.C.E. to as recently as the beginning of the twentieth century. Its contents were not early on circumscribed and defined as were those of the Western Bible or the Qur'an."[7]

But Thompson then makes the common mistake of referring to this shapeless mass as "the Taoist canon." The Bibliotheca Taoica *was never canonized.* The same objection applies to other phrases such as the "Confucian canon," the "Pali canon," or the "Tibetan Buddhist canon." Not one of these semifluid, boundless, evolving conglomerations of sacred texts was ever canonized by a religious elite gathered for that specific purpose.

No Canon of Scripture at Qumran

The manuscripts found at Wadi Qumran, including both biblical texts and sectarian writings, provide a perfect illustration of my point. Ask any Qumran expert to give a definitive list of the writings the covenanters regarded as scripture: for example, did the covenanters regard the Book of Jubilees as having scriptural authority?[8] What about the Temple Scroll?[9] How many Psalms were in their "Bible"? Answers vary, depending on which expert you ask.[10]

The same lack of clear-cut boundaries is visible in the varieties of the text of the biblical manuscripts found at Qumran.[11] This multiplicity of texts ranges from minor differences to different editions of whole books. Eugene Ulrich describes two editions of Exodus, two of Joshua, and two of Jeremiah, and there are other examples.[12] The Israeli textual authority Emanuel Tov "has divided the entire corpus of the so-called Qumran biblical manuscripts and fragments into five textual categories: texts written with the special orthographic practices of Qumran scribes (ca. 25 percent); proto-Masoretic texts (ca. 40 percent), pre-Samaritan texts (ca. 5 percent), texts close to the Hebrew model for the Septuagint (ca. 5 percent), and nonaligned texts (ca. 25 percent)."[13] This leads Tov to the conclusion that, in view of the evidence at Qumran, it is impossible to decide which was "the original text" of any book of the Hebrew Bible, and that it may be time to abandon the whole idea of "reconstructing the original text."[14]

Likewise, we cannot speak of a "canon of scripture" at Qumran. The variety of manuscripts treasured there indicates the semifluid character of the process through which scripture accumulated over time. Eugene Ulrich describes the result using the image of baklava:

> The books [of Scripture] were the result of a long literary development, whereby traditional material was faithfully retold and handed on from generation to generation, but also creatively expanded and reshaped to fit the new circumstances and new needs that the successive communities experienced through the vicissitudes of history. So the process of the composition of the Scriptures was organic, developmental, with successive layers of tradition. Ezekiel was commanded to eat a scroll and found that it was as sweet at honey (Ezek. 3:1-3), so perhaps I may be permitted to use the image of baklava for the composition of scriptural texts: many layers were laid on top of earlier ones by successive generations over the centuries, as the traditions were handed on faithfully but creatively adapted, and formed into a unity of the honey—sometimes heated—of the lived experience of the community over time.[15]

Using the Qumran evidence as a springboard, scholars writing in the important volume *The Canon Debate*[16] went on to other, more far-reaching conclusions: "There was no *canon* of scripture in *Second Temple Judaism*";[17] *rabbinic Judaism* did not operate with a *closed canon*;[18] early Christianity *never intended to have a closed canon* of scripture.[19] These scholars drew their unprecedented conclusions with considerable hesitancy. One scholar, James A. Sanders, who has been exploring the "dialogic character of scripture" and probing the riddle of the canon for decades,[20] has this explanation: "Shedding the 'Jamnia mentality,'" i.e., the idea that the rabbis closed the canon at the "Council of Jamnia," "has not been easy for the Western mind."[21] In Sanders's view, canonization was a problematic development from the start; he now sees it as an unfortunate attempt to "freeze the text,"[22] which was, in any case, doomed to failure since "the Bible is dialogical literature. . . . No closure [of the scripture collection within a canon] can curb the dialogue that is at the heart of Scripture."[23]

The unbounded quality of the collection of scriptures at Qumran, and the wide variability of the text of these same scriptures in rabbinic Judaism and early Christianity as well, are precisely the characteristics observed by others in the sacred scriptures of Hinduism, Buddhism, the Chinese Confucian tradition, and indeed of any religion having oral or written normative traditions. From this perspective, the way the Qumran covenanters, the rabbis, and early Christians treated their sacred texts was quite normal.

Misleading Use of Novel Terminology

If some scholars have failed to distinguish canon and scripture clearly, others have confused the issue by employing novel terminology. For example, comparative religions scholar Wilfred Cantwell Smith described the processes, from the second through the seventh centuries C.E., by which the early Christian, rabbinic Jewish, Gnostic, Mandaean, Zarathustrian [sic], Manichaean, and Muslim communities accumulated and selected their respective scriptures as "the Scripture movement . . . in the process of *crystallization*."[24] Smith rightly recognized that something significant and unusual was going on, but—because he used the ambiguous concept "crystallization"—he failed to pierce the riddle. He observed that "Hindu, Buddhist, and Chinese counterparts, teasingly similar in other respects, have *little or none of this particular notion,* [namely the] creation of a limited collection or a book of sacred writings from the 'founder.'"[25] But Smith left it at that without attempting to discover what it was that prompted a few Middle Eastern religious communities to produce a *canon* of scripture, i.e., an officially sanctioned, officially limited collection of sacred writings.

Over the past two centuries of biblical studies, scholars have shown little awareness of the uniqueness of the Christian canon of scripture compared to the scripture collections in the other world religions.[26] One reason is that biblical scholars, too, tend to use novel terminology. For example, in his essay, "Christianity, Scripture and Canon," H. Y. Gamble Jr. sees nothing strange in the Christian canon of scripture even though he realizes that *scripture* and *canon* are not quite the same thing. He explains their conjunction by saying, "The development of a canon of Christian scripture was part of a larger movement in the ancient church towards religious self-definition."[27] In the 1970s, Gamble had taken part in a three-year interdisciplinary seminar at McMaster University in Hamilton, Ontario, on the theme "normative self-definition in Judaism and early Christianity." The project, which drew dozens of scholars from North America and Europe, produced a wealth of insights regarding the ongoing redefinition of religious communities in the Greco-Roman world. Constant re-self-definition is a typical, ongoing feature of all religious traditions, Middle Eastern or other; it is a good way to characterize their ordinary active, organic vitality. But a *canon* of scripture is not an ordinary event. Gamble's focus on the category of religious self-definition obscured precisely what was distinctive about the Christian canon of scripture (and its Jewish and Muslim equivalents).[28]

Recent secular Western historians who specialize in Greco-Roman history have also failed to notice the peculiarity and uniqueness of the many *kanones*—canons—that appeared in Greek culture after the fourth century B.C.E., but for a different reason: they simply take for granted a rather vague understanding of what these *kanones* are. Typical is H. Beyer's discussion of *kanōn* in Kittel's *Theological Dictionary of the New Testament,* which consists primarily of an idealization of "the Greek": "[*Kanones*] becomes the 'norm,' i.e., the perfect form and therefore the goal to be sought or the infallible criterion by which things are to be measured. . . . For the Greek seeks what is perfect, balanced and harmonious, i.e., the ideal." As we shall see below, a *kanōn* has little to do with a supposed aesthetic appreciation of "perfect form."[29]

A Look Ahead

We lose sight of something truly important if we use the term *canon* as a synonym for any and every conglomeration of scripture. In what follows, I will demonstrate that the legal imposition of a *kanōn* (Latin: *regula,* a rule, regulation) upon Christian scripture along with a *kanōn* of the correct summary of doctrine (the creed), and the enforcement of both with the full power of the Roman government, was a phenomenon unique to fourth- and fifth-century Christianity. This set of phenomena also occurred in a brief but decisive way in seventh-century Islam under the third Caliph, 'Uthman, and to an even lesser extent, and with important rabbinic modifications, in third-century rabbinic Judaism under Judah the Prince. The appearance of canons of scripture (or in Judaism, a canon of halakah) within just these three religious traditions was no accident. Why just these three?

A common feature of discussions of canonization is the search for "factors" that caused, or provoked, canonization.[30] This study will begin its search for "factors" long before Marcion, Montanus, or Valentinus in second-century Christianity. I suggest that a much more holistic, comparative-religions approach is needed to provide the historical background for the original meaning(s) of the term *canon* and to explain why a desire for canons arose in the first place.

To answer these questions, I will begin by examining, in chapters two and three, the revolutionary new Greek *polis* ideology with its insistent demand for order, precision, and clarity. The ideal of the Greek *polis* was carried by Alexander the Great across the ancient world, and we will witness its influence especially on Second Temple Judaism and the early Christian church, observing the many uses of *canon,* along with the closely related emergence of church orders. In chapter four, I continue the story by examining the Greek philosophical schools and their common emphasis upon the life and teachings of a Founder, their reliance upon a carefully chosen succession of subsequent leaders of the school whose main responsibility was preserving accurate copies of the genuine writings of the Founder and his disciples, and their emphasis on interpreting these writings accurately. With this survey of the Greek schools as background, I turn to evidence of the emergence of similar concerns in second- and third-century Christianity—that is, the quest for genuine writings of the first disciples of the Founder of Christianity, the effort to hand them down in carefully preserved and unbroken successions in the church, and the emphasis on maintaining the correct interpretation of these writings.

In chapter five, I describe how Eusebius of Caesarea wove together all of these threads in his monumental *Ecclesiastical History*. There we can see, much more clearly than in any previous writing in the (orthodox) church's history, exactly how the scripture selection process worked—in detail, that is, book by book. Why was this book excluded and that book included in the embryonic, just-forming New Testament? If there were so many writings (more than one hundred) considered as divinely inspired, potentially scripture, circulating in all parts of the Christian movement by the year 300, why did only twenty (plus seven, more or less) make it into the charmed circle? Chapter five will answer that question.

Chapter six explains the enormous impact the first Christian emperor had on the church's scripture selection process. Working closely with the grateful, eager, and willing collaboration of the Christian orthodox bishops, Constantine fundamentally transformed orthodox, Catholic Christianity* into imperial Christianity, quickly stamping out all other factions and types of Christianity. Once the bishops and priests began to receive salaries from the state, once church councils could be called and their business personally directed by the emperor, once huge new buildings were built at the emperor's personal expense and given to the Catholic Christians for

---

*In the pages that follow I use the term *Catholic* to distinguish orthodox Christianity in the third and fourth centuries C.E. from various alternative forms of Christianity deemed heretical. I do not mean to imply any identification with what would later come to be called Roman Catholicism.

Sunday worship, once the emperor had personally ordained Sunday as the universal day of rest, it was just a matter of time before canon law became inextricably intertwined in the process of deciding which writings of the Lord's disciples should be read at Sunday worship (the Holy Scripture) and what was the proper interpretation of the doctrines contained in them (the Creed).

In chapter seven, an epilogue, I offer a few reflections on the historical survey just completed and briefly look at the history after Constantine: the Reformation, the Enlightenment, and modernity, with its widespread assault on the biblical canon.

Chapter 2

THE GREEK *POLIS*
and the Demand for Accuracy

In order to understand the original range of meaning of the Greek word *kanōn,* we must briefly review the rise of the ancient Greek city-state, the *polis.* It was in ancient political discussions of this radical innovation—rule by citizens, without a king—that *kanōn* first became an important category.

The Emergence of Democratic Structures in the Ancient Greek *Polis*

When one looks for the beginnings of the revolutionary Greek *polis,* one encounters an era described by Karl Jaspers as "the Axial Age."[1] During this age, a whole range of new values and new institutions mysteriously emerged across Asia, led by thinkers whom later ages regarded as prophets and saviors. One of these institutions was the revolutionary Greek *polis.*

Historians of civilization distinguish among successive stages in the emergence of ancient cities.[2] There is evidence of tiny settlements by hominids going back more than a million years.[3] The emergence of homo sapiens is far more recent.

The Rise of Cities

Farming, including irrigation and the domestication of certain animals, followed, providing the base for the rise of the first archaic cities some ten thousand years ago, in northern China, the Indus River area, Mesopotamia, Palestine (Jericho), and Egypt. After the last ice age, some fifteen thousand years ago, the planet's average temperature rose sufficiently (approximately 5°C) to make possible the domestication of wild plants.

The design of these archaic cities was roughly similar. A sacred walled precinct (which could double as a defensive fortification) enclosed a temple complex where the king and priestly families lived. Large farms spread outside the walls, owned by the baronial families and worked by slaves, peasants, and tenant farmers.[4] Many of the basic inventions we associate with "civilization" appeared in these archaic cities: for example, pictogram writing and the wheel. These, in turn, provoked still other technological developments: the lever, the siphon, the screw, and all sorts of military inventions.[5]

Each of these archaic city cultures regarded some written and/ or oral texts as sacred and gave them into the charge of a religious elite who cared for them and used them on appropriate occasions. None of these cities had canons, except possibly the original kind: a ruler, that is, a rod, made out of cane.

In the ninth century B.C.E.—the time of Homer—"Greek" inhabitants of Ionia were not very different from their contemporaries around the eastern Mediterranean. Then an extraordinary change took place over the following two or three centuries. As the British classical historian Gilbert Murray has put it:

> The historian of early Greece must find himself often on the watch for a particular cardinal moment, generally impossible to date in time and sometimes hard even to define in terms of development, when the clear outline of what we call classical Greece begins to take shape out of the mist.[6] . . . If we wish for a central moment as representing this self-realization of Greece, I should be inclined to find it in the reign of Peisistratus (560–527 B.C.E.), when that

monarch made the first sketch of an Athenian empire based on alliances, and took over to Athens the leadership of the Ionian race.[7]

The brilliant reign of Peisistratus was built upon the legal reforms of Solon (ca. 640–560 B.C.E.), which gave his government the internal rhythms of the radical new concept of democracy even while it retained the outward appearances of monarchy. This period paved the way for the democratic party under Cleisthenes (ca. 570–508 B.C.E.) to sweep away the institution of monarchy in Athens, setting up in its place the earliest example of representative government in world history.

The writings of Plato (427–347 B.C.E.) and Aristotle (384–322 B.C.E.) on this new form of government are well known. As they looked back at the tumultuous events of the previous century, they tried to decide which combination of kingship (monarchy), baronial league (oligarchy), and citizen self-rule (democracy) would produce the most stable combination of government types in the new, democratic *polis.* There were many options available, but on one thing they did agree: the vacuum created by the removal of the hated *tyrannos* (tyrant) and his court of sycophants and armed thugs should be replaced forever by (written) law and the will of the (male) citizens, as expressed in the radical new concept of voting. Aristotle described Athens's revolutionary new *polis* as consisting of a body of citizens (*politeia*),[8] united by agreements and laws they had voted into existence (the *politeia,* "constitution")[9] and led by a people's assembly, the *ekklēsia,* which was responsible for all decisions pertaining to internal and external policy. The Athenian *ekklēsia* numbered some six thousand citizens, was selected by lot on a rotation basis, and met some forty to fifty times a year. A people's court, the *dikastēria,* consisted of panels of two hundred members selected by lot. A council of elders, or *boulē* (in Sparta, it was called a *gerousia*), typically consisted of five hundred men, fifty from each tribe, chosen by lot. The *boulē* set the agenda to be voted on by the *ekklēsia.*[10] Each body in the government and all suborganizations were presided over by elected officials (variously termed *prytanis* or *prostatēs*), whose term in office could last one day, or a month, or a year, depending on the needs and requirements of that body.[11]

These and many other features made up the revolutionary new *polis*, supplanting the traditional institutions of monarchy. The changes were sweeping and exhilarating, especially the sense of freedom citizens obtained in leaving behind the hated institution of monarchy, adopting by popular vote their own laws, and drawing their own officials from their peers. Here is the comment of Plato's younger contemporary, the famous public orator Aeschines (ca. 390–314 B.C.E.):

> It is acknowledged that there are in the world three forms of government: autocracy [*tyrannia*], oligarchy [*oligarchia*], and democracy [*dēmokratia*]. Autocracies and oligarchies are administered according to the tempers of their lords, but democratic states [*poleis*] according to established laws. And be assured, fellow citizens, that in a democracy it is the laws that guard the person of the citizen and the constitution of the state [*politeia*] whereas the despot [*tyrannos*] and the oligarch find their protection in suspicion and armed guards.[12]

And again:

> The question of right involved [in this lawsuit] is not an indefinite [*aoriston*] one, but is defined by your own laws. For as in carpentry, when we wish to know what is straight and what is not, we apply the carpenter's rule [*kanōn*] which serves as our standard, so in indictments for illegal motions, there lies ready to hand, as a rule [*kanōn*] of justice, this tablet containing . . . our laws.[13]

A striking feature of the new democratic rhetoric was the frequency with which the carpenter's ruler or canon (*kanōn*) was used as a metaphor for accuracy, definiteness, and truth. Whence this sudden thirst for order, clarity, and accuracy?[14]

"Canon" as a Metaphor for Mathematical Accuracy, Clarity, and Precision

During the same period in Greek history that witnessed the first halting steps toward democratic government, with all of the explorations of novel and bewildering mechanisms for voting and obtaining elected officials and combinations of oligarchy, monarchy, and democracy, there understandably arose a powerful countertrend toward order, stability, and clarity. And not just any kind of order and clarity: the advocates of the new *polis* began to turn more and more to *mathematically based* conceptions of order and precision. A classic example from this period is the bronze statue by the fifth-century sculptor Polykleitos of Sikyon (active 450–420 B.C.E.). Now known as "The Spear Carrier" (*Doryphoros*), it was accompanied by an unprecedented table of exact measurements (i.e., numerical ratios) for each part of the statue's body, so that anyone could make an exact replica. Later writers referred to it as *Kanōn*, "Guide," because so many sculptors copied it, believing that it expressed the ideal proportions of the human form.[15]

A century earlier, the great mathematician Pythagoras (ca. 569–ca. 475 B.C.E.) was said to have applied mathematical calculations to music, comparing the lengths of the vibrating parts of lyre strings (determined by the location of the finger on the string) with the pitch of the notes produced, expressing these as a series of fixed mathematical ratios. These ratios he termed *kanōnikoi*, "standards" (i.e., standard tones).[16]

Similarly, Hippodamos of Miletus (mid-fifth century B.C.E.) introduced the concept of straight streets at right angles to each other, or the "gridiron" pattern, into cities of Greece and southern Italy. He designed Pericles' colony at Thurii, refurbished part of the port city of the Piraeus (Athens) in this new fashion, and laid out the design for the new city of Rhodes.[17]

Also at this time, rhetoricians began to insist that the well-crafted speech should have exactly the same number of words in each part and sentences should contain exactly the same number of syllables.[18] In his play, *Frogs*, Aristophanes (ca. 405 B.C.E.) ridiculed his rival Euripedes (ca. 480–406 B.C.E.) for indulging in this new fad. He has the old and revered Aeschylus say concerning the upstart Euripedes:

AESCHYLUS. Why you'll see poetry weighed out and *measured!*

XANTHIAS. What? Will they *weigh* their tragedies?

AESCHYLUS. Yes, they will, and with their rulers [*kanones*] and compasses they'll measure and examine and compare and bring their plummets and their lines and levels to take the bearings—for Euripedes says he'll take a survey, word by word![19]

The Quest for Accuracy, Precision, and Clarity in Greek "Philosophy"

One of the most far-reaching attempts to obtain geometrically precise conceptions of things occurred in a movement to extend the *polis* revolution to other aspects of culture, including religion, politics, education, commerce, art, medicine, sports, and theater, each of which saw profound innovations. In this new ideology, it was believed that geometry was the ideal of truly accurate knowledge. The movement that gave concentrated expression to this novel idea called itself "philosophy"—the love of wisdom—and it embarked upon an endless quest for precision, clarity, and universality of terminology in ethics, politics, natural history (what we today would call the sciences), art, and metaphysics.[20] In this ancient Greek understanding, the term *philosopher* could refer to any of a whole spectrum of roles: teacher, healer, political consultant, public conscience, scientist, musician, or wandering street-corner preacher. (Later applied in Christian contexts, it would refer to what we would now call a *theologian*.) When I use the word *philosophy* in this book, it is this particular quest for mathematical precision in various aspects of human relations that I have in mind.

Many passages could be cited to illustrate this development, but one classic passage is in Plato's dialogue *Philebus* (composed around 360 B.C.E.).[21] Toward the end of this dialogue, after a lengthy examination of the essential components of the "good life" (i.e., a mixture of prudence and pleasure), Socrates and Protarchus turned to consider an obvious ancillary issue, namely whether precise conceptions were even possible in such a nebulous topic (55d–59e). Socrates answered by passing in review those "arts" where real precision is evident, finding that "the art of building employs the greatest number of measures and instruments. This gives it great accuracy [*akribeia*] and makes it more artful [*technikōteros*] than most knowledge [*epistēmē*]" (56b).

However, continues Socrates, the most precise field of all is mathematics, especially geometry, while the least accurate fields are music and poetry. For this reason, the former are much to be preferred, since they confer greater clarity of knowledge (57d). Then he asks Protarchus which art (*technē*) "has the greatest regard for clearness [*saphēs*], exactness [*akribeia*], and truth [*alētheia*]?" (58C). Protarchus answers: "Philosophy." Socrates then asks what kinds of things the art or skill of "philosophy" can properly be said to know exactly. Protarchus's answer: "[Only] things which are fixed [*to bebaion*] and pure [*to katharon*] and true [*to alēthes*] and unalloyed[22] [*to eilikrines*]. . . . Things which are eternally the same without change or mixture" (59c).

Socrates responds: Since the physical world bombards the senses with constantly changing impressions, where can the mind encounter objects possessing the attributes just mentioned? The answer: only in the mind itself, where it perceives the eternal forms (or ideas), concepts possessing the clarity and distinctness of the forms and patterns of geometry.

Why was Socrates (or should we say Plato, who wrote the dialogue) drawn to such clear-cut, fixed mental concepts? Perhaps we have a clue in Aristotle's *Metaphysics*. Commenting on the intellectual odyssey of his elder colleague, Plato, Aristotle said that, at first, Plato was a follower of the exact opposite point of view, namely, that of Heraclitus, who said that all things were in constant flux. During this period, Plato held the view that certain knowledge of external things was impossible because they were constantly changing. Later, however, Plato abandoned the doctrines of Heraclitus and became a disciple of Socrates. Socrates differed from Heraclitus in one major way: he paid no attention to cosmology, questions regarding the origin and nature of the universe. Socrates spurned such "big questions," leaving them to the naturalists, such as Heraclitus, Democritus, and Empedocles, who were famous for their theories regarding the origin of the universe, what the universe is made of, and how it maintains itself. Instead, Socrates focused his attention on things where he could make a difference, namely, on the nature of human society and right conduct.

This was an arena, said Socrates, that urgently needed attention anyway, given ceaseless civil wars, terrible economic injustices, and rampant religious superstition on all sides. Socrates insisted that there had to be some way to gain greater stability and clarity in all of these areas, and he spent years searching for clear-cut definitions, modeled on the universal "ideas" (or forms) of geometry, of such key concepts as "truth," "justice," "the good life," and so on. If just a few of Athens's leading citizens would jointly adopt clear, accurate, and consistent definitions of these terms, Socrates taught, they would gain great power and their efforts could produce a new influx of justice and tranquility in Athenian society.[23]

We must remember that Socrates and his disciples did not merely intend to rid Athens of corrupt and tyrannical kings in order to have good kings. They meant to dethrone monarchy altogether. That radical agenda meant rethinking every aspect of Athens's way of life—a daunting task. For one thing, throwing out monarchy meant abandoning the central role of the king in society, with his intimate bond with all sorts and classes of people in and around the city who depended on him for stability, prosperity, and leadership. It meant jettisoning the great, complex web of religious rituals, officials, and institutions devoted to maintaining the king's bond with the living fields and mountains around and about Athens, radiating into the Heavens above and down into the Underworld below. If the king were to be disposed of, then all of the gods, goddesses, temples, rituals, priests, temple virgins, sacred groves, and holy mountains, in the equally monarchical pantheon, would have to go too.

As it turned out, these were among the first to go. We can understand the search, by the seventh- and sixth-century Ionian naturalists (Thales, Anaxagoras, Anaximander, Anaximines, Pythagoras, Heraclitus), for alternatives to the traditional Greek gods as the concerted attempt to conceive of a resolutely nonmonarchical deity. Once the unpredictable (not to say, outrageous), anthropomorphic deities of the traditional, geographically restricted religious cults were replaced by universal, orderly, nonanthropomorphic forces of nature, all sorts of new possibilities opened up before the human world, including a revolutionary new way to conceive of man's habitation in the universe: the *polis*.

The radical innovation of the *polis* was thus part of a larger cultural revolution, characterized by a penchant for mathematically based precision in various fields of human relations. Alexander the Great and his armies carried the Greek *polis* ideology and Greek "philosophy" across the length and breadth of western Asia, from Egypt to the Indus River.[24] To the extent that Hellenism penetrated the host cultures in the many cities he refounded, the radically different Greek *polis* concepts, methods, values, and institutions replaced the traditional monarchy-oriented political structures, along with the rituals and social elites that went with them. Of course, none of this happened smoothly and evenly everywhere, nor did these changes always take place voluntarily. Alexander often had to enforce the adoption of the new Greek *polis* culture with the sword.[25]

Chapter 3

GREEK *POLIS* IDEOLOGY WITHIN SECOND TEMPLE JUDAISM AND EARLY CHRISTIANITY

Having described the desire for accurate, reliable, rational or legal standards in the ancient Greek city-state, we turn now to examining how this important legacy influenced strategies of community formation among Jews and, later, Christians living in the Greco-Roman world.

In the early spring of 332 B.C.E., Alexander the Great, fresh from his victory over the Persian king Darius at the Battle of Issus, led his armies down the eastern coast of the Mediterranean until he reached the ancient walled city of Tyre. He sent his emissaries out to the island city to demand that the Tyrians submit to him. He was on his way to Egypt for personal religious reasons, but he knew that the time had come for him to neutralize the powerful Tyrian navy, allies of the Persians, before he could continue his attack on the main Persian force in the north. The proud Tyrians scoffed at Alexander's demand—what land army could defeat the Tyrian navy? But scorn turned to consternation when they saw Alexander's response. Conscripting thousands of workmen from the surrounding regions, *he began filling in the sea,* building a causeway out to their island. The tables were turned as the Tyrian navies frantically and unsuccessfully tried to block the causeway. After the causeway was completed, Alexander ran battering rams and siege towers out to the walled city and destroyed their fortifications. Once he had captured the city, he slaughtered all of the men, sent the women and children off into slavery, and burned it to the ground. The message was stark: do not oppose Alexander.

Reports of Alexander's astonishing siege preparations spread up and down the coast. Terrified ambassadors from nearby cities and territories hastily came to his camp to pay homage. Although the story must be carefully pieced together[1] (Josephus gives a characteristically glowing account), this much can be ascertained: the Judean leadership in Jerusalem also came and offered submission to Alexander. The result was an advantageous treaty for both sides. They gained favorable terms, and he gained an ally sitting astride the strategic land-bridge connecting Africa and Asia. Thus it was that some time in 331, Greek *polis* ideology and Greek philosophy took up residence in Jerusalem.

Signs of Greek *Polis* Ideology within Second Temple Judaism

Scholars have devoted considerable attention to the changes introduced into postexilic Hebrew culture as a result of Greek influence.[2] For the purposes of this book, we can see the clearest signs of Greek *polis* ideology during the first century c.e. in the rise to power of the quasilegal, quasicultic, quasipolitical movement known as Pharisaism,[3] with its two "schools of thought" (Beth Shammai and Beth Hillel) and its prominent chain of succession.[4] The Pharisees' power base was a radically new institution called the "synagogue," which resembled a Hellenistic private association (*thiasos*) and school, resembling those of the Greek philosophical sects (*didaskaleion:* in Hebrew, *beth ha-midrash*, lit. "house of study").[5] Synagogues were independent centers of political action and community worship, and the schools were devoted to Torah study. They were the locus of many rituals and activities originally rooted in the Temple cultus but operated independently of the Temple, and as such were not under the control of the powerful and conservative priestly families controlling the Temple (the Sadducees). When Titus and the tenth

Roman legion destroyed the Jerusalem Temple in 70 c.e., many elements of the older monarchy-oriented religious polity (including the Sadducees) disappeared. The Pharisees, or "rabbis" as they came to be called, were left as the de facto religious and political leaders of the shattered Hebrew nation, thanks to the adroit last-minute negotiations conducted by Jochanan ben Zakkai with the soon-to-be emperor Vespasian.[6]

By the time Judah the Prince created a standard edition of the *Mishnah* during the third century c.e.[7]—a significant development to which I will return in chapter seven—the use of Greek styles of argument in rabbinic legal disputes had become common.[8] Outside Jewish Palestine, the powerful influence of Greek culture and philosophy on Jewish intellectuals and communities in Egypt, greater Syria, Asia (Minor), and Rome was obviously much more pronounced.

Greek *Polis* Structures in Early Christianity and the Appearance of the First Church Orders

Earliest Christianity sprang from this potent mixture of Jewish culture thoroughly permeated by Hellenic culture and philosophy. As was the case with the synagogue before them, Greek *polis* structures and terminology can also be seen already in the first-generation Christian house-churches.

Most significant in my estimation was the designation of the Christian congregation by the term "assembly" (*ekklēsia*),[9] which, as we saw above, was the name of the popular assembly in a Greek *polis* responsible for all decisions of internal or external policy. This term came into the early Christian movement from two sources: The first is the Greek Old Testament, where *ekklēsia* is the translation for Hebrew terms for "assembly" more than one hundred times.[10] The second source is the Diaspora synagogue culture, with its customary use of the LXX and its own combined private association/ *polis* structure. Before long, it was not unusual to see a Christian *ekklēsia* governed by an elected *boulē* or council, with an elected (or appointed) presiding officer or overseer (the preferred Christian term was *episkopos*). When Paul wrote to the Christians at Philippi not to be concerned over the harassment directed at them by the local citizens of that Roman garrison city, he could assure them that such tribulations meant nothing to them since they had their citizenship—their *politeuma*—not in Philippi but in heaven,[11] from whence their savior (*sōtēr*)[12] would soon come to save them (Phil 3:20). In short, these little Christian congregations—like the synagogues before them—had many of the institutions and procedures of miniature Greek *poleis*.

And as we noted in chapter two, in the context of so much radical rethinking and reconstituting of traditional institutions and customs, an obvious need of the new Greek *polis* was constant infusions of order and control—based on written laws they had adopted by vote and not on the arbitrary whim of some tyrant. In the Diaspora synagogue context, something of the same ferment was occurring, and thus we can understand better the rabbis' assiduous attention to issues of halakah—communal order.

In the Christian *ekklēsia*, the ferment was, if possible, even more pronounced. Some Christians drawn from the Hebrew nation were trying to reject certain aspects of traditional Judaism (such as the Temple cult). Others, drawn from the surrounding Gentile world, were jettisoning large elements of their pagan culture (bloody sacrifices, polytheism). Both groups were attempting to invent or create a uniquely Christian ethos and a new set of institutions—all the while waiting eagerly for the Lord to return and put an end to the old world of sin, death, and despair. Partly as a direct result of the Christian proclamation of grace and forgiveness, which could (and did) produce a kind of anarchy, and partly because converts came into the churches from so many diverse backgrounds, there was constant struggling to be true to their newfound faith and, at the same time, not simply burst into dozens of splinter groups, each following its own vision. Hence, there arose within the Christian *ekklēsia* powerful impulses toward greater order and standardization, accompanied by written regulations dealing with church doctrine and church polity.

The oldest example of the new trend toward written church regulations are the late first-century pseudo-Pauline epistles known to us as the Pastoral Epistles (1 and 2 Timothy and Titus) with their emphasis on qualifications for ordination, acceptable conduct for church officers, and general stance of avoiding innovation while adhering strictly to the received doctrine (1 Tim 1:3, 6:20; cf. Jude 3: guard "the faith which was once for all delivered to the saints" [RSV]).

Closely related to the Pastoral Epistles, in spirit if not in content, is the late first-century church order having the title *Teaching of the Lord through the Twelve Apostles to the Nations,* or simply *Didachē* (Greek for "teaching"). It opens a fascinating window onto late first-century Syrian Christianity struggling to establish the mechanisms necessary for long-term stability, through standards of personal behavior, church order, and liturgy. The *Didachē* in turn became the ancestor of a whole succession of church orders, among which the best known are the *Didascalia,* the *Apostolic Constitutions,* and eventually Canon Law.[13]

1 Clement is a striking example of attempted cross-congregation regulation, in the form of a letter sent from the church at Rome to the church at Corinth. In fact, it is actually a legal brief,[14] warning certain "insanely rash" men to restore the bishop and other officials to their rightful positions (44:4-6) after they had illegally deposed them (44.1). The great reverberations of this "abominable and unholy schism" had caused the Corinthians' "good name . . . to fall into the gravest ill repute" (1:1). Word had even reached Christians in Rome, stirring up mockery and derision among "those who dissent from us" (47:7) at a very sensitive time—the church in Rome had just weathered a bout of intense persecution brought on by the demented Emperor Domitian (1:1). The Roman congregation felt obliged to write to the Corinthians because their "contention and rivalry, touches on matters that *bear on our salvation*" and because the *whole church* now stands threatened now that "the Lord's Name is being blasphemed [polluted] because of your stupidity" (44:6, 47:7).[15] The author appeals to the Corinthian rebels to return to the tradition they had received: "Give up [your] empty and futile concerns and turn to the glorious and holy rule of our tradition" (7:2).[16] This tradition was the bedrock of the church and everyone had to remain faithful to it, for it was handed down from the Apostles, who in turn received it from Jesus, the Son of God:

> The apostles received the gospel for us from the Lord Jesus Christ; Jesus, the Christ, was sent from God. Thus Christ is from God and the apostles from Christ. And so the apostles, after receiving their orders . . . went out in the confidence of the Holy Spirit to preach the good news that God's Kingdom was about to come. They preached in country and city, and appointed their first converts, after testing them by the Spirit, to be the bishops and deacons of future believers. (*1 Clem* 42:1-3)

Any deviation from the tradition that the church received was a dire threat to the whole church.

As might be expected, this powerful legal brief in defense of duly elected church officers served to solidify Rome's reputation as a bastion of orthodox church order and itself became a part of the tradition that was handed down. The fourth-century church historian Eusebius of Caesarea could report that this letter was still being occasionally read on Sunday as part of the church's Scripture more than a hundred years after it was received.[17]

The early second-century orthodox bishop Ignatius of Antioch (ca. 50–ca. 107) also gave additional momentum to the trend toward increasing church order. At the end of his life, while being hauled in chains from Antioch to Rome to face certain martyrdom, he could dictate letters to numerous churches along the way urging them to be obedient to their bishops and to adhere to the apostolic tradition. For instance, to the church at Tralles he wrote: "Be subject to the bishop as to the Lord . . . whatever you do, do nothing without the bishop. And be subject also to the presbytery (the council of elders), as to the apostles of Jesus Christ."[18] To the Magnesians he wrote: "The bishop presides in the place of God and the elders in the place of the assembly of the apostles and your deacons are entrusted with the ministry of Jesus Christ."[19]

The Use of the Ruler *(Kanōn)* Metaphor as Part of the Orthodox Christian Demand for Accuracy, Correctness, and Truth

As I pointed out in the last chapter, the word *ruler—kanōn—*appeared frequently in the formative years of the Greek *polis* as a metaphor for accuracy, correctness, and truth. It occurred in a wide range of applications, such as in politics, where the laws were held to be "rulers" or "yardsticks" for right conduct in society, or in sculpture where a book of mathematical ratios could provide a "ruler" or "yardstick" for the right way to construct the perfect replica of the human body, or in music, where charts of mathematical ratios made it possible for musicians to have a "ruler" or "yardstick" for the right notes of the five musical scales. As Greek *polis* culture permeated early Christianity and contemporaneous Judaism, a similarly wide range of applications of the "ruler" metaphor—*kanōn*—appeared in them as well.

There are occurrences where the metaphor *kanōn* is extended to mean something like a general rule, in the sense of a broad spiritual principle. The Apostle Paul could exhort his Galatian churches: "Neither circumcision nor uncircumcision is anything; but a new creation is everything! As for those who will follow this rule [*kanōn*] . . . peace be upon them" (Gal. 6:16).[20] A contemporary mid-first-century Pharisee proposed a similarly broad "rule" (*kanōn*): "Philosophizing piously is the whole rule [*kanōn*] of philosophy."[21] We have just heard 1 Clement's advice to the rebels at Corinth: "give up your empty and futile concerns and turn to the glorious and holy rule of our tradition."[22] In all these references we have become accustomed to the translation "rule," but the original sense of the metaphor—a "ruler" or standard of precise measurement—is never far away.

The use of the *kanōn* metaphor to point to the church's apostolic tradition as the basic guideline or "ruler" for right Christian belief appears more and more frequently in the writings of second-century orthodox church fathers. Irenaeus of Lyon could criticize the Valentinians for departing from "the rule of truth . . . [which says] that there is one God Almighty, who created all things by His word" (here Irenaeus begins to paraphrase the baptismal creed).[23]

Tertullian (ca. 160–230) also makes use of the same "ruler" metaphor when he offers a creedal summary in his *On the Prescription of Heretics*: "With regard to this rule of faith [*regula fidei*] . . . it is that which prescribes belief that there is one God, and that He is none other than the Creator of the world, who produced all things out of nothing through His own Word, etc." (Here Tertullian also begins to summarize the baptismal creed.)[24]

Clement of Alexandria (died ca. 215), a contemporary of Tertullian, was the successor to the converted Greek philosopher Pantaenus as head of the Christian Catechetical School in Alexandria. He tended to use the "ruler" metaphor in a very broad "guideline" sense: " 'All things are right,' says the Scripture, 'for those who understand,' that is, those who receive and observe, according to the church's guideline [*kanōn*], [namely] the exposition of the Scriptures explained by Him [Jesus Christ]. And the church's guideline [*kanōn*] is the concord and harmony of Law and Prophets in the covenant delivered at the coming of the Lord" (my translation).[25] And again a few lines later: "These things the Lord said in the Gospel, 'Whoever leaves father and mother and brothers and everything for my sake and on account of the Gospel. . . .' Blessed is such a person, for he acts like a citizen who is living according to the guideline [*kanōn*] of the Gospel because of love for the Lord."[26]

Clement's successor as head of the Catechetical School in Alexandria was the brilliant young Origen (185–254). Where Clement had been drawn primarily to the mystical, "gnostic" side of Christianity, Origen was extraordinarily prolific in a whole range of fields: text-critical studies on the Old Testament, commentaries on books of the Bible, homilies on books of the Bible, speculative theology (*On First Principles*), and lengthy defenses of the Christian faith against pagan critics (*Against Celsus*). He used the "ruler" metaphor frequently, especially in his favorite expression *kanōn tēs pisteōs*, which is routinely translated "rule of faith." This did not mean for him something set and definite, like a baptismal creed. Rather, Origen seems to have thought in terms of a kind of general basic belief held by all orthodox Christians. In an allegorical exposition of John 4:21, "neither on this mountain nor in Jerusalem . . . ," Origen wrote:

> We, on the other hand, understand the phrase, "neither on this mountain," to mean the piety expressed by the heterodox in their fantasy of Gnostic and supposedly lofty doctrines. And we take the words, "Nor will you worship the Father in Jerusalem," to refer to the Church's *rule of faith in the majority of churches.*[27]

In his important theological treatise, *On First Principles,* Origen complained of Christians who did not interpret the Bible correctly, saying they needed to "hold fast to *the rule of Jesus Christ's heavenly church according to the succession of the apostles.*"[28] Thus, for Origen, as for Clement before him, the "ruler" or "yardstick" [*kanōn*] of the church referred to the central core of the Christian faith based on the Bible.[29] In their writings, "ruler"—*kanōn*—never referred to a set collection of doctrines in a formal creed, nor did either Origen or Clement ever use the metaphor to refer to an officially approved collection—what we should properly call a *canon*—of Scriptures.[30]

In addition to using the "ruler" metaphor as a way of characterizing normative tradition, *kanōn* could also refer to an individual as a model of behavior. Thus Philo of Alexandria (20 B.C.E.–50 C.E.) held up Abraham as "the model of nobility [*kanōn tēs eugeneias*] for all proselytes."[31] In the same way, the pagan author Lucian of Samosata (second century C.E.) could point to the Athenian lawgiver Solon as the model of "Greekness" for all foreigners who desired to emulate things Greek: "Look! There you have a model [*kanōn*] of Greekness, the very image of Greek philosophy! How blessed you are to meet Solon!"[32] This way of using the term *kanōn*—holding up an individual as an exemplar or model—went on to become enshrined in the Roman Catholic Church's practice of beatifying its saints, a process known (not surprisingly) as *canonization.*

After the legalization of Christianity in the early fourth century, it became common for church councils to use the term *kanōn* to refer to individual ecclesiastical rules and regulations. This legal sense had been hovering in the background since the beginning. We can see it in the late first-century writing of *1 Clement's* use of the term *kanōn* when insisting that officeholders should stick to their appointed duties: "Each of us, brothers, in his own rank [an army metaphor], must win God's approval and have a clear conscience. We must not transgress the rules [*kanones*], laid down for our ministry, but perform them reverently" (*1 Clem* 41:1).[33]

And from an even earlier period, we have this quasilegal formulation from the Apostle Paul: "We do not boast beyond limit, that is, in the labors of others; but our hope is that, as your faith increases, our sphere of action [*kanōn*] among you may be greatly enlarged, so that we may proclaim the good news in lands beyond you, without boasting of work already done in someone else's sphere of action [*kanōn*]" (2 Cor 10:15-16).[34]

Conclusion

As was the case in the older Greek *polis* culture out of which it sprang, the word *kanōn* had a wide range of uses in early Christianity. Surprisingly, no second- or third-century Christian writer ever used the term *kanōn* in the sense of an official list of scripture sanctioned by the church. There are plenty of references to a "canon of faith" and a "canon of truth" and a "canon of our holy tradition," but no "canon of sacred scripture." This is all the more surprising because the term *kanōn* was widely used by pagans and Christians alike for lists of all kinds.[35] The Alexandrian grammarians created "canons" of noun declensions and canons of the correct spellings of proper names (for example, kings and countries). Greek astronomers created "canons" of astronomical information. Poets and literary critics created "canons" of meter, and musicians prepared "canons" of the appropriate chords for different kinds of music. Historians, pagan and Christian, created "canons" of comparative chronology to keep straight the dates of parallel events in different countries using different calendars (which they all had)—such as the chart of comparative chronology involving six different nations that Eusebius created, called *Chronological Canons* (*chronika kanones*). But there is no mention of a "canon" of sacred scripture. Why not?

The reason appears to be that so far no official ecclesiastical body had met to determine which writings to accept and which to reject in Holy Scripture. That act did not occur until the latter part of the fourth century (see Chapter Six). Before then, bishops and orthodox theologians never thought of Holy Scripture in that manner.[36] It was just the Scripture read on Sunday morning, and different regions read different things. At the same time, the range of applications of the term *kanōn* went from a broad "spiritual guideline" notion to narrow, specific "rules" or "guides" for practical applications. In fact, this latter sense is where the modern term "handbook" came from. Some of these ancient charts were called *procheiroi kanones,*[37] "handy guides" to their subject. When Eusebius created a chart of gospel parallels to aid in finding similar passages in them,[38] he was creating precisely this sort of "handy guide for scholars." The "Eusebian Sections and Canons," as his chart came to be known, were widely imitated and expanded and copied into countless manuscripts of the gospels.[39]

These handy charts of canons were meant to contribute to the increase of exact, accurate knowledge and were a symptom of the thirst for order, precision, and objective truth found in the Greek *polis.* In none of these uses of the Greek word *kanōn* was there any reference to regulations or laws. It was not until the fourth century, after the Roman emperor stepped in and—with the whole-hearted assistance of the orthodox bishops—took de facto charge of aspects of the Catholic church's doctrine, polity, and scripture selection, that the first occurrence of the term *canon of scripture* appeared, consisting of a list of the approved writings of the Old and New Testaments, and the Greek term *kanōn* came to be increasingly used in the narrow Latin sense of *regula* = law.[40]

Before we examine that historic development (in chapter six), several other pieces of the puzzle must be put on the table, all coming from Greek philosophy: a powerful emphasis upon the teachings and example of the Founder, which, in turn, necessitated the acquisition of genuine copies of the writings about him by his disciples. In the case of Christianity, these were obtained and preserved by bishops in churches that claimed apostolic succession in the major centers of Christianity, assuring the accurate and consistent interpretation of the Gospel of the Lord throughout the orthodox church.

Chapter 4

THE INFLUENCE OF
GREEK PHILOSOPHY UPON
EARLY CHRISTIANITY

Historians are accustomed to discussing the development of "the New Testament canon" in terms of the orthodox church's defense of its faith and its sacred writings against innovations and impostures. As we will see in this chapter, the very particular context of Greek "philosophy," which (as discussed in the previous chapter) so decisively shaped the metaphorical use of the term *kanōn,* also played a decisive role in shaping second- and third-century discussions of Christian scripture—though (as we shall see in a later chapter) the term *kanōn* was not yet being used in these discussions.

We saw in the previous chapter how scholars have worked for several generations examining and clarifying the influence of Greek *polis* culture and philosophy on late Second-Temple Palestinian Judaism. Relatively less work has been done on the influence of Greek philosophy and Greek culture on the genres, doctrines, and structures of early Christianity.[1] This influence became evident during the second century, when a number of converts who had received philosophical training prior to becoming Christian put that training to work in their new religious affiliation. For instance, it is during the middle of the second century that Christian philosophers[2] wrote the first dialogues defending the Christian philosophy against Jewish and pagan critics.[3] Public defenses of the faith, *apologiai* in Greek, began to appear, setting the Christian philosophy in as favorable a light as possible and appealing for a fair hearing from indifferent and hostile outsiders. A good example of the tone and attitude adopted in these apologies/public defenses is the *Apology for the Christian Faith*, addressed to the emperor Marcus Aurelius (161–180) by Melito, the second-century orthodox bishop of Sardis. Note the interchangeable use of the terms *philosophy* and *religion* in his statement:

> Our *philosophy* became a good omen to your Empire, for from that time [of Augustus Caesar] the power of Rome has increased in size and splendor. You are now his happy successor and shall be, along with your son, if you protect the *philosophy* which grew up with the Empire and began with Augustus [namely, Christianity]. Your ancestors held it in honor together with other *religions*.[4]

One of the prominent philosophical Christian defenders of the Christian faith during the mid-second century was Justin Martyr (ca. 100–165). Although he was never ordained, Justin spent a lifetime teaching, writing dialogues and apologies, and debating both pagans and Jews in defense of his understanding of the Christian faith. Justin was born in Flavia Neapolis in Samaria (modern Nablus). He wrote that, as a young man, he studied the philosophical systems of Stoicism, Pythagoreanism, and Platonism before "a certain old man" persuaded him of the superiority of the Christian philosophy.[5] Justin taught for several years in Athens before going to Rome, where he continued to teach and write philosophical defenses of Christianity until he was arrested and executed after arguing too vigorously with one of the powerful court philosophers.[6] A memorable aspect of Justin's rhetoric was his way of referring to the four biblical Gospels as "memoirs of the apostles," so that his learned audience would think of them in the same category as the cherished memoirs written by Pythagoras's disciples.[7]

Contemporary with Justin Martyr were the famous Christian Gnostic teachers of the mid-second century: Valentinus of Alexandria

and Rome (died. ca. 160) and Basilides of Alexandria (active 120–
130). Less well-known Christian philosophers of the time included
Miltaides the rhetorician (mid-second century), probably a disciple of Justin Martyr; Theophilus (ca. 118–181), the sixth bishop
of Antioch and a converted pagan philosopher; and Athenagoras
of Athens (latter part of the second century), whose skillfully pol-
ished diatribe, *Embassy on Behalf of the Christians,* as well as his
scholarly disputation, *On the Resurrection of the Dead,* bear eloquent
testimony to his rhetorical training. The famous second-century
Christian reformer Marcion of Pontus and Rome (active 140–160)
also flourished at this time and will be discussed in greater detail in
a moment.

These Christian philosophers taught their brand of Christian
philosophy to their disciples, wrote polemical tracts attacking rival
"schools" (Christian and other), and even composed new "gospels"
(for example, Valentinus's *Gospel of Truth*), where the term *gospel* was used in its original sense of *good news.* They purified their
sacred scriptures of interpolations and claimed that their opponents
relied on forged or tainted writings. These activities were exactly
what their fellow philosophers among the Greeks and Romans were
doing at the same time. In other words, we can see that second-
century Christianity in all its forms exhibited the first clear signs
of a widespread and powerful trend. The earlier Palestinian Jewish
apocalyptic Christianity was being transformed into a new hybrid
whereby the Christian church was indigenized or enculturated in
the thought patterns, methods, and objectives of Greek *polis* culture
and Greek philosophy. This trend brought with it an unusual ambition: to identify the actual author of every writing.

Greek Philosophy's Unheard-of Demand
to Identify a Writing's Actual Author

Part of Greek philosophy's quest for accuracy in all things[8] was
the unprecedented idea that every writing in their libraries should
be identified not just by a title but also by the name of its actual

author—not some imaginary author, or some famous ancient figure, or, most commonly, no author at all. Achieving this ambition was more difficult than one might think. Greek parents typically gave their children only one name, leading to a lot of confusion since many parents gave their children the same name. A place-name would be appended to your name if you were famous enough, to distinguish you from others with your name: for example, "Eusebius of Caesarea" or "Eusebius of Nicomedia."

The idea of putting the actual name of the author on a writing does not seem peculiar to us, but it was a very peculiar, indeed offensive, idea back then. It was the complete opposite of a centuries-old custom of anonymous or pseudonymous authorship found throughout the ancient world. Think of "the five books of Moses" or "the Psalms of David" or *The Epic of Gilgamesh* or the *Bhagavad-Gita:* who were the actual authors of these works? The only modern equivalent that comes to mind are our traditional folk songs. When someone sings a folk song like "Greensleeves" we do not wonder who the original composer was or get upset if the performer doesn't sing it "accurately." The same is true of most of the books in the Bible. Scholars have long realized that for most of them, like Deuteronomy or Job, it is no longer possible to identify the original author.

Greek philosophy rebelled against this ancient custom of anonymity and pseudonymity on the grounds of a new, positive evaluation of the unique creativity of each individual person. An example of the transition from ancient anonymity to this new kind of individually named authorship can be seen in the Old Testament (apocryphal) book *Ecclesiasticus* (not Ecclesiastes).[9]

The most important early implementation of this radical innovation came with Callimachus of Cyrene (305–240 B.C.E.), who was appointed chief librarian at the great library in Alexandria, which had been founded by the Greek ruler Ptolomy II Soter in 283 B.C.E. and was known as the Museum, or shrine of the Muses. Callimachus the librarian set about creating a comprehensive catalogue or index (Greek: *pinax*; Latin: *tabula* = list, register) of the thousands of scrolls in his library, identifying them by title and author.[10] Along with other resident librarian-scholars—at its peak, there may have been as many as a hundred scholars working full time to catalog, make accurate copies, and comment on the classics—Callimachus expanded the Index to include a biographical sketch of each author, along with a list of his genuine (*gnēsioi*) writings, followed by a list of spurious (*nothoi*, illegitimate, counterfeit) writings, and, occasionally, cases of mistaken attribution, i.e., genuine writings by other authors with the same name.[11]

This novel practice spread and was imitated by others. In the first century B.C.E., a Greek historian and teacher of rhetoric, Dionysius of Halicarnassus, produced a biography of the Athenian orator Deinarchos that concluded with a list separating genuine (*gnēsioi*) from false (*pseudepigraphoi*) writings ascribed to Deinarchos. Similarly, the great medical doctor Galen of Pergamum (ca. 130–200 C.E.) wrote a biography of the ancient "father of medicine," Hippocrates of Cos (ca. 460–370 B.C.E.), and concluded with a list of some sixty writings ascribed to him, though accepting only thirteen as perhaps "genuine."[12]

Many other individual examples could be mentioned. Instead, let us look at the historical survey written by Diogenes Laertius (native of Cilicia and active ca. 230 C.E.), entitled *Lives and Opinions of Eminent Philosophers*. This compendious review of more than eighty Greek philosophers is basically divided into two geographical branches, the Ionians (Books 3–7) and the Italians (Books 8–10), and contains numerous judgments regarding genuine and spurious writings. Laertius's writing will enable us to get a more complete picture of the different elements of a practice that was subsequently adopted by Christian scholars in the second century and afterward.

In Book 3, Laertius presents the life and work of "the divine Plato." He begins with Plato's genealogy, then gives us an account of his miraculous birth, followed by his extensive education, selected teachings and biographical anecdotes, and, finally, an account of his death, his will, and several epitaphs. Next comes a list of Plato's chief disciples and then—citing different authorities—a list of Plato's "genuine dialogues,"[13] followed by a list of dialogues "acknowledged to be spurious."[14] Looking at these lists, one is struck by several features: (a) Laertius's constant reliance on the testimony of other experts—"some say . . . but so-and-so says"; (b) the occasional sweeping judgment—"all agree that X is *genuine*"; (c) and a cautious, provisional tone—"so far as we know, the following are considered *spurious.*"

Laertius and the scholars he cites divided all writings into two groups: *genuine* and *spurious.* However, when they could not report a consensus vote one way or the other (genuine or spurious), they would fall back on a third category: *doubtful* (*distazein*) or *disputed* (*antilegomenoi*) (see Table 4.1). For example, at one point Laertius has listed all the authors that experts agreed wrote dialogues with Socrates as the key speaker, adding: "Panaetius thinks that, of all the Socratic dialogues, those by Plato, Xenophon, Antisthenes and Aeschines are the only *genuine* [*alētheis*] dialogues; but he is *in doubt* [*distazei*] about those ascribed to Phaedo and Euclides, and he *rejects* all the others [as pseudonymous, i.e., as forged imitations]."[15]

TABLE 4.1. Laertius's Terms for Genuine or False Authorship

genuine or *true*	Gk. *gnēsioi, alētheis*
spurious (rejected)	*pseudepigraphoi*
disputed or *doubted*	*antilegomenoi, distazomenoi*

After he has completed a biographical sketch of Plato's life, teachings, and writings in Book 3, in Book 4 Laertius lists the succession of philosophers who were the heads of Plato's Academy or "School" after his death. These successors worked to keep the Academy alive and functioning and to train new students. To accomplish their objective of keeping the Academy going, they had two primary responsibilities: first, to create and hand on *accurate copies of Plato's writings.* Laertius tells us that Plato's successors hired copyists who took extra care in reproducing Plato's genuine dialogues. They placed special marks above the letters in the text to inform the reader that this or that word was not a mistake, or other marks to indicate that this or that word or phrase probably was a mistake or an interpolation.[16] Secondly, they saw to it that the

Founder's writings were *accurately interpreted,* and Laertius lists specific guidelines to follow to obtain the correct interpretation of Plato's dialogues.[17] Laertius concludes Book 4 with a biographical sketch of each of Plato's successors, with lists of *their* genuine writings.

In Book 5, Laertius describes the life and teachings of the great Aristotle, taking many pages to list the titles of his genuine writings,[18] i.e., about four hundred, "counting only those the *genuineness* of which is *not disputed.*"[19] In making this claim, Laertius did not cite any experts; he just gave the blanket judgment: these four hundred are unanimously "acknowledged as genuine," adding that there were many other writings attributed to the famous Aristotle that scholars regarded as spurious.[20] Some of them are cases of mistaken attribution since there were many other men named Aristotle— Laertius lists seven.[21] After the catalog of genuine writings, Laertius presents *a three-page summary of Aristotle's main ideas:* "In [these writings] he puts forward the following views."[22]

In Book 6 he describes the history of the Cynic School and in Book 7 that of the Stoics, all according to the same pattern: biography of the Founder, summary of his main teachings, list of genuine writings, and succession of heads of each one's school. In Book 8 he describes the Pythagoreans, pointing out that the Pythagorean succession continued unbroken "until the ninth or tenth generation" (8.45). Book 10 is devoted to Epicurus's teachings and genuine writings.

Key Aspects of Diogenes Laertius's Account of the Greek Philosophical Schools

Key aspects of Laertius's history of the Greek philosophical schools can help us better understand the second- and third-century Christian scripture selection process and the parallel debate over correct interpretation (see Table 4.2).

First, it is obvious that Laertius did not expect his history to *end the discussion* regarding the various philosophical schools, their founders, their successors, their doctrines, or their judgments

TABLE 4.2. Aspects of Laertius's Account of the
Greek Philosophical Schools
*(as They Illuminate the Christian Process of Scripture Selection
in the 2nd and 3rd Centuries)*

---

1. He reported the "state of the question": he didn't intend to end discussion.

2. He followed the order: Founder (biography, summary of main doctrines, list of genuine writings); successors (biographies, doctrines, list of genuine writings).

3. He always listed the genuine writings of founder and successors alike.

4. He depended on an objective report of past evidence accepted in his own day.

5. He took care to examine the most accurate copies of writings available.

6. (Correspondingly, the schools took care to preserve accurate copies in order to ascertain correct interpretation.)

7. He trusted the ongoing philosophical discussion rather than the application of external authority to determine questions of interpretation.

---

regarding genuine and spurious writings. Laertius is *just reporting* what he has been able to glean from others' discussions for the benefit of all educated readers. His history merely summarizes the state of the question: "This is the situation as best as I can ascertain it, having read countless other authorities, many of whom I cite by name, who in turn have read countless other authorities." His book is clearly intended as a scholarly contribution (think of the German *Beitrag*) to the general, ongoing discussion of the theme, "lives and opinions of eminent philosophers." It was a well-known genre.[23] This point may seem too obvious to bear discussion, but its relevance will become clear in Chapter Six—when we see what happened to the Christian church's debate over right scripture after the Roman government intervened. That intervention shut down further discussion by issuing laws regulating church doctrine, apostolic succession, behavior of bishops, *choice of scripture,* liturgical practices, and church governance.

Second, there seems to be a basic order that Laertius followed in his account of each major *school:* first a description of the *founder* (biography, summary of his main doctrines, list of his genuine writings), followed by a description of his *successors* (briefer biographies), a summary of their *doctrines,* (or just a few anecdotes illustrating their teachings), and a list of *genuine writings* (if any). This Founder-successor aspect is clearly the "spine and skeleton" of each philosophical school. It was what maintained a school's intellectual vitality and doctrinal accuracy—in short, its fidelity to the founder's aims and teachings. The successors (always identified by name when known) were the fundamental control network ensuring the school's perseverance and dedication to the founder's vision for the school. Not that this always happened, of course—Plato's Academy evolved into complete skepticism—but that was the original intention.

Third, closely related to the foregoing, Laertius always mentioned the *genuine writings of the founder of each school* and the *genuine writings of the disciples and successors.* It was widely recognized that elements of the truth revealed by the founder would continue to come out in the writings of the disciples and successors as they continued to probe and explicate his original insights.

Fourth, how did Laertius know which writings were genuine and which were spurious? He lived several hundred years after the death of all of these famous philosophers, so he had no firsthand knowledge. His solution was to consult *named experts,* especially the (genuine) writings of the original disciples of each founder, as well as the (genuine) writings and opinions of the successive heads. These "experts" were obviously in the best position to know which writings were genuine and which were spurious. This meant that Laertius's stance was essentially *backward-looking:* he was examining *the past* for his key evidence. If the sources provided a unanimous opinion one way or the other, he could confidently report that, but if there was a split opinion, or uncertainty, he had to be cautious, objective, ready to change his report if new evidence should be presented.

It is very important to not be misled by what seems to be Laertius's casual tone or vague manner: "Some say . . . , but others say. . . ." The vague *some say* is scholarly shorthand. Most of his readers knew full well who these unnamed voices were, as well as the relative value of the "experts" he cites by name. It was not that large a group to begin with, and, moreover, the other histories he cites for this or that school repeated the same evidence he gives. In other words, Laertius is citing well-known judgments. These characteristics will help us understand Eusebius's seemingly casual tone of voice and vague manner when we look at his history of the Christian church's disputes over selecting some scripture and rejecting others.

Fifth, everyone believed it was essential to have *accurate copies* of the founder's and successors' genuine writings. How could anyone prove anything from corrupt copies of the original? Special care was taken to preserve the most accurate copies possible. Grammarians spent hours studying the texts and debating whether this or that wording or spelling should be corrected or accepted in the ongoing effort to establish the *correct text*.[24]

Sixth, the succession of heads of the Schools relied on these accurate copies of the genuine writings of the Founder and/or his disciples in order to preserve the *correct interpretation,* as successive generations of disciples joined the school.

In short, Laertius's history of the Greek philosophical schools reveals a basic three-fold structure: the over-all control mechanism was the school's *succession of heads,* who, generation after generation, handed on the scrupulously *correct texts of genuine writings* from the earliest days of the school, in order to remain true to the *correct interpretation,* i.e., the Truth as that school perceived it. We will need to keep these component parts in mind and remember how they fit together, because each component—true succession, genuine writings (with accurate texts), and accurate interpretation—became focal points of great stress and increasingly bitter disagreement in the Christian church, until they were all unexpectedly resolved by the forceful intervention of the Roman emperor on the side of the orthodox Catholic faction in the fourth century and after.

Seventh, to come back to a point made at the outset: Laertius's *History* was *a contribution to ongoing dialogue.* It was never intended to end it or become the "final word" that everyone had to agree with. At no point did Laertius appeal to government officials or local politicians to step in and enforce some "correct" interpretation or decision regarding a specific genuine writing or certify a contested succession. Involvement of the government was the farthest thing from Laertius's mind, as it was for all of the scholars cited by him. These issues belonged entirely to the realm of the Quest for Truth, which was understood as the special purview of the philosophers. How could ignorant laypeople, much less public officials (whose chief concern was staying in power, not ultimate Truth), decide anything pertaining to philosophy? After all, most laypeople did not know how to read, much less know how to compare the good Greek style of one writing with the bad Greek style of another, to ascertain if the same author wrote both. We should note, by way of comparison, that Eusebius never speaks of consulting laypeople in the Christian scripture selection process.

The Greek Philosophical School Model in Second- and Third-Century Christian Disputes over Scripture

Increasingly, many Greek-style philosophers, including Syrians, Phoenicians, Jews, Egyptians, Ionians, Italians, and others, converted to Christianity during the second and third centuries, bringing their Greek-style philosophical education and values with them. They naturally employed philosophical goals and methods against each other. Setting up little philosophical schools, they debated the rationality of each school's doctrines, accused each other of not having the genuine writings of the founder's life and teachings, insisted that their opponents based their ideas on inaccurate or incomplete texts, and claimed that their succession of "heads of the church" (i.e., bishops) was an unbroken chain going back to the founder (Jesus Christ) and his disciples, while their opponents had long since strayed from the "true succession." Having said that, it is equally important to remember that Christians used these philosophical methods in startling new ways: after all, the Christian church was a much larger operation numerically, with a huge geographical reach compared to any Greek school; furthermore, it pursued these issues with a visceral intensity quite foreign to the Greek schools.

There is no better illustration of the emergence of these Greek philosophical school techniques in second-century Christianity than the brilliant, mid-second-century reformer Marcion of Pontus. Although he may have started off as an orthodox Christian,[25] before long Marcion was insisting that the orthodox church of his day was riddled with "Judaizers," who forced Christians to use the false and spurious Gospels of Matthew, Mark, and John, as well as a number of non-genuine epistles of Paul (1 and 2 Timothy and Titus). Marcion quoted Paul's statement in Gal 1:8f. — "But even if we or an angel from heaven should proclaim to you a gospel contrary to what we proclaimed to you, let that one be accursed. As we have said before, so now I repeat, if anyone proclaims to you a gospel contrary to what you received, let that one be accursed" — a verse that was widely believed to refer to an actual *written gospel* in Paul's possession. Marcion claimed that there had always been only one *genuine* apostolic account of the life of the Lord, and that it had been written by Paul's assistant Luke. The trouble was, said Marcion, that all existing copies of Luke had been *corrupted* by "Jewish interpolations." As proof, he pointed to the first two chapters, where Jesus is portrayed as having been born of Jewish parents, which was a lie (he said), and as going to the Jerusalem Temple to be circumcised, which was another lie (he said). These horrible things never happened, claimed Marcion. To the contrary, Jesus' earthly career began when he "came down from heaven" (cf. Luke 4:31) as a full-grown man, "in the twelfth year of Tiberius Caesar"[26] and suddenly appeared — poof! — in the synagogue at Capernaum and healed a man with a demon. Moreover, existing copies of Luke contained other falsehoods and Jewish interpolations, such as the horrible lie that Jesus Christ was crucified — an abomination, asserted Marcion. Jesus had not been crucified; the Romans mistakenly crucified someone else (possibly Simon of Cyrene, who carried his cross).[27]

Based on his rigorous theological filter, Marcion accepted as *genuine* only ten of the epistles of Paul. Two parts formed his scripture: the first part was named simply *Euangelikon* — the expurgated version of Luke's Gospel (minus his name)—followed by the second part, *Apostolikon*—the "Apostle"—the (ten) genuine letters of Paul. Beyond that, Marcion rejected everything, including the entire Old Testament.

One might think that Marcion's drastic truncation of Christian scripture to one abbreviated version of Luke and ten letters of Paul would deeply offend the Christians of his day. Just the opposite was the case: it was incredibly popular. Of course, those in the orthodox church were offended and immediately wrote a whole series of attacks on Marcion. Indeed, the series of orthodox refutations of Marcion and his writings continued for two hundred years. But his message certainly struck a chord with many others: scholars estimate that the Marcionites were more numerous than any other Christian factions at that time.[28] From the perspective of the methods and practices of the Greek philosophical schools, it is readily apparent how Marcion's campaign to base Christianity only on the genuine text of the original writings would have been seen as perfectly legitimate.

As the second century progressed, an even clearer example appeared. Indeed, in many ways, the orthodox bishop of Lyons (ancient Lugdunum), Irenaeus (120–202), most clearly exemplifies the three-fold philosophical school model: standing in the *true succession of leaders* back to the founder, possession of the only *genuine writings* written by the founder's disciples (with accurate texts), and adhering to the *correct doctrine.*

In his youthful days in Asia Minor, Irenaeus had been a disciple of the venerable Polycarp, Bishop of Smyrna (69–155). Polycarp, in turn, had heard the Apostle John teach and preach in person at Ephesus (around the turn of the first century) when he was a young man. This experience gave Irenaeus a special appreciation of the concept of the bishops in apostolic succession—he never forgot that he was only one step removed from the living voice of one of Jesus Christ's actual disciples, John, the son of Zebedee.

As his teacher, Polycarp, had done, Irenaeus resisted all attempts to modify the Christian message. This led him to resist vehemently the teachings of other Christian schools, such as the doctrines of the self-styled People of Knowledge, or gnostics, as they were known. Irenaeus had met them in Rome, where they were led by the learned Egyptian Christian philosopher Valentinus.[29] What especially angered Irenaeus was Valentinus's accusation that the orthodox Christians' gospels were incomplete and were interpreted with a childish literalism. The Valentinians taught that the Lord Jesus had bestowed esoteric doctrine secretly upon a few specially chosen disciples, and that this secret, more advanced teaching had been brought to Alexandria, where Valentinus learned it.[30]

Irenaeus responded to the Valentinians on each point, beginning with their claim to secret teachings of the Lord. For Irenaeus, the *succession of bishops* was the ultimate court of appeal:

> Suppose there arise a dispute relative to some important question among us [such as what is the true doctrine or whether there were secret gospels], should we not have recourse to the most ancient Churches with which the apostles held constant intercourse, and learn from them what is certain and clear in regard to the present question?[31]

Of course we should, continued Irenaeus, and in the present case we should ask the Valentinians to show us *their* succession or produce an original apostolic writing that supports their outrageous beliefs. As far as we are concerned, Irenaeus continued, anyone can see that

> it is within the power of all in every Church, who may wish to see the truth, to contemplate clearly the tradition of the apostles manifested throughout the whole world. We are in a position to reckon up *those who were by the apostles instituted bishops* in the Churches and [to demonstrate] *the succession of these men to our own times*; those who neither taught nor knew of anything like what these [heretics] rave about.[32]

Irenaeus claimed that the orthodox Church preserved "the whole truth"—not just part of the truth—because it alone had handed down the true message of the apostles through *unbroken successions* of duly authorized bishops going back to the holy apostles, Peter and Paul in Rome and John in Ephesus.[33] Listing by name the ten successive bishops of the church at Rome, Irenaeus concluded that it is "*by this succession,* that the ecclesiastical [orthodox] tradition from the apostles and the preaching of the truth have come down to us. This is the most abundant proof that there is one and the same vivifying faith which has been preserved in the [orthodox] Church from the apostles until now and handed down in truth."[34]

Meanwhile, Irenaeus went on, the Valentinians and the other heretics do stand in successions, but not back to Jesus Christ. They are descended from the arch-heretic, Simon the Samaritan.[35] From the beginning they have not accepted the orthodox Church's four genuine apostolic writings but have claimed to have secret gospels and mysterious writings.[36] They "boast that they possess more gospels than there really are," such as their comparatively recent writing, the *Gospel of Truth*[37] and the *Infancy Gospel of Thomas.*[38] The orthodox Catholic Church, on the other hand, has "learned from none others the plan of our salvation than from those [four apostles] through whom the Gospel has come down to us, which they did at one time proclaim [verbally] in public and at a later period by the will of God handed down to us in [writing], to be the ground and pillar of our faith."[39]

Then Irenaeus listed the four *genuine* gospels written by Jesus' disciples or their assistants: Matthew, Mark, Luke, and John.[40] He followed this with *a short summary of the doctrine* they contained, which was a paraphrase of the first two sentences of the baptismal creed. This "rule of truth"[41] is held in common by orthodox Christians everywhere: "The [orthodox] church though dispersed throughout the whole world, even to the ends of the earth, has received from the apostles and their disciples this faith."[42] As for the "School of Valentinus,"[43] they have "deviated far from the truth" (1.22.1), even though they style themselves "people of knowledge" (Greek: *gnōstikoi*).[44] Their system of thought is one "which neither the prophets announced, nor the Lord taught, nor the apostles delivered" to us.[45]

These quotations from Irenaeus clearly indicate the power and resilience of the Greek schools' three-fold structure when used by a master of polemics: insisting upon the unshakeable, combined witness of a number of apostolic successions back to the founder; proving that the orthodox church possessed the full set of genuine writings from the founder's disciples (with correct texts); and insisting that upon them is erected the full, correct doctrine, or, in Irenaeus's phrase, the *rule of truth* (*kanōn alētheias*).

A younger contemporary of Irenaeus, the Roman lawyer Tertullian (160–240),[46] adopted the same three-fold structure in his polemics against the followers of Marcion and Valentinus: "The heretics say that the adulterations of the scriptures and false expositions [*adulteria Scriptuarum et expositionum mendacia*] thereof are introduced by us. . . . They maintain that Truth is on their side [*sibi defendant veritatem*], not ours."[47] The disagreement could not be more complete: "I claim that my [version of the] Gospel [of Luke] is the true one; Marcion that his is. I affirm that Marcion's gospel has been adulterated; Marcion that mine is. Who shall decide between us?"[48] Tertullian argues that the only objective answer is to ask this question: Where did Marcion's "Gospel" come from? Did he in fact "single out Luke to mutilate,"[49] "openly and expressly using the knife . . . to make an excision of [the offensive portions of Luke] to suit his theology?"[50] If so, Tertullian argues, that means that our version is older than his and therefore is closer to Luke's original text. This could explain why "Marcion's gospel is not known to most people"[51]—it is of such recent origin. In other words, *it is a brazen forgery*. If it is not a forgery, then why won't Marcion put anyone's name on it as the author, so that we may know who the author was? Answer: he's afraid to. "I argue . . . that a work ought not be recognized that will not hold its head erect . . . [and publicly announce] its author."[52]

The Catholic Church does not need to worry, Tertullian concludes, when the Marcionites or others accuse it of corrupt doctrine and corrupt sacraments. The Catholic Church can have complete confidence in these matters because of the consistency of its teaching across its *multiple international apostolic successions* in each of the great centers (Jerusalem, Alexandria, Ephesus, Rome) of the Christian faith. Contrary to the heretics' repeated accusation that the Catholic Church is filled with error, the exact opposite is the case: the churches belonging to the apostolic successions teach pure apostolic truth. And how can one objectively verify this contention? Precisely by the fact that they do not have any variation or contradiction among them in what they each teach and believe. Nor is this impressive consistency an accident:

> It is not likely that so many churches, and they so great, should have [accidentally] gone astray into one and the same faith. No casualty [or accident] distributed among so many men issues in one and the same result. . . . When, therefore, that which is deposited among many is found to be one and the same, it is not the result of error but of tradition.[53]

The basic apostolic tradition has been carefully handed down in all of the Catholic churches in the world, from bishop to bishop back to Christ, who taught the twelve disciples and then instructed them to go out and teach all nations:

> [The Apostles] then founded churches in every city, from which all the other churches, one after another, derived the tradition of the faith. . . . It is on this account that they are able to deem themselves apostolic. . . . Therefore the [apostolic succession] churches, although they are so many and so great, comprise but one primitive church founded by the apostles.[54]

The Marcionites and the Valentinians have nothing comparable to this massive, concurrent witness, Tertullian holds. They cannot point to any successions of bishops in any of their churches:

> Let [the Marcionites and Valentinians] produce the original records of their churches; *let them unfold the roll of their bishops,* running down in due succession from the beginning in such a manner that [the first] bishop shall be able to show for his ordainer and predecessor one of the apostles or apostolic men.[55]

They cannot do it. They have no "apostolic churches in which the very thrones of the apostles are still pre-eminent in their places, in which their own *authentic writings* are read, uttering the voice and representing the face of each of them."[56] The Catholic church alone has "the rule of faith,"[57] "taught by Christ"[58]—and at that point Tertullian begins to give a paraphrase of the baptismal creed, which to him is a summary of correct doctrine unanimously held by the true Church.[59]

Bishop Hippolytus of Rome (active 210) was a disciple of Irenaeus and, like his master, also went to great lengths to combat what he considered to be false or aberrant systems of thought within the Christian movement.[60] His *Refutation of All Heresies* also relied heavily on the argument from *true succession*, but he pursued it a little differently. Although his general aim was the same as Irenaeus's, namely, to distinguish The True (Christian) Philosophy from all aberrant versions of it, he established this distinction by seizing on specific doctrines put forward by the heretics and arguing that they were brought in from various Greek philosophies rather than going back to the teachings of Jesus Christ.[61] Otherwise, the central structure of his position is identical with that of Irenaeus: As bishop, he stands within the authoritative succession of (orthodox) bishops back to Christ; his church is positive it possesses *genuine* writings composed by Christ's disciples; and from them he proclaims the Divine Truth every Sunday.[62]

Origen's Decisions Regarding Genuine and Spurious Apostolic Writings

The third-century orthodox Alexandrian biblical scholar and theologian Origen is an especially clear-cut example of the application of the methods and goals of the Greek philosophical school—and is all the more important since he was the predecessor and model for Eusebius of Caesarea, the subject of the next chapter. Origen's predecessor in the Catechetical School was Clement of Alexandria (died ca. 215). He, like the other Alexandrians Valentinus and Basilides, believed that humans could know Divine Truth by looking within, more or less independent of tradition. Not that Clement disregarded the orthodox tradition: he just was not focused on it the way Irenaeus had been. As a result, when it came to the issue of *genuine apostolic writings,* Clement was more blasé. Truth, he believed, could be received from many sources.[63]

Origen (185–254) was a very different person. Uniquely among orthodox Christian scholars in the entire ancient church, Origen was deeply concerned with establishing an *accurate text* of the Greek Old Testament and with pinpointing its relation to the original Hebrew text of the Old Testament. Why did Origen decide to make this seemingly obscure project his lifework?

By the third century, the Christian church was plagued by a plethora of differing versions of the Old Testament, causing all sorts of confusion, uncertainty, and ridicule. Jewish scholars derided the Christians for stealing their scripture and then debasing it with omissions and Christian interpolations. These corruptions of the Greek Septuagint translation of the Old Testament (the LXX) were one reason they dismissed the central doctrines of the Christian faith. Moreover, there were rival Greek translations circulating among the Jews, each one claiming to be "the more accurate text," adding to the confusion. Origen felt it was imperative to put an end to this confusion. Accordingly, he created a monumental research project intended to ascertain once and for all the precise differences between the original Hebrew text and the LXX, on one side, and the precise differences between the most important competing Greek translations and the LXX, on the other. Out of this complex chart would come presumably the most accurate and reliable text of the Old Testament humanly possible.

His huge chart was called Hexapla ("six-fold") because it had six columns. The Hebrew text (which Hebrew text he used is not known) is in the left column. Next to it was the Greek translit-eration, to make sure of the pronunciation of the Hebrew. Then came the Septuagint (which text is not known), and then three columns containing the rival Greek translations. The final manu-script (there was only one) was physically enormous, more than 6,500 pages, because each column was only one or two words wide to facilitate comparison. In the Septuagint column, Origen inserted special signs—the same as those used by the Alexandrian grammar-ians in their textual analyses—to indicate where it differed from the Hebrew: An obelus (÷) indicated words in the Septuagint that were not in the Hebrew. An asterisk (✳) indicated words missing in the Septuagint that were in the Hebrew.[64] He and his assistants worked on this massive project for years. One very significant outcome was the use made of this carefully revised Greek Septuagint text, long after he was dead, by Eusebius, his successor in the library at Caesarea, in preparing fifty copies of the Old and New Testament for the Emperor Constantine to use in the Christian churches of his brand new imperial capital, Constantinople.[65]

This monumental project was by far the most complex and the largest textual analysis in all of antiquity, dwarfing anything done by any of the Greek grammarians. As such, it clearly demonstrated Origen's desire for precision and accuracy as regards the biblical text.

Another illustration of his commitment to accuracy was his analysis of the genuine apostolic gospels. These he wrote commentaries on, trying to explicate their deeper meaning for his learned readers. Along the way, Origen would take up the issue of whether this or that writing was *genuine* or *spurious*. For example, in his *Commentary on Matthew,* Origen had this to say about the small number of apostolic gospels the entire orthodox Catholic church acknowledged as genuine:

> As I have understood from tradition, respecting the four gospels, which are the only *undisputed* ones in *the whole church of God under heaven.* The first is written according to Matthew, the same that was once a publican, but afterwards an apostle of Jesus Christ, who having published it for the Jewish converts, wrote it in the Hebrew. The second is according to Mark, who composed it, as Peter explained it to him, whom he also acknowledges as his son in his general Epistle. . . . And the third according to Luke, the gospel commended by Paul which was for the converts from the Gentiles, and last of all the gospel according to John.[66]

This kind of sweeping judgment, reporting a unanimous verdict regarding the genuineness of a writing without citing any specific authority, is what often occurs in Laertius's *Lives and Opinions of Eminent Philosophers.*[67] More intriguing is the rarely seen name for the entire international Christian network Origen uses here: "*the whole church of God under heaven.*" This intentionally formal, all-inclusive designation was one way to refer to the entire international network of orthodox congregations. "Catholic church" (*katholikē ekklēsia*) was more common, and the shortened version "assembly" (*ekklēsia,* usually translated as "church") was the most common of all.[68]

Again, like other philosophers, Origen could express doubt or uncertainty in some cases. In his *Commentary on John,* he paused at one point to take up the question of the genuineness of the epistles said to be written by Peter and John and widely used (in worship) in the Catholic Church: "Peter upon whom the church of Christ is built, against whom the gates of Hell shall not prevail, has left one *acknowledged* epistle.[69] We might allow [as many claim] that Peter also left a second epistle; but this is *doubtful.*"[70] Here Origen reports, without citing any authorities, a unanimous verdict on one epistle of Peter but expresses considerable doubt regarding the second. He does not simply shut the door; he leaves it open just a bit, obviously because many brethren whom he respects disagree with this view and think 2 Peter is genuine. Hence he adopts a very tentative tone of voice. This also is appropriate in discussions of genuineness where the verdict is split, as we saw in Laertius. Eusebius adopts precisely the same tentative tone when discussing these same epistles.[71]

Origen continues, commenting on the writings ascribed to the Apostle John:

> What shall we say of him who reclined upon the breast of Jesus, I mean John? Who left one Gospel, in which he confesses that he could write so many that the world would not contain them. He also wrote the Apocalypse. . . . He has also left an epistle consisting of very few lines. We might allow also a second and a third epistle are from him [as many claim], but *not all agree that they are genuine.* Anyway, there aren't a hundred lines between the two of them.[72]

I will end with one final example from Origen that beautifully illustrates what I have been saying. In his *Homily on the Epistle to the Hebrews,* Origen stops to inquire who wrote the Epistle. This was an especially touchy question because (a) it was a very popular writing that had been circulating in the orthodox church for a long time, hence it must have been written very early; but (b) there was no evidence at all as to the identity of the original author. Some said the Apostle Paul wrote it, but Origen was too good a linguist to accept that opinion:

> The *style* of the Epistle with the title "To the Hebrews" has not that roughness of diction which is typical of the apostle [Paul,] who confesses that he is but common in speech, that is, in his phrase-ology. But that this epistle is more pure Greek in the composition of its phrases, every one will confess who is able to discern the difference of style. On the other hand, it is obvious that the *ideas* of the epistle are admirable and not inferior to any of the books acknowledged to be apostolic. . . . But I would say that *the thoughts are the apostle's but the diction and phraseology belong to someone else* who recorded what the apostle said, . . . [and revised] at his leisure what his master dictated. If then, any church considers this epistle as coming from Paul, let it be commended for this, for nei-ther did those ancient men deliver it as such without cause. But who it was that really wrote the epistle, God only knows.[73] The explanation that has been current before us is, according to some, that Clement who was bishop of Rome wrote the epistle; accord-ing to others, that it was written by Luke, who wrote the gospel and the acts.[74]

This explanation captures perfectly the mild, judicious, learned, candid tone of a Greek philosopher discussing the authenticity of a writing that many experts consider sacred and believe to be genu-ine, but that others, impressed by the obviously non-Pauline style of the writing, refuse to admit is by the apostle—leaving the issue squarely on the fence. In the next chapter, we can see Eusebius fol-lowing closely the model of his revered mentor, Origen, as he sifts through the many candidates for Christian scripture, using many of the same critical terms in the process.

Chapter 5

AGAINST PAGANS AND HERETICS:
Eusebius's Strategy in Defense of the Catholic Scriptures

Forty years of uninterrupted peace and tranquility followed the brief but intense persecutions of the Christian church, first under the emperor Decius in 250, when Origen was tortured and died, and the second under the Emperor Valerian in 258–260.[1] After this period, the many different Christians sects and factions thrived and grew as never before, spreading to all of the great cities of the empire—Rome, Alexandria, Antioch, and Carthage—and to countless smaller towns and cities.

By now, there were distinguishable regional types of Christians: Jewish Christians, with their preferred gospels and anti-Trinitarian Christology, originally living in numerous small communities throughout Syria-Palestine (but greatly reduced by the end of the third century). Marcionites, with their tiny scripture of "Gospel and Apostle" and doctrine of two gods, outnumbered most other Christians in Asia Minor and northern Syria (especially in the late second century). Montanus and his prophetic daughters, with their ecstatic followers and no scripture at all (since they had the Holy Spirit), were numerous (especially in the late second century) in the province of Phrygia in eastern Asia Minor. And Gnostic conventicles, with their esoteric doctrines and distinctive gospels and mystic tracts, could be found in secretive suburban house-churches throughout Egypt, Syria-Palestine, and Italy in the second and third centuries. During this time period, i.e., the latter half of the third century, missionaries sent by the Persian visionary and religious reformer Mani (ca. 210–275) came into the eastern provinces of the Roman Empire with their scriptures (including the Christian Gospels) and made numerous converts in Syria, Egypt, and even as far west as Carthage in Proconsular Africa (most famously, the theologian Augustine, who was a devout Manichaean before he converted to Christianity). Last but not least, the large international network of orthodox Christian congregations, who liked to refer to themselves by the collective designation "the universal assembly" (*katholikē ekklēsia*), was slowly but surely becoming more well-organized and financially secure. The process by which these Christians, over time, evaluated and selected their scriptures is the subject of this chapter.

Pagan Critique . . .

As might be expected, the increasingly prominent Christian activity everywhere excited periodic cries of alarm. "Christians are building up great houses," cried the Neo-Platonic "philosopher" Porphyry, "where they can assemble for prayer, and no one is preventing them from doing it! The whole world has heard of their Gospels."[2]

Porphyry was not the first pagan philosopher to focus critical scrutiny on the Christian religion. In the latter part of the second century, a philosopher named Celsus, otherwise unknown to us, published a sophisticated philosophical attack upon the Christian religion, entitled *True Religion*. Origen was urged to write a refutation, for which historians today are deeply grateful, since his answer consisted of a paragraph-by-paragraph, line-by-line refutation of everything Celsus wrote. Origen's response is so detailed that one can form a fairly accurate idea of what Celsus said.[3]

One of Celsus's main objections was that it was impossible to tell what Christians believed, since they disagreed among themselves so completely. "When they were beginning . . . they were few and of one mind, but since then they have spread to become a multitude and are divided and rent asunder because each wants to have his own party [*stasis*]."[4] He went on:

> Some of them will agree that they have the same God as the Jews while others [the followers of Marcion] think there is another God to whom the former is opposed and that the Son came from the latter. . . . There are some, too, who profess to be Gnostics. . . . And some who accept Jesus although they still want to live according to the law of the Jews [i.e., the Ebionites]. . . . And there are some who are Simonians who reverence . . . Helena, . . . [and] Marcellians who follow Marcellina and Harpocratians who follow Salome and others who follow Mariamme and . . . Marcionites who take Marcion as their leader. . . . And these [different sects] slander one another with dreadful and unspeakable words of abuse . . . for they utterly detest each other.[5]

Celsus's tract was mild compared to the powerful denunciation issued at the end of the third century by the noted Neoplatonist philosopher Porphyry of Tyre (ca. 233–304). Entitled *Against the Christians* and written in fifteen books, this work combined elements taken from Celsus and earlier pagan critics with harsh points garnered from the equally bitter denunciation composed by Marcion in his *Contradictions,* all mixed with Porphyry's own criticisms.[6] Scholars agree that it was the single most damaging critique in the history of the ancient church. Porphyry was a trained philosophical critic and, at the time of writing, had been for years a student of the famed Neoplatonic philosopher Plotinus (ca. 205–269), writing a biography about him and editing his doctrines (the *Enneads*). Before that, Porphyry had studied Christianity in the school of Origen in Alexandria, learning Origen's theology and distinctive biblical criticism.[7]

In his earlier works such as *Philosophy from Oracles,* Porphyry had been mildly approving of elements in Christianity, but at some point between 270 and 300 C.E., during his stay in Sicily, he seems to have changed his mind drastically. He published the sweeping attack, *Against the Christians,* which began with a mocking tirade aimed at Jesus and his disciples (Books 1 and 2). This was followed by a list of the inconsistencies and absurdities in the Genesis account

(Book 3), then by a lengthy, detailed list of dozens of inconsistencies and contradictions between the Gospel accounts (Books 5 through 7), followed by a scathing attack on the absurdities of the book of Daniel (Book 12), and so on.[8] For the purposes of this chapter, Porphyry's four main objections to Christianity were:

Objection #1. Christians are social outcasts and traitors who reject our ancient and proud cultural heritage in order to adopt the obscure and alien tradition of the Jews. Why would anyone want to believe that the Highest God showed particular favor to that detestable nation?

Objection #2. Shamelessly abandoning their native heritage for the Jewish, Christians inconsistently go on and reject the Jewish tradition as well, concocting for themselves monstrous fables about a crucified Savior, which even Jews regard with disgust.

Objection #3. Having separated themselves from all civilized society, Christians have made a mockery of the teachings of their Founder by fighting and opposing each other more than they do those of us who do not share their insane beliefs. It is impossible to tell exactly what the Christians believe.

Objection #4. Their sacred writings are riddled with contradictions and inconsistencies, especially the stupid legends called gospels, where Christ heals others but could not save himself from crucifixion. It is common knowledge that Christians brazenly alter their sacred writings to make them conform to their theological whims.

Porphyry ended with a resounding plea to the emperor to rid society of the scourge of Christianity.[9]

... and Christian Response

This sweeping indictment by a reputable intellectual was immediately answered by several prominent Christian leaders. Jerome mentions Methodius of Lycia and Eusebius of Caesarea.[10] They hoped to nip Porphyry's onslaught in the bud, lest it gain a receptive hearing at Nicomedia, the eastern imperial court, and add fuel to the smoldering embers of anti-Christian hatred. They were right to worry. Before long, in 301 or 302, a second high-profile attack on the Christian religion appeared, this time composed by someone obviously well connected at court: Sossianus Hierocles, a newly appointed governor in Bithynia.[11] Drawing extensively on Porphyry's work, Hierocles focused on the person of Jesus Christ, portraying him as a pitiful and pathetic person around whom extravagant lies had been spun by his followers, in comparison with the noble and impressive late first-century Cappadocian savior and wandering prophet, Apollonios of Tyana, who had been given a laudable biography by the professional writer Philostratus of Lemnos.[12]

These polemical writings, amplified by certain provocative actions on the part of Christians at the imperial court, had their desired effect. A flood of imperial rage at the Christians burst over the eastern empire in February 303. The signal for all-out war was given when imperial storm troopers bashed in the door of the central church in Nicomedia and, within hours, had razed it to the ground.[13] The Great Persecution of 303 had begun. Official edicts appeared in cities throughout the eastern provinces, depriving Christians of all civil offices and ordering houses of worship to be destroyed and scriptures to be burned.[14] Further edicts followed in swift succession, stepping up the violence, as Christians sought to protect their churches and conceal their sacred writings from official destruction. Mass arrests took place, followed by bloodshed, as torture failed to coerce bishops, priests, and believers into performing the required sacrifices of the state cult. Finally, in December of 303, Galerius prevailed upon Diocletian to pass a fourth edict commanding all citizens to offer sacrifice to the Emperors on pain of death.[15] Large numbers of Christians accepted death rather than comply.

In Caesarea, birthplace of Eusebius (ca. 260–341), the wave of arrests and executions reached into the little scholarly circle around Pamphilus, the leader of the local school and library. Eusebius soberly notes that the "first of the martyrs of Palestine" was one of their group, a young man named Procopius, who bravely refused to sacrifice and was beheaded on the spot.[16] Eusebius began keeping records of those who suffered and died, some of whom were his dear friends, including his revered mentor Pamphilus, who was arrested and cast into prison.[17] For some reason, Eusebius himself was spared and quickly resolved to do more than keep a tally of those who confessed Christ and died. Before long he had embarked upon a comprehensive refutation of the intellectual bases of the persecution—focusing specifically on the writings of Porphyry and Hierocles—the results of which have made him world famous (see Table 5.1).[18]

Eusebius dashed off a refutation of Hierocles[19] while he laid out his strategy for answering Porphyry at great length. The first step was to create a Christian chronology that would directly challenge Porphyry's claim, in Book 4 of *Against the Christians*, that Moses had been a comparatively recent figure of history, not the source of Hebrew and Greek wisdom as Jewish apologists—and Christians after them—claimed.[20] These *Chronological Canons* consisted of two parts: summaries of the ethnic histories of different peoples (Chaldeans, Greeks, Hebrews, Assyrians, Egyptians, and Romans), followed by a chronological table of parallel events in the nations of the world. Eusebius used this chronological chart in his later writings as a way of keeping his dates straight.[21] He then dictated a writing entitled *Against Porphyry,* in twenty-five books. This work has not survived, nor does Eusebius ever refer to it, possibly because it, like Origen's *Against Celsus,* was a lengthy refutation whose structure was based on the order of Celsus's argument.

Eusebius then started over and decided upon a much broader, more comprehensive refutation,[22] involving four separate publications. The first defended the Christian rejection of the confused, immoral, and self-contradictory Greco-Roman tradition, entitled *Preparation for the Gospel* (in fifteen books). This was followed closely by a second, even larger writing, *Proof of the Gospel,* in twenty books, defending the Christian adoption and modification of the Jewish tradition.[23] The third publication, the *Ecclesiastical History,* today consists of ten books but was originally published in seven. That work is the focus of this chapter. In it, Eusebius demonstrated the coherence, consistency, and reliability of the orthodox Christian set of sacred writings and of the orthodox interpretation of them.

Table 5.1. Eusebius's Writings in Refutation of
Hierocles and Porphyry

The Treatise of Eusebius, the son of Pamphilus, against the Life of Apollonios of Tyana *written by Philostratus, occasioned by the parallel drawn by Hierocles between him and Christ*	Eusebius lays out his strategy for answering Porphyry at greater length and gives the remarkable argument in his reply to Hierocles that everyone naturally looks to the goodness of God for those "rays of light sent from God called Saviors."
Chronological Canons	Eusebius creates a Christian chronology that would directly challenge Porphyry's claim that Moses was a comparatively recent figure of history, not the source of Hebrew and Greek wisdom as Christian claimed. Eusebius used this chart in his later writings as a way of keeping his dates straight.
Against Porphyry (not extant)	A lengthy refutation of Porphyry.
Preparation for the Gospel and *Proof of the Gospel*	Eusebius defends the Christian adoption and modification of the Jewish tradition.
Ecclesiastical History	Eusebius demonstrates the coherence, consistency, and reliability of the orthodox Christian set of sacred writings and of the orthodox interpretation of them.
Sections and Canons	Eusebius provides a table of Gospel pericopes with single, double, or triple parallels, to provide a guide for scholars interested in verifying the essential harmony and concord of the Gospel accounts about Jesus, the better to answer claims that the Gospels contradicted each other.

It was probably written in four successive editions, to take quickly changing current events into account.[24] The fourth publication, known to us as Eusebius's *Sections and Canons,* provided a table of Gospel pericopes with single, double, or triple parallels to provide a guide for scholars interested in verifying the essential harmony and concord of the Gospel accounts of Jesus, the better to answer claims that the Gospels contradicted each other.[25]

In what follows, I will focus on Books 1 through 7 of *Ecclesiastical History*—and specifically on what these books have to tell us about the way the churches went about selecting what would become Christian scripture.

Eusebius's Defense of Catholic Scripture

I will restrict my discussion to a careful examination of those passages where Eusebius explicitly describes the criteria used to evaluate and select the church's scripture, the key terms and methods of which, as I have shown in the previous chapters, he inherited from Origen, Irenaeus, and other orthodox authorities, and, behind them, the Greek philosophical schools. Let us begin with a particularly clear example in his discussion of the writings of the Apostle Peter.

> As I proceed in my history, I shall carefully show with the successions of the apostles what ecclesiastical writers in their times respectively made use of any of the *disputed* writings and what opinions they have expressed, both respecting the *incorporated* [*endiathēkōn*] and *acknowledged* [*homologoumenōn*] writings and also what respecting those that were not of this description. (*Hist. eccl.* 3.3.3)[26]

Comments

"I shall carefully show ... the successions of the apostles ..."
Eusebius says he is going to identify, for each of the major centers of the orthodox Christian faith, the specific names and dates of the chain of succession of bishops there, all the way back to the apostle who founded each of those churches. Given the kinds of resources at Eusebius's disposal, this would have been an enormous undertaking![27] As it turned out, Eusebius's narrative does not even come close. He managed to give complete successions (with more or less accurate dates) for four major churches (Rome, Alexandria, Antioch, and Jerusalem) and pieces of the successions for many

other churches. Given his resources, the completeness and accuracy he did manage to accomplish is astonishing—and a boon to church historians ever since.

But why go to all this trouble regarding these bishops? Because, as Irenaeus and Tertullian had said, it was the bishops in these churches where a chain of apostolic succession could be demonstrated which were responsible for deciding which apostolic writings should be used in their worship services and liturgies.[28] This was the key question: which writings should be used in holy worship? Answer: *Apostolic* writings—the ones closest to Jesus Christ. But that raised a second question: Which ones, out of the great number of writings bearing apostles' names, were genuine? Who was in a position to answer that? Answer: the bishops in apostolic succession churches, because they had received the genuine apostolic writings directly from the hands of the apostles in the first place and had passed them down from bishop to bishop.[29]

"what ecclesiastical writers"—Eusebius, and all orthodox writers all the way back to the Apostle Paul, used the word *ecclesiastical* (from the Greek *ekklēsia*) to refer to the orthodox Catholic branch of Christianity. They never used it to refer to any heretical group. Eusebius never refers to the Marcionites or Montanists or Gnostics or any of the other heretics as "ecclesiastical writers." He consistently puts these outside the sphere of Christian orthodoxy and calls them by the name of their originators: Marcionites, Valentinians, Montanists, etc., or generically, heretics (i.e., deviants).

"in their times"—The plan of Eusebius's *Ecclesiastical History* is roughly chronological.[30] Book 1 focuses on God's revelation in Jesus Christ; Book 2 treats events from Tiberius (14–37) through Nero (54–68); Book 3 begins with Vespasian (69–79) and continues to Trajan (98–117); Book 4 continues the history down to Marcus Aurelius (161–180); Book 5 goes from Aurelius to Septimius Severus (193–211); Book 6 continues from Severus to Decius (249–251); Book 7 goes from Gallus (251–253) to Gallienus (260–268); and Book 8 focuses on the suffering of Palestinian Christians under the persecution of Diocletian (284–305), ending with the deathbed edict of Galerius (305–311), which halted the persecution. Books

9 and 10 treat contemporary ecclesiastical history, ending with Constantine's total victory over all other claimants to the empire and his edicts in favor of the (orthodox) Christian church. As he worked through the historical record, Eusebius tried to give as many actual names, dates, and locations for every apostolic church founder, orthodox bishop appointed by him, and orthodox theologian associated with that succession as he could. In many cases, he gave a quote or excerpt from their writings regarding what they thought of the genuineness of the writings thought to be by apostles. In some cases, Eusebius even appended a short list of their own genuine writings. As I have said, it was a huge undertaking. If modern scholars find fault with Eusebius's results (and many have), it is often because they have forgotten the limited resources he had at his disposal.[31]

"*made use of any of the disputed writings and what opinions they expressed both respecting the acknowledged writings and those that were not of this description.*"— "Made use of" means, first and foremost, "used in orthodox worship." It also can mean "quoted or cited as an authority in a letter or theological treatise." I will say more about the meaning of "acknowledged" and "disputed" in a moment.

On *The Shepherd of Hermas*

Illustrating the points I have just made is a passage that occurs a few lines later in this same context about a writing known today as *The Shepherd of Hermas*.

> But as the same apostle [Paul], in the addresses at the close of the Epistle to the Romans, has made mention among others of Hermas, of whom they say we have the book called *Pastor*, it should be observed that this too is *disputed by some* on account of whom it is not placed among those [writings] of [unanimously] *acknowledged* authority. By others, however, it is judged most necessary, especially to those who need an elementary introduction. Hence, we know that it has already been in public use in our churches, and I have also understood by tradition that some of the most ancient writers made use of it. (*Hist. eccl.* 3.3.6)

Comments

"made mention of Hermas..."—Note how Eusebius provides a historical cross-check, going from an already known and dated apostolic writing (Paul's Epistle to the Romans 16:14) to an otherwise unknown person named "Hermas." Eusebius's purpose here is to locate "Hermas" within the same category as "Luke," "Clement," and "Silvanus," other assistants and coworkers with the Apostle Paul. If you read attentively, you will notice Eusebius employing this "historical cross-check" technique frequently as a means to verify the dates of people and writings in his history.

"they say..."—This vague reference actually means something very specific: the orthodox Catholic authorities. A vague "they" like this never refers to heretical writers—their opinions are of no value in Eusebius's discussion.

"disputed by some"—Again, he is referring to the opinions of orthodox authorities, not heretics.

"not... acknowledged"—Only a few writings were unanimously accepted by all Catholic bishops and writers, all the way back to the beginning. This writing was not one of them.

"By others..."—That is, by other ecclesiastical authorities in the apostolic succession churches.

"public use"—That is, read as Holy Scripture in public worship services.[32]

"I understood by tradition..."—Judging by the preponderance of evidence cited by Eusebius throughout the *Ecclesiastical History*, his library had more source material from eastern centers (Syria, Palestine, Egypt) than from western centers (Italy, North Africa, Gaul, or Spain).

"made use of it"—He probably means "quoted from it."

ON THE EPISTLES OF PETER

We can examine another example of Eusebius's method by going back to an earlier part of the same discussion to see what Eusebius had to say about the First and Second Epistles of Peter:

As to the writings of Peter, one of his epistles called the first is *acknowledged as genuine*. This was anciently used by the ancient fathers in their writings as an *undoubted* work of the apostle. But that which is called the second, we have not, indeed, understood to be embodied [*endiathekon*] with the sacred books. Yet, as it appeared *useful to many*, it was studiously read with the other Scriptures. (*Hist. eccl.* 3.3.1)[33]

Comments

"acknowledged as genuine... by the ancient fathers"—First Eusebius says that 1 Peter is *universally acknowledged as genuine*, that is, by every orthodox bishop and theologian in the whole Catholic church everywhere in the Roman Empire, from Eusebius's day back to the time of the *palai presbyteroi*, the ancient elders; not a single orthodox authority ever cast a negative vote on this writing. His use of the term "acknowledged" (*anōmologētai*) is precisely the same word Origen used in his discussions of authenticity—and the Greek grammarians and philosophical schools before him. It was a standard term for this kind of discussion.

"useful to many... studiously read"—On the other hand, Eusebius had to report that this kind of unanimous consensus did not extend to another epistle ascribed to the Apostle Peter, called the Second Epistle of Peter; nor does he ever explain why. He merely reports the split opinion and adds immediately that "many" bishops and theologians of the orthodox Catholic faith found it "useful," and therefore it was "studiously read," i.e., regularly and intentionally used in worship and elsewhere—along with the other accepted epistle of Peter. My assumption is that it was joined to 1 Peter early on and that later orthodox authorities were loathe to leave it out in the face of widespread acceptance.

We begin to see how best to interpret Eusebius's language. Let us go now to the very first sentence of the whole book. There Eusebius tells the reader the main subjects of his history.

ON EUSEBIUS'S PURPOSE IN THE *ECCLESIASTICAL HISTORY*

It is my purpose to record the successions of the holy apostles together with the times since our Savior down to the present, to recount how many and important transactions are said to have occurred in ecclesiastical history, what individuals in the most noted places eminently governed and presided over the church, and what men also in their respective generations, whether with or without their writings, proclaimed the divine word. I will also describe the character, times, and number of those who, stimulated by the desire of innovation, and advancing to the greatest errors, announced themselves [as introducers of Knowledge (*gnōsis*) falsely so-called], like grievous wolves, unmercifully assaulting the flock of Christ. (*Hist. eccl.* 1.1.1)[34]

Comments

"record the successions of the holy apostles"—church historians have noted that Eusebius's *Ecclesiastical History* is unique for a number of reasons but primarily in that it is the first history to focus on persons, events, and developments in the Christian church. Previous histories tended to focus on the lives and accomplishments of the Roman emperors.[35] Eusebius says here that he will, as his prime objective, establish a comprehensive record of the historical chain of succession of the names, dates, and locations of all bishops who presided over churches that were founded by Jesus' apostles.

"together with the times since our Savior down to the present"—Eusebius will locate these various apostolic successions of bishops within their historical contexts, a task he prepared for by first compiling a complicated comparative chronology, the *Chronological Canons,* to keep his historical record consistent as he went along (note the reference to it at *Hist. eccl.* 1.1.6).[36]

"to recount how many and important transactions are said to have occurred in ecclesiastical history, what individuals in the most noted places eminently governed and presided over the church ..."—Eusebius was severely restricted in what he was able to cover by the resources of his library. Hence, he does not in fact preserve the names of all bishops in all apostolic succession churches within the Christian religion. Here he admits as much, saying that he will focus on the major centers of Catholic orthodoxy (which he does not name, but which we can ascertain—by looking at his narrative—as Rome, Antioch, Alexandria, and Jerusalem). Even here his records of successions are not complete.[37] Having said that, it is remarkable how many individuals, writings, and cities Eusebius did manage to record something about, beyond the great centers of orthodoxy.

"I will also describe the character, times, and number of those who, stimulated by the desire of innovation, advanced to the greatest errors . . ."—Not only will Eusebius name the most important bishops in their respective cities and generations, as well as the most important orthodox theologians (ordained or not), together with a list of their genuine writings, but Eusebius will also provide lists of the successions of the heretics and their main writings and teachings, so that all may clearly distinguish one from the other. In this way, Eusebius hoped to counteract Porphyry's smear of the Catholic name which associated it with the many deviant forms of Christianity. The heretics, Eusebius argues, had long mixed their religion with all sorts of extraneous doctrines and rituals. His effort was all the more important now that "the Christian corporation" had been elevated to a position of legitimacy in the Edict of Toleration issued by Constantine and Licinius in 313. Eusebius did not want there to be any doubt in the government's mind as to who belonged to the true "Christian corporation."[38]

So far, Eusebius has brought together the three main themes in his depiction: the unbroken chain of orthodoxy and its scripture as contrasted to the false successions and false scriptures of the deviant forms of Christianity. But he is still not finished with his introduction. There are four more topics to add to his agenda.

> It is my intention, also, to describe the calamities that swiftly over-
> whelmed the whole Jewish nation in consequence of their plots
> against our Savior; how often, by what means, and in what times
> the word of God encountered the hostility of the nations; what

eminent persons persevered in contending for it through those periods of blood and torture, beside the martyrdoms which have been endured in our own times; above all, to show the gracious and benign interposition of our Savior. (*Hist. eccl.* 1.1.2–3)

Comments

"It is my intention, also, to describe the calamities that swiftly overwhelmed the whole Jewish nation in consequence of their plots against our Savior. . . ."—In the eyes of Eusebius and his contemporaries in fourth-century orthodox Christianity, the crucifixion of Jesus of Nazareth had brought a series of terrible catastrophes upon the Jewish nation, culminating in their expulsion from Jerusalem in the days of Hadrian and the renaming and refounding of the city as a Roman colony named Aelia Capitolina. As he proceeds through his narrative, Eusebius periodically pauses to note these calamities.[39]

"how often, by what means, and in what times the word of God has encountered the hostility of the nations; what eminent persons persevered in contending for it through those periods of blood and torture . . . in our own times, and the benign interposition of our Savior [to end the persecution]."—Eusebius will also document each of the many persecutions that occurred in the church's 250-year history, which emperor instigated it, and which eminent bishops and theologians suffered martyrdom. His history will conclude with the complete triumph of the Christian church, as the Christian God brings about the complete collapse of the chief persecutors of the Great Persecution of 303–313—Diocletian, Galerius, Maxentius, and Maximian—and raises up a new Moses[40] in the form of the emperor Constantine, who will not only stop all further possibility of persecution, but through imperial edicts and personal example raise the Christian church to levels of advantage and power unheard of in all previous generations.

"These are the proposed subjects of the present work"—Eusebius asks the reader's indulgence concerning the many shortcomings of his narrative. No one has ever tried to write a history like his—he is attempting to walk "a trackless and unbeaten path" (*Hist. eccl.* 1.1.3).

Results of the Orthodox Scripture Selection Process

Having gained a better idea of the methods by which the orthodox assessed the various scriptures available to them, as reconstructed from Eusebius's discussion, let us now consider his statement of the results of this endeavor. Keep in mind that Eusebius and his predecessors sifted through more than 100 writings that had been cited or used as supposed apostolic writings, by some person or group, during the previous 250 years (for a fairly complete annotated list, see Appendix B). There were more than three dozen gospels, half a dozen acts, many additional letters of Paul (for example, *3 Corinthians*, the *Epistle to the Laodiceans*, a letter *To Mary*, an *Acts of Paul and Thecla*, and so on), many additional writings of Peter (a *Preaching of Peter*, a *Revelation of Peter*, an *Acts of Peter*) and John (a *Secret Teaching of John*, an *Acts of John* and several letters of John), and others, such as an *Epistle of the Apostles*, a *Teaching of the Apostles to the Nations* (now known by the first word, in Greek, *Didache*), and more. Although Eusebius does not discuss them all, in Books 2 through 7 he does comment on many of them repeatedly, citing authorities and quoting their comments, providing historical cross-checks where possible, and in general gathering all the evidence he could on the main candidates.

After a detailed discussion of many of the most likely writings in *Ecclesiastical History*, Books 2 and 3, at 3.25.1-7 Eusebius pauses to give a summary statement of the results of the selection process so far. After this passage, Eusebius will spend most of his energy discussing the "disputed" books, i.e., those that were neither fully accepted nor fully rejected. This summary, *Hist. eccl.* 3.25.1-7, is the most detailed list of approved and nonapproved writings of the New Testament to appear in the church up to that time. (See Table 5.2.)

"Genuine" or "acknowledged" writings

This appears to be the proper place to give a summary statement of the books of the New Testament already mentioned. And here among the first must be placed the holy quaternion of the Gospels; these are followed by the Book of the Acts of the Apostles; after this must be mentioned the Epistles of Paul, which are followed by the *acknowledged* First Epistle of John, as also the first of Peter, to be admitted in like manner. After these is to be placed, if proper, the Revelation of John, concerning which we shall offer the different opinions in due time. These, then, are *acknowledged as genuine.*[41]

Comments

"The holy quaternion of the Gospels"—Eusebius has carefully prepared for the first part of this summary in the preceding two books. He has assiduously given detailed reports about each Gospel—who its author was (by name), with date and reason for writing it; what his credentials were; who in the orthodox tradition had commented on it (quoting the comment in most cases)—and otherwise trying to determine the authorship, date, and orthodox content of each one as securely as possible. Why Eusebius refers to the four Gospels with the strange term "holy quaternion" (*hagia tetraktys*) is evidently a mystery to most translators, since neither "quaternion" nor "quartet" (as in choral quartet) is the right translation. The Greek is *tetraktys,* and it was the famous term used by the Pythagorean School for the set of their four sacred numbers, $1 + 2 + 3 + 4$ ($= 10$, ten being the perfect number).[42] Eusebius may have been thinking that the four Christian Gospels were like the Christian "perfect number": Jesus Christ. In any case, to my knowledge, this allusion to Pythagorean numerology is Eusebius's own invention; I am unable to find any use of this term in Origen or after Eusebius.

"Acts of the Apostles"—Eusebius does not so much verify the reliability and apostolic authorship of this writing in the foregoing chapters as draw heavily on it for much of his own historical narrative of the early period.

"Epistles of Paul"—This phrase is intentionally vague so as to be able to mean thirteen or fourteen letters, depending on whether one considers the Epistle to the Hebrews as genuine or not. Later, Eusebius will report on many authorities pro and con about this epistle.

"First Epistle of John" and "First (Epistle) of Peter"— He has briefly discussed the unanimous opinion regarding the complete authenticity of these two epistles earlier in *Hist. eccl.* 3.3.[43]

"Revelation of John"—At this point, we must note that here Eusebius is seriously inconsistent with his method. He says that the Revelation of John is accepted by some and not accepted by other apostolic succession authorities—which obviously means it is "disputed." Why Eusebius does not list it among the disputed writings, instead of here among the acknowledged writings, cannot be explained, except to say that Eusebius is occasionally inconsistent.

"acknowledged"—As we have already noted, "acknowledged" (*homologoumenoi*) is a shorthand expression that has a very precise meaning for Eusebius. It is important to remember its full meaning whenever we see this shorthand expression: it means unanimously *acknowledged* by all orthodox bishops in apostolic succession churches throughout the empire, all the way back to the beginning. (Eusebius's fuller expression for "church" was "the whole church of God under heaven" or "all the churches under heaven": *Hist. eccl.* 3.24.2.[44])

"genuine"—That is, authentic, in Eusebius's view: a writing that was actually produced by one of Jesus' disciples or their immediate assistants (Luke, Mark). These two terms, "acknowledged as genuine," taken together, mean that, according to all the evidence Eusebius has presented or has in his library, there is not a single dissenting vote by any Catholic bishop or orthodox scholar anywhere in the far-flung Catholic churches in Rome, Alexandria, Antioch, or Jerusalem, or in any lesser places, from the beginning all the way down to his day, regarding authorship of any of these twenty writings. It represented a historic, unanimous consensus regarding each writing.

Note that this judgment does not include the opinions of the various Gnostic sects, or the Marcionites, or the Jewish Christian Ebionites, or any of the other heretical groups, who all denied that the orthodox Catholics were in possession of genuine apostolic writings. But that is precisely the question, as we saw Tertullian

say earlier.[45] How do people on either side know they are right?
Who is to judge which of us is telling the truth? Tertullian's answer,
as Irenaeus before him, and Origen and Eusebius after him, was
to point to the apostolic succession churches and say, in effect:
"Because those churches are based upon the apostolic tradition,
those bishops are more likely than anyone else to know which writings are genuine writings of Jesus' apostles and which writings are
not. What is the combined verdict of all of the bishops in apostolic
succession?"

"DISPUTED" WRITINGS

Eusebius next lists the books that are in the category that Greek
grammarians and philosophers called "doubtful" or "disputed" —
writings where there was a split vote, with some bishops on record
as saying the author of the writing in question actually was an apostle, while other bishops or orthodox theologians were on record as
denying this claim.

> Among the *disputed* books, although they are *known* and *approved*
> *by many*, is reputed that called the Epistle of James and [the Epistle]
> of Jude. Also [disputed are] the Second Epistle of Peter and those
> called the Second and Third [Epistles] of John, [because some
> authorities cannot decide] whether they are by the evangelist
> [Gospel author] or by some other [person with] the same name.
> (*Hist. eccl.* 3.25.3)

Comments

"known and approved by many"— Again, Eusebius is stating the
facts as they have come to him, or as he chooses to present them.
By modern standards, we may be in a position to know far more
than he did about the actual evidence that had accumulated in all
branches of the Christian church during its first 250 years,[46] but
by ancient standards, and given the admittedly limited scope of
the library at Caesarea, Eusebius's openness and accuracy of cita-
tion were much higher than the norm for his day, whether among
pagan or Christian historians. "Known" means that orthodox bishops and theologians have given written evidence that they knew of

it and used it as an authentic apostolic writing. "Approved" means approved for use in worship or cited in writing as an authority in Catholic theological writings.

"is reputed"—Eusebius is relying on records and traditions from the orthodox fathers, not named.

"Epistles of James and Jude"—These are epistles thought by some to have been written by Jesus' brothers James (in Hebrew, Jacob) and Jude (in Hebrew, Judah). These men were not apostles or disciples of Jesus but were believed to be Jesus' brothers or half-brothers. James rose to prominence after Jesus' resurrection and ascension to become the head of the congregation in Jerusalem (Acts 12:17; 15:13; 21:18), but Jude is scarcely attested anywhere in earliest orthodox Christianity. Eusebius mentions both men earlier in his history, but why these writings were rejected (by some) he does not say.

"2nd Peter and 2nd and 3rd John"—These writings suffered from a similar problem. Orthodox bishops and theologians rarely (if ever) made use of these writings, hence they were not well known. They were not unorthodox in their content; they were just not well attested by any writer in the apostolic orthodox tradition.

A Second Group of "Disputed" Writings

Eusebius now takes up another subset of the "disputed" writings, a group he designates as "spurious" (*nothoi*). This term was widely used in Greek discussions of literary authenticity and had a very specific sense: "illegitimate," as in a "bastard" child, that is, a child who may look like one of the parents but is in fact known to be not a "genuine" offspring of both parents. Like a counterfeit coin, something that is spurious *looks* like the real thing, until you look closer.[47] I will explain in a moment what Eusebius meant by setting this group apart from the preceding group of "disputed" writings.

> Among the *spurious* must be numbered both the books called the Acts of Paul and that called Pastor, and the Revelation of Peter. Besides these, the books called the Epistle of Barnabas and what are called the Institutions of the Apostles. Moreover, as I said before, if it should appear right, the Revelation of John, which some, as

before said, *reject* but others *rank among the genuine.* There are
also some who number among these the Gospel according to the
Hebrews, with which those of the Hebrews who have received
Christ are particularly delighted. (*Hist. eccl.* 3.25.4-5)

The first four writings have in common that they were each
reputed to be compositions of or about actual apostles or their
assistants: the *Acts of Paul,* the *Pastor* (better known as *The Shepherd
of Hermas*), the *Revelation of Peter,* and the *Epistle of Barnabas.*
Although Eusebius earlier has briefly mentioned the persons
Hermas[48] and Barnabas,[49] he does not discuss these writings elsewhere, except to cast doubt on their apostolic origin.[50]

But that doubt applied as well to all of the "disputed" writings.
Why is this second group of writings separated from the first and
designated as *spurious,* that is, counterfeit? None of the writings in
this or the previous group is accused of lacking orthodox *content.*
The problem seems rather to be uncertainty regarding whether
these writings were really written by apostles (or their assistants). I
suggest that what distinguished these writings from the previously
discussed "disputed" writings can be seen in the phrase "approved
by many." The first group of "disputed" writings were well known
in all of the major Catholic churches, and a significant proportion of the bishops (though not all) thought they were genuine.
On the other hand, this second group of "disputed" writings, which
Eusebius calls "spurious," were scarcely known or used by any of
them, as we can see from Eusebius' scanty or non-existent references elsewhere in his *History* to the *Epistle of Barnabas* or the
Institutions of the Apostles. That is, these particular writings were
not "well-known and approved by many," and thus they appear here
in Eusebius' catalogue as a distinct subset of the "disputed" writings.
He declares them "spurious," by which he apparently means that
they are writings with orthodox content but probably composed
by someone else in the name of an apostle—and not well known
or widely approved among Catholic authorities.

Eusebius's mention of the Apocalypse of John presents a peculiar case. He declares that "some reject it but others rank it among the genuine" writings of the apostle. This is confusing. We should have expected him to discuss it earlier, with the first group of *disputed* writings, rather than here, with the *spurious* writings: it was hardly unknown, after all. As we will see from Eusebius' repeated references to it later in his *History*, it had a long history of affirmative support from some of the most eminent bishops and theologians in the orthodox Catholic network: Irenaeus, Justin Martyr, Melito, and Origen.[51]

So why does Eusebius mention it here, among the *spurious* writings? The best answer I can offer is that Eusebius discusses the Apocalypse of John among writings he considers a subset of the *disputed* writings (rather than as a completely different set of "rejected" writings: more on those in a moment). But there is more here than meets the eye.

The Apocalypse of John was uniquely troubling for Eusebius and some of his fellow scholars within the Catholic Church. Prominent among them was Dionysius, bishop of Alexandria and a contemporary of Eusebius. Dionysius waged a powerful campaign against the tradition that the Apocalypse of John had been written by the Apostle John, author of the Gospel. Eusebius quotes page after page of Dionysius's argument, almost in full, in his *History*.[52] Dionysius ended with the ringing declaration that there is no doubt *someone* named John received a revelation, but it was not John, the son of Zebedee, the disciple of the Lord. Equally damaging was the contention of Dionysius and others that the Apocalypse of John was orthodox only if it were interpreted *allegorically*.[53] If taken literally, they argued, it expressed the heresy of Cerinthus (whom some alleged to be its actual author). Cerinthus had been a second-century heretic who had taught that Christ would return, set up a physical kingdom of God upon the earth, and rule for 1,000 years.[54] Although Eusebius does not record any opponent of the Apocalypse saying so, the problem may have been that the sort of this-worldly, realistic eschatological hope it expresses, though once acceptable among the orthodox, was no longer so in Eusebius's day. Now that the Christian God in his providence had raised up a Christian emperor to be his champion on earth, and now that this "rod of God's anger" was busily laying waste to the church's foes and simultaneously strengthening and enriching the Catholic church itself, it simply would not do to speak of Christ coming back to destroy the evil Roman empire along with all the other powers destined for wrath (see Rev. 19:17f.), and setting up a physical Kingdom of God on earth which would necessarily supplant the newly triumphant Catholic church! In short, despite a long period during which few orthodox leaders found anything objectionable in the Apocalypse of John, in Eusebius's day it had suddenly become hotly contested both in terms of authorship and orthodoxy.

Eusebius concludes his discussion of *spurious* writings by referring to the *Gospel of the Hebrews,* which he does not discuss anywhere else. Here again, the problem may have been uncertainty as to the identity of the author and a lack of widespread acceptance of the writing. We know from modern scholarship that the *Gospel of the Hebrews* may have been related to the Gospel according to Matthew. We have no indication that a lack of orthodox content was its problem. Like others in the *spurious* group, however, there was no record of its being a genuine apostolic writing, and no support for it outside Syria-Palestine.

At this point, Eusebius rounds off what he has said so far about the *acknowledged* writings (total 20), the *disputed* writings, including those that were well known but of uncertain apostolic authorship (total 5), and those that were, in his view, *spurious* (total 7) (see Table 5.2):

> These [writings I have just been discussing] may be said to be all concerning which there is any *dispute.* We have . . . added here a catalogue of these [disputed writings], in order to distinguish those [in the first list] that are *true, genuine,* and *well-authenticated* writings from those others [in the second two lists] which are not only not embodied in the canon [*endiathēkoi*]*[55] but likewise *disputed,* notwithstanding that they are *recognized* by most ecclesiastical writers (*Hist. eccl.* 3.25.6a).[56]

Comments

"These may be said to be all concerning which there is any dispute."—Note that Eusebius here classes *both* of the immediately preceding groups under the general category of *disputed* (*antilegomenoi*).

"We have ... added here a catalogue ... recognized by most ecclesiastical writers"—The key to understanding this confusing sentence is to realize that it refers backward to the two categories of writings so far discussed:[57] first, to those writings whose apostolic authorship was universally *acknowledged* by orthodox Catholic

TABLE 5.2. Eusebius's catalogue at *Hist. eccl.* 3.25.1-7

Acknowledged as genuine by all	The "holy quaternion" of Gospels (Matthew, Mark, Luke, John)
	The Acts of the Apostles
	The (13) Epistles of Paul
	1 John
	1 Peter
	("if proper") the Revelation of John
Disputed—(a) "though known and approved by many"	James
	Jude
	2 Peter
	2, 3 John
Disputed—(b) and "spurious," i.e. not known or approved by many	*Acts of Paul*
	Shepherd of Hermas
	Revelation of Peter
	Epistle of Barnabas
	Institutions of the Apostles
	("if it should appear right") the Revelation of John
	Gospel according to the Hebrews
Rejected by all as not genuine, i.e., not having apostolic authorship; also other heretical writings	*Gospel of Peter*
	Gospel of Thomas
	Pseudo-Matthew and other Gospels
	Acts of Andrew
	Acts of John and other writings

authorities, and second, to two sets of "disputed" writings concerning which bishops in apostolic succession and orthodox Catholic scholars were divided in their opinions.

To anticipate our discussion in Chapter 7, many of the writings in the first set of disputed writings (but *not* those Eusebius regards as "spurious") will eventually be included in the New Testament. In particular, they will be included by Jerome in his officially sanctioned Latin version of the New Testament after approval by several church councils in the fourth century. Eusebius, on the other hand, like a good philosopher reporting the state of the question, is content to leave them perched squarely on the fence, neither in nor out.

"True, genuine, and well authenticated": Eusebius's Three "Tests"[58]

Eusebius writes, in a paragraph discussed earlier (*Hist. eccl.* 3.25.1-2), about the group of "universally acknowledged" writings. In the paragraph just discussed (3.25.6), he reveals that all of them had met three distinct, make-or-break tests: each one was *"true, genuine, and well authenticated."* That is, each of these writings—according to the consistent, universal judgments of all of the orthodox authorities Eusebius had available to him (including bishops in all the apostolic succession churches, as well as authorities in many lesser centers)—were stated to be (1) *true,* that is, accurately and fully teaching the Gospel of Jesus Christ. I call this the *test of theological orthodoxy.* Moreover, this far-flung network of orthodox testimony also bore unanimous witness that each and every one of these writings was (2) *genuine,* that is, had been written by one of Christ's twelve apostles and Paul (or their immediate assistants). I call this the *test of genuine apostolic authorship.* A third test—whether a writing was (3) *acknowledged* by regular and consistent use by orthodox churches—will be discussed below. (See Table 5.3.)

THE FULL MEANING OF "GENUINENESS"
The second test—concerning whether a writing was held to be "genuine"—merits further discussion. The fundamental purpose of the

TABLE 5.3. Eusebius's Three Tests—the "Three-Layer Sieve"

"True" (*the theological test*)	Does it accurately and fully teach the Gospel of Jesus Christ?
"Genuine" (*the test of genuine apostolic authorship*)	Was it actually written by one of Christ's twelve apostles or Paul?
"Well-authenticated" (*the use test*)	Was it used by bishops in churches of apostolic succession, in public worship and as a source for theology and church governance?

entire orthodox Scripture selection process was to identify, with all the certainty their methods would permit, exactly those writings bequeathed to posterity by Jesus' apostles. If we compare the second- and third-century Catholic church's methods to those of the Greek philosophical schools, we might imagine that they would eagerly have preserved any writing by the Founder, Jesus, as well; but since (like Socrates) he had not written down his teachings, identifying and carefully preserving what his own disciples (and their followers) wrote would necessarily have become the secondary goal.

Even here, few of Jesus' disciples had put what they had known into written form. In fact, writing down Christ's teachings and actions appears not to have been a priority for any of the disciples at first, since they expected Jesus to return on the Day of Judgment almost immediately. They reportedly waited for him in the Temple (the obvious place to wait: Acts 2:46, 3:1). But Jesus did not return as they expected. To the contrary, as weeks and months stretched into years, several things the early disciples did not expect happened instead:

- The Gentile mission was gaining converts rapidly, which posed a number of problems for the Jewish leadership of the Jerusalem church. The Gentile Christians ate all manner of unclean foods; they were uncircumcised (and resisted getting circumcised); they were ignorant of Torah, and had little aptitude for learning proper halakah. Most embarrassing of all, they were responding to the Good News in Jesus Christ in greater numbers than were their Jewish neighbors. The earliest records bear ample witness to the tensions between these two groups.

• Suddenly, in 66 C.E., rebellion broke out in Jerusalem as Jewish freedom fighters, outraged by the Roman prefect's theft of money from the Temple treasury, destroyed the Roman garrison and liberated the city. Wanting no part of the ensuing strife and turmoil, the Christian Jews in Jerusalem—including the remnants of Jesus' family—fled across the Jordan and, according to a tradition that Eusebius transmits (see *Hist. eccl.* 3.5.3), settled in a little Jewish community named Pella, in the Decapolis. Not long after that, they dropped from sight; we have no further record of them.

• At about the same time, during the early to mid-60s C.E., both Peter and Paul were arrested and executed by the Roman emperor Nero in Rome. When word of these executions reached the East, the little Christian congregations everywhere must have been stunned: their two most active leaders had been executed! How could the Christian God have allowed this to happen?

Such powerful shocks, coming hard on the heels of the public lynching in the year 62 C.E. of James, the brother of Jesus and the leader of the Jerusalem Christians, must have struck terror into their hearts. It may also have galvanized the remaining leadership to begin writing down some of their traditions, lest the whole first generation die off and take their memories with them.[59]

In the ensuing years, some of Jesus' disciples (and their assistants) put what they remembered about the Lord into writing. Books 2 and 3 of Eusebius's *History* attempt a painstaking reconstruction of who these apostles were.[60] As time went by, however, more and more writings allegedly by "apostles" began mysteriously to surface so that, by the middle of the second century, there were more than a dozen gospels allegedly authored by the apostles, numerous letters of Paul (many more than what we have in our New Testament today), and many more letters and tracts allegedly by Peter and John, such as the *Gospel of Peter* and the *Secret Teaching of John*. This proliferation of writings claiming to be "apostolic" was experienced by the Catholic churches as a problem requiring diligent discernment. Eusebius describes a common pattern: when a bishop in one of the apostolic churches encountered a previously unknown writing, he would examine it, and if he determined that it was a forgery, he sent warning letters to fellow bishops in other orthodox Catholic churches in the region.[61]

Meanwhile, the Jewish people staged two great revolts against Roman domination in the eastern Roman Empire and Palestine in 113–115 and 132–135. These revolts were bloodily suppressed at great cost and, after the second such revolt in less than a generation, a furious Roman Senate under Hadrian passed an edict banning all Jews from Jerusalem on pain of death, made the city a colony of Rome (effectively destroying the shekel-based economy), and renamed it Aelia Capitolina (after the gods worshiped in the Capitoline temple in Rome and Hadrian's family name). They canceled all Jewish privileges and demanded harsh annual tribute from every Jew living under Roman jurisdiction.

Since at this time the civil authorities often could not tell the difference between a Jew and a Christian, sometimes these punishments also fell on Christians. Such confusion is understandable, since neither group would participate in the official sacrifices to the gods. Both believed in only one god, and that all others were idols, and both groups tended to live together in little communities within their urban locales. To make matters worse for the Christians, they worshipped a crucified Jewish felon as their "king"—something the Roman authorities never understood, and something that gave rise to the popular idea that Christians were insane. By the middle of the second century, Christians had a huge PR problem on their hands. How could they prove that they were neither Jews, nor traitors to the Roman state?

Different versions of Christianity handled these complex problems differently. Some retreated into greater secrecy and arcane ideas understood only by the initiated. Others tried to find safety in living in more remote areas. Among Catholic Christians, one way of making clear that they neither were Jews nor had any rebellious intentions regarding the Roman government came in the form of open letters to the emperor that began to appear around the middle of the second century. A classic example of this genre was the *Apology* (or Defense) by Justin Martyr, in which he proclaims to the Emperors Antoninus Pius and Marcus Aurelius that "we Christians are your best allies and subjects," while "the rebellious and blood-thirsty Jews" deserved everything they had gotten in the brutal sup-pression of their revolts.[62]

Other Christian attempts to distinguish themselves from the Jews took an even more radical bent. Around mid-century, the charismatic Christian leader Marcion of Pontus insisted that Jesus had never been Jewish to begin with and that the Christian gospels that portrayed him as the son of Jewish parents were infected with "Jewish blasphemy." Marcion went on to claim that the god of the Jews was a demon while the god of Jesus had previously never been heard of. He called for a sweeping rejection of all orthodox Christian leaders who had allowed the Christian message to become tainted with "Jewish corruption." As we have seen, Marcion insisted the only accurate historical narrative of Jesus of Nazareth was his own version (apparently the Gospel of Luke, once the "Jewish interpo-lations"—all of chapters 1 and 2, plus many other passages—had been removed). Moreover, Marcion insisted that the only true apos-tolic letters were ten letters of Paul (omitting the Pastoral Epistles), with Paul's stridently anti-Judaizing letter to Galatians featured prominently in the first position. He rejected the Old Testament in its entirety as the worship of a demon. Though they seem extreme to us today, Marcion's ideas about authentic Christian scripture, his fundamentally anti-Jewish message, and his insistence upon a pure and ascetic lifestyle attracted a huge and sympathetic following.

Meanwhile, certain learned "philosophers" from the Gnostic branch of the Christian church, named Valentinus and Basilides, showed up around mid-century in Rome claiming that the orthodox Catholic authorities were relying on deficient accounts of the Lord Jesus, while they themselves were in possession of secret gospels that were far superior. Several orthodox Catholic bishops and theolo-gians took up the challenge, such as Irenaeus, bishop of Lugdunum (Lyons) in southern Gaul (ca. 120–ca. 200). He sought to demon-strate the groundlessness of the Valentinians' claims, by pointing to the chain of orthodox Christian bishops with their unbroken tradi-tion going back to the time of the apostles and Jesus Christ. Irenaeus maintained that since these bishops had handed down whatever writings the apostles had composed, there was no reason to think there were any secret gospels, filled with previously unheard-of ideas. Secret teachings that Jesus never told the Apostle Peter, the chief of his disciples? Secret rituals that Jesus never revealed to John, his most beloved disciple? Irenaeus called the Gnostics' claim absurd and baseless. The Lord Jesus' authentic teachings had been deposited in the apostolic succession churches, he insisted, and were in wide circulation among the orthodox Catholic church.

The complex and tumultuous history I have just summarized included developments that defied the expectations of the earliest churches and the challenge of distinguishing orthodox faith from Judaism, on one side, and Gnostic Christianity, on the other. These challenges highlight the urgency with which orthodox Catholic leaders approached the task of identifying "true, genuine, and well-authenticated" writings from among the multitude of anonymous and pseudonymous writings available.

"WELL-AUTHENTICATED" WRITINGS

Finally, we come to the third test, "well-authenticated." This test I call the "use" test. For Eusebius, it meant this: Was the writing in question actively used by the orthodox Catholic bishops in all of the main apostolic succession churches in public worship and as a source for theology and church government, from earliest times down to Eusebius' own day? If not, the writing either went into the "disputed" column, or, if there was explicit or open rejection of a writing, or total silence regarding it (indicating that none of the orthodox Catholic bishops had ever heard of it), it went into the "rejected" column.

These three tests functioned individually and collectively as a "three-layer sieve"[63] to screen out fraudulent, fictitious, or heretical writings. They were applied with intense determination: by the time Eusebius wrote his *Ecclesiastical History,* only twenty writings out of more than 100 candidates[64] had made it through this rigorous screening process into the charmed circle of the New Testament.

"REJECTED" WRITINGS

And what of the writings judged not "well authenticated"? Here is what Eusebius has to say about the great pile of "rejected" writings:

> Thus we have it in our power to know both those books [which are universally accepted as genuine writings of the apostles or at least partially accepted] and those that are adduced by the heretics under the name of the apostles, such as, namely, the Gospel of Peter, the Gospel of Thomas, [pseudo-]Matthew, and other [Gospels] besides them, or such as contain the Acts . . . of Andrew, the Acts of John, and still other [writings not having apostles' names in their titles], of which no one of those writers in the ecclesiastical succession has condescended to make any mention in his works. (*Hist. eccl.* 3.25.6b)

Comments

Eusebius seems to distinguish two sub-groups in the "rejected" category. First, he names pseudonymous writings, that is, writings forged in the name of one of the apostles as if to convey their teachings. He mentions a few of these: the *Gospel of Peter*; the [Coptic] *Gospel of Thomas*;[65] another gospel with the name "Matthew" in the title, the identity of which is no longer clear, "and other [gospels] besides them," such as the *Gospel of Judas*[66] or gospels purporting to be by close associates of Jesus and the apostles, such as the *Gospel of Mary* (Magdalene) and the *Gospel of Nicodemus,* or about important figures in Jesus' life, e.g., the *Acts of Pilate.*[67] Eusebius also names various Acts, still speaking of books that had apostles' names in their titles, such as the *Acts of Andrew,* the *Acts of John,* and other Acts (he may have had in mind the *Acts of Peter,* the Acts *of Paul and Thecla,*[68] or the *Acts of Thomas*). Second, Eusebius's reference to "*still others*" may refer to writings that do *not* have apostles' names in their titles (such as the *Gospel of Truth*).

Concerning both kinds of "rejected" writings, Eusebius says, no bishop or theologian or historian in all of the orthodox, Catholic apostolic succession churches ever mentioned them in his works. Here we must be on guard against Eusebius's rhetoric. Modern scholarship can easily show that some of his orthodox Catholic predecessors did in fact mention them repeatedly: Irenaeus did, as did Clement of Alexandria and, certainly, Origen. I think Eusebius was simply reaching here for a resounding conclusion. We can agree that most of these writings were not cited positively by any orthodox Catholic authority. Even so, Eusebius has not finished the discussion just yet: he adds one very significant paragraph.

Two Corroborative Criteria

Eusebius next introduces two additional tests, that serve to corroborate the earlier criteria: *style* and *theological consistency.*

> Indeed, [in these "rejected" writings] the character of the *style* itself is very different from that of the apostles, and the sentiment and the purport of those things that are advanced in them, deviating as far as possible from *sound orthodoxy,* evidently proves that they are the fictions of heretical men. Therefore, they are [not even] to be ranked among the *spurious* writings but are to be rejected as altogether absurd and impious. (*Hist. eccl.* 3.25.7)[69]

Eusebius does not explain why he mentioned these two tests at the end of his discussion, which is unfortunate, since they played a very significant role. I see them operating as a kind of "double-check" regarding the fateful decision to reject such a great number of writings. He provides two additional tests (after the "three layer sieve" used earlier) to make sure that the decision to reject in each case was well founded.

The need for these additional criteria is apparent enough, if we give the matter some thought. Imagine a situation in which, by some accidental lapse of tradition or breakdown in communication over time, a genuine apostolic writing somehow ended up preserved way out in the boondocks, far from the major Christian centers, so that the orthodox leaders who played so important a role in the selection process were unaware of its existence. On the principles of the "three-layer sieve" just described, we can imagine that such a writing would have been completely overlooked, or not mentioned favorably by anyone, despite the fact that it was genuine.

We might imagine that Eusebius proposes these two additional tests as criteria that might be used in the case just such novel writings were brought forward from the "hinterlands," so to speak. We cannot demonstrate that Eusebius was planning for such an eventuality, but these criteria would have proven useful in such a circumstance by allowing authorities to measure the style and theological content of the "new" writing against that of the tried and tested "genuine" writings. In fact Eusebius gives two examples of these tests actually being applied within the *Ecclesiastical History* itself.[70]

The first additional test was to consider the *Greek style* of the writing: its *distinctive vocabulary,* its *phraseology* (grammatical peculiarities and characteristic turns of phrase), the *sophistication* of its Greek (was it written in good Greek or the Greek of someone whose primary language was something else, like Syriac, Coptic, or Latin?). This was very important, and Catholic scholars well knew of the great variety of sophistication in the Greek of New Testament writers, even within the Pauline corpus. Thus, if a writing were to turn up claiming to be a long-lost letter of Paul (e.g. "third Corinthians"), or if someone unexpectedly discovered a fragment of Acts not in the canonical version, the test of Greek style would mean that these unknown fragments must mirror the Greek style of one of the universally accepted writings by that same author. (Modern scholars apply just such tests in comparing the Greek style of the Gospel of John with the First Epistle of John, or Paul's Epistle to the Galatians with 1 Corinthians.)

The trouble is, this test has the same shortcoming as the "three-layer sieve": the writing in question has to match something already accepted in order to make it into the "inner circle." But what if the writing in question were in a totally unknown or unique Greek style, like a writing claiming to be from the apostle Nathaniel or Andrew, the brother of John? The question is not far-fetched, after all: Eusebius discovered what he considered to be a genuine letter of Jesus to Abgar (Agbar), king of Edessa, in that city's archives. The logic of the test of style was such that the letter would have failed the test, even though it might well have been the sort of genuine, but "unknown" writing suggested above.

The second test could function as a partial remedy for this flaw in the first one. Examine the theology, or, in Eusebius words, ascertain whether "the sentiment and the purport of those things that are advanced in them, deviate . . . from sound orthodoxy."[71] In other words, the unknown writing must not represent a radical departure, but in one way or another make the same kinds of theological points in the same ways as the combined testimony of the already approved writings. Note that the "loophole" in the three layer sieve and the test of style does not apply to this theological test. It is difficult to imagine Paul writing one kind of theology in his acknowledged letters and then suddenly coming up with a radically different theology in a newly discovered letter. This principle applies in particular to the unexpected appearance of allegedly genuine, long-lost gospel accounts of the teachings of Jesus, such as the Coptic *Gospel of Thomas* or the *Gospel of Judas*. The church already has a number of universally acknowledged gospels which they contain a wide spectrum of Jesus' teachings. If a gospel were to emerge from the sands of Egypt that portrayed a Jesus Christ very different from the combined portrait in the four Gospels, it would fail Eusebius's theological test. The acknowledged Synoptic Gospels and John offer depictions of Jesus Christ that are quite different at many points, yet there are also strong points of contact among all four, especially regarding the Passion narrative. From the time of Irenaeus at least, the four have been taken by orthodox Catholic authorities to represent a genuine, combined, apostolic witness that any new writing would have to match.

Excursus: Ways Not Taken

What kinds of tests or methods did Eusebius and the orthodox authorities *not* use?

One way to learn more about something is to find out what it is not. In this case, we are in a position to learn many things about the orthodox selection of scripture by examining different sorts of methods and tests that, although normally used for serious religious issues and decisions, were *not* used in deliberations over scripture.

One can read through all the pages of Tertullian's attempt to prove that the orthodox version of the Gospels—especially Luke—

are the true, authentic versions of the apostolic originals, or Origen's lengthy analysis of the true text of the Old Testament, or the arguments of Eusebius himself, and one will never find any mention that *they used divination*—examining the flight of birds, entrails of a sheep, or any of the other methods commonly accepted in the Roman world—to decide which books were genuine apostolic writings and which were not. Such a suggestion may strike us as absurd today; these authorities were, after all, Christians! But *Christian scriptures themselves* provide an example of a sort of Christian divination: *casting lots*—similar to the modern custom of flipping a coin to obtain the answer to a crucial decision (from God) when humans feel the decision should be out of human control.[72] According to the Acts of the Apostles, the eleven apostles implored God to give them a sign indicating whom to choose to fill Judas' vacant place:

> Then they prayed and said, "Lord, you know everyone's heart. Show us which one of these two you have chosen to take the place in this ministry and apostleship from which Judas turned aside to go to his own place." And *they cast lots* for them, and the lot fell on Matthias; and he was added to the eleven apostles. (Acts 1:24-26)[73]

But we have no evidence, either in Eusebius or any of his predecessors in the orthodox churches, that anyone ever cast lots to determine which of the hundreds of writings bearing apostles' names were genuine or counterfeit.

We have no evidence that anyone ever relied on dreams, visions, portents, signs, omens, or voices from heaven, to get help in deciding which writings to accept and which to reject. All of these were common enough in the biblical records and in the Christian culture of the time. Yet we never hear of anyone, confronted by the bewildering array of more than 100 writings, all bearing apostle's names (or close to it), praying, "Oh Lord, thou who canst see through the evil stratagems of the Adversary, give us a sign! May lightning strike the books created by the Enemy and burn them up—but preserve the rest!" No such action was ever taken. And yet we do know of several cases where visions were received by Peter and Paul, helping them make major decisions regarding on where to go in the early days of the Christian mission, or what to eat.[74] Why didn't the later authorities ask God or the Holy Spirit to help them decide which writings were genuine and which were counterfeit? It was an obvious thing to do, but we have no evidence that they did so.

Neither did they ever ask the question, "Is this writing inspired or not?" as part of their deliberations in deciding which writings to keep and which to reject.[75] This fact may seem surprising, since one would think that this was the real issue at stake. Christians today regularly say that the Bible is inspired of the Holy Spirit: wouldn't that have been the first question the early Catholic authorities would have asked? The problem was, inspiration was thought to be widely active in all branches of the Christian religion, not just among the orthodox—inspiration being exclusively what the Montanists relied on, for example—so that *every* writing was thought by *someone* to be inspired. (Indeed, the idea of consciously producing an inspired writing was not that uncommon: the *Shepherd of Hermas* explicitly claims to be inspired by God.) Since inspiration was a common, wide-spread phenomenon among Christians of all types, it could hardly help the orthodox in the critical task of separating genuine from forged apostolic writings.

In fact divine inspiration was so often claimed by heretics that orthodox Catholics learned to disregard such claims as utterly fraudulent and groundless. Eusebius says about a certain Menander, the "successor" of Simon Magus, that he

> exhibited himself as an instrument of diabolical wickedness . . . reveling in pretensions to miracles, saying he was the Savior sent from the invisible worlds for the salvation of men [and that everyone] should participate in the baptism imparted by him. (*Hist. eccl.* 3.26.1).

On another occasion, Eusebius quoted a second-century orthodox writer's complaint[76] regarding a rival Christian leader, a certain Cerinthus, that Cerinthus, "by means of revelations which he pretended were written by a great apostle [namely, John], also falsely pretended to wonderful things, as if they were shown to him by angels . . ." (*Hist. eccl.* 3.28.1). The same applied to the orthodox Catholic reaction to the Montanists' claims to possess the Holy Spirit. One of the best examples of this is Eusebius' quote of an unknown late second-century orthodox writer from eastern Asia, an associate of Bishop Claudius Apollinaris of Hierapolis, about the extravagant claims to possess the Spirit among the Montanists:

> . . . A recent convert, Montanus by name . . . was carried away in spirit and wrought up into a kind of frenzy and irregular ecstasy, raving and speaking and uttering strange things, and proclaiming what was contrary to the institutions that had prevailed in the church as handed down and preserved in succession from earliest times. . . . Others, as if elated by the holy spirit and the gift of grace . . . [made similar outrageous claims, etc.]. Those that were deceived were Phrygians; and the same inflated spirit taught them to revile the whole church under heaven, because it gave neither access nor honor to this false spirit of prophecy. (*Hist. eccl.* 5.16.7, 9)

The orthodox bishops in the region banded together and sent letters of warning out to their brethren in the region (*Hist. eccl.* 5.19). In short, claims to inspiration, no matter how extravagant, were of no avail unless what was inspired coincided with received orthodoxy.

Concluding our catalogue of procedures or tests that were not applied by the orthodox Catholics in the scripture selection process, we come to martyrdom. Was martyrdom ever used as an argument to support claims to which writings were genuine and which were not? The answer is a quick and decisive *No*. Here again, the orthodox were not impressed by the fact that many followers of Montanus or Marcion were willing to die for their beliefs. An anonymous Catholic writer, an associate of Apollinaris, bishop of Hierapolis, put it this way:

> But since they [the Montanists] are at a loss what to reply to the refutation of their errors, they attempt to take refuge in their martyrs, saying they have many martyrs and this is one sure evidence of the power of that spirit which they call prophetical. But this [claim] is nothing the more true on that account. For some of the other heresies also have a vast number of martyrs, but neither

> do we [orthodox Catholics] the more on that account agree with
> them, nor acknowledge that they have truth on their side. Indeed,
> they who are called Marcionites say that they had vast numbers
> that were martyrs for Christ, but they do not confess Christ in
> truth. (*Hist. eccl.* 5.16.20–21)

That may seem cold-hearted but it is quite logical. The mere fact
that people are willing to die for something does not prove that
it is true. History is full of individuals and large groups who have
fallen prey to great delusions for which they are willing to die, and
sometimes they do die for them. Nazi Germany is one example,
Jonestown is another, Heaven's Gate in California (where people
committed suicide believing they would be translated to alien space-
ships afterward) is another, of many that we could mention.

The argument cuts both ways, of course. Christians sometimes declare that the Gospels *must* be true because the people
who wrote them were willing to die for them. Unfortunately, that
argument falls to the ground for the same reason that the orthodox
Catholic church rejected the many martyrs of the Montanists and
the Marcionites. Unless the idea is true in itself, dying for it won't
make it true.

Conclusion

We may summarize the orthodox scripture selection process as
reflected in the pages of Eusebius' *Ecclesiastical History*. First of all,
Eusebius cites public tradition, explicitly names his sources, and
frequently quotes them verbatim and at length—a fairly uncommon thing to do in his day.[77] His writing is clearly meant to be part
of a public, collaborative search for an objective historical decision
as to whether a particular writing was actually written by one of
Jesus' disciples or not. Secondly, this very public search went on for
at least 150 years—more like 200—as hundreds of scholars and
bishops in the apostolic succession churches vigilantly defended the
few genuine writings known to them. Thirdly, these same bishops
sought not only to identify and preserve these writings, but interpret them accurately.

In his *Ecclesiastical History,* Eusebius patiently compiled the detailed verdicts as to genuine or spurious authorship across the far-flung network of orthodox Catholic bishops and scholars in the apostolic succession churches. To warrant the coveted verdict "acknowledged," these authorities all had to agree on a candidate writing over the entire 200 year time period. A single "no" vote was sufficient to doom a writing forever, as happened with the *Gospel of Peter,* which the orthodox Bishop Serapion of Antioch rejected.[78] Given such painstaking, lengthy, far-flung collaborative efforts, and Eusebius' standard that "acknowledged" meant 100% acknowledged, not 80% or 90%, it should not surprise anyone that the resulting list of "acknowledged" writings in *Hist. eccl.* 3.25.1-3 is so small. The margin for error was made as small as Eusebius and his predecessors could possibly make it.

We now have a minimalist collection of scriptures, but one that is as hard as granite. As Eusebius presents the evidence, all regional agendas have been intentionally ignored; all personal preferences of prominent theologians and bishops set aside; every possible evidence of pressure politics and manipulation of the process rigorously suppressed.

When it was first published, Eusebius's *Ecclesiastical History* was widely regarded as a brilliant achievement, one that so impressed his contemporaries and subsequent generations that no fewer than four other church historians wrote imitations of it, copying out large parts of it into their histories.[79] In our day, Eusebius has rightly come to be known as "the father of church history." The report he gave of the orthodox Catholic scripture selection process immediately passed into church law in the form of numerous conciliar decisions regarding the contents of the Christian scriptures, based on Eusebius' findings.

For our part, we may note especially the "open-ended" nature of his results: a small number of universally acknowledged, *genuine* writings, followed by another short list of *disputed* writings awaiting further consideration, and finally a large number of *spurious,* rejected writings. Like the good philosopher he was, Eusebius left the question of *disputed* writings at that—open to the ongoing deliberations of fellow scholars and the providence of God.

As we shall see in the next chapter, the orthodox Catholics received, as a gift from Heaven, something they had never thought they would see, and for which they were totally unprepared: the sudden appearance of an emperor who claimed to be a Christian and a defender of the Catholic Church.

Chapter 6

AN EMPEROR INTERVENES:
Constantine Reshapes Catholic Christianity and Its Scriptures

In the middle of the bloodiest, most destructive persecution Roman officials had ever inflicted on the Christian Church, the new young emperor Constantine, son of Constantius, decided to appeal to the Christian God for supernatural protection in his civil war against Maxentius. That audacious decision must rank as one of the most ironic, consequence-laden events in western history.

Constantine's "conversion" to Christianity remains the subject of considerable debate. While complete skepticism regarding the depth or genuineness of the emperor's faith is not justified, we should recognize that—in keeping with the popular syncretistic worship of the sun (*Sol Invictis*) practiced by his family, and like other emperors before him who received and publicized auspicious dreams and visions before going into battle—Constantine seems to have adopted a form of Christianity that proved particularly serviceable for his political ambitions.[1]

If there was shock at the ease with which Constantine defeated and killed Maxentius, there was astonishment at the speed and extent of the newly Christian emperor's efforts to influence virtually every aspect of his newfound ally, Catholic Christianity[2]—from building new churches to paying clergy out of the state treasury, to intervening in church disputes, to convening councils of bishops and issuing edicts and making their decisions the law of the realm, to helping to determine the date for celebrating Easter, to mandating Sunday as the universal day of worship, to outlawing heresy, to de facto implementation of Eusebius's "acknowledged books" as the standard Bible of the Catholic Church.

Surely some astonishment must be reserved for the role played in all this by the Catholic bishops and theologians at the time. We look in vain for any record that any bishop or theologian ever objected that Constantine—who was not baptized, had never joined a church, knew little theology, and was not ordained—had no right or authority to do any of these things. After decades, indeed centuries of resisting imperial harassment and sporadic persecution, why did church authorities all acquiesce in Constantine's extension of imperial authority now, when he suddenly began to ingratiate himself to them? The reason appears plain: to a man, they welcomed the emperor's interventions because they were convinced that he had been given the authority to do all these things by their God. And the reason for that belief is equally obvious: at great risk to himself and to his family, Constantine repeatedly rescued the church from certain destruction and actively sought to support, extend, and enrich the Catholic Church, relentlessly pressing everyone in the Roman empire to convert to Catholic orthodoxy—actions from which the bishops all benefited and for which they were profoundly grateful, to him and to their God.[3]

Constantine risked everything time and again, trusting the Christian God to lead and protect him. At the same time, his Christian advisors coached and guided him every step of the way. Thus a flexible, symbiotic relationship grew between emperor and Catholic church. As that symbiotic relationship grew and matured, what had been the persecuted Church of the Martyrs underwent a period of *rapid enculturation*[4] during which it shed its original antagonistic, otherworldly posture in favor of the values, concerns, and—if it is not putting the matter too strongly—the god of Mighty Rome. Catholic theology and church politics became thoroughly imbued with Roman imperial ideology. The effects of this enculturation are too numerous to detail here. In general, the Catholic church adopted the geographical divisions (dioceses) of Roman administration, and Catholic clergy took on the official titles of Roman government. They began to think and act like Roman officials, living in stately villas and conducting public worship services, not in the little house-churches they were previously accustomed to, but in huge new temples or basilicas, packed with masses of half-converted parishioners. These new Christian temples were decorated by Roman craftsmen with glorious mosaics in the dome or apse at the front that depicted the Lord Jesus Christ in the posture and clothing of the Roman emperor[5]—which made sense, since the Sunday morning service was now conducted as if everyone was in the presence of Christ the emperor.

This period of rapid enculturation coincided with the last thirty years of the life of Eusebius of Caesarea, i.e., from 312 to 339. Along with the prominent north African rhetorician and philosopher Lactantius, Eusebius played a key role in transforming what had been a persecuted minority religion with little outward power, relying entirely on its superior moral example and reasoned persuasion to attract adherents and periodically pleading with the government for freedom of worship, into the official cultus of the empire, willing to use force on any who would not conform to its standard of orthodoxy and bent on eradicating pagan polytheism by all means necessary: prison, torture, exile, the mines, death.[6]

Let us resume the historical narrative at the fateful moment in the spring of 311 when the winds of change first began to blow. Mighty Rome was just about to choke the life out of the Christian Church (in the eastern provinces at least), when suddenly the brutal campaign stopped and the edicts outlawing Christianity were revoked.

What had happened?

The Great Persecution Grinds to a Halt

The government's campaign to exterminate Christianity first began to unravel in 305 when Galerius, the eastern Caesar and most rabid of the Christian-haters, successfully pressured Diocletian, his senior and leader, to abdicate because of old age. The timing seemed opportune. Christians were being caught and killed by the hundreds. The church's infrastructure lay in ruins throughout the cities and towns of the eastern provinces and north Africa. Diocletian's far-reaching political and military reforms were holding up well, and the economy was reviving. When Galerius chose Gaius Valerius Licinianus to be Diocletian's successor, it seemed possible to look forward to a Second Tetrarchy more powerful than the First. Unfortunately, events did not unfold as expected. The western junior emperor, Constantine son of Constantius, stubbornly followed his father's example and refused to destroy the Christian Church. The new eastern junior emperor, Licinius, likewise seemed reluctant to seek out and kill Christians.

Then, around the middle of the year 310, three of the four emperors in the original tetrarchy died in terrible and humiliating ways:[7] Constantine forced Maximian to hang himself when he discovered his plot to overthrow him.[8] That same summer, the eastern Augustus, Galerius, was struck by a horrible disease.[9] Christians loudly announced that the Christian God was finally wreaking vengeance on those responsible for the Great Persecution. This rumor may have reached the imperial bedchamber: the dying Galerius suddenly issued an edict, in the spring of 311, stopping the persecution and urging Christians to pray to their god for his recovery. Here is a fragment of that edict (notice the Porphyry-style criticisms in italics):[10]

THE EMPEROR CAESAR GALERIUS . . . to [my] subjects in the provinces, greeting. Among other matters which we have devised for the benefit and common advantage of our people, we have first determined to restore all things according to the ancient laws and public institutions of the Romans. And to make provision for this, that also the Christians, who have *left the religion of their fathers,* should return again to a good purpose and resolution. But . . . such *arrogance* had overtaken and such *stupidity* had beset them, that they would not follow the principles anciently prescribed to them . . . that they began to make and follow laws, each one according to his own purpose and his own will, . . . [creating] *different opinions*

and different sects. . . . [But] having regard to our clemency and our
invariable practice whereby we grant pardon to all, we most cheer-
fully have resolved . . . [that Christians] may restore their houses in
which they were accustomed to assemble . . . and they are obligated
to implore their god for our safety as well as that of the people and
their own. (Eusebius *Hist. eccl.* 17.3-10)

Galerius's edict may not have persuaded many Christians to pray
to their god on his behalf. He soon died in wretched agony. When
Diocletian learned of the deaths of his former colleagues, he became
convinced that everything he had tried to accomplish in his career
was falling into ruin and he apparently lost his desire to live. He
stopped eating and died in December of 311.[11]

Constantine Prays to the Christian God
for a Magic Charm (and Gets It)

Licinius was now peacefully ruling as the senior emperor in the east,
but his junior colleagues, Maxentius in Rome and Constantine in
Gaul, were preparing for civil war to determine who would control
the western half of the empire.[12] As he advanced toward Rome,
Constantine became obsessed with the idea that he could not defeat
Maxentius's larger armies and superior strategic position inside the
heavily fortified city of Rome without supernatural assistance.[13] He
was especially disturbed by reports that Maxentius planned to use
some sort of black magic on him. In a first-person account related to
Eusebius many years later, Constantine explained that he became

> convinced that he needed some more powerful aid than his
> military forces could afford him, on account of the . . . magical
> enchantments . . . practiced by the tyrant [Maxentius]. . . . He con-
> sidered therefore on what god he might rely for protection and
> assistance. . . . The thought occurred to him that, of the emper-
> ors who had preceded him, those who had rested their hopes in
> a multitude of gods . . . had been deceived . . . and met with an
> unhappy end. . . . But the [emperor] who had pursued an entirely
> opposite course [namely, Constantine's father] . . . and honored

the Supreme God . . . had found him to be the Savior and Protector of his empire and giver of every good thing.[14]

Constantine began to pray and to beseech "the god of his father" for help. Sure enough, Constantine told Eusebius years later, around noon the next day a supernatural portent in the shape of a "cross of light" appeared in the heavens, accompanied by an inscription in the sky: *hoc signo victor eris,* "by this sign you will be victor."[15] Constantine told Eusebius that the sign left him amazed and uncertain as to what it might mean.

> He was, he said to me, wondering what the manifestation might mean. Then, while he meditated and thought long and hard, night came on. As he slept, the Christ of God appeared to him holding the sign which had appeared in the sky [a shining cross], and urged him to make himself a copy of this sign [Greek: *sēmeion*] which had appeared in the sky, and to use it as protection [*alexēma,* safeguard] against the attacks of the enemy.[16]

The next morning, Constantine sprang up and immediately assembled his goldsmiths and jewelers, giving them instructions to make what he had seen in his vision. First of all, as Eusebius later recounts the story Constantine had told him, he took a lance and fastened a short crossbar to it, a short distance from the top, forming a cross. Then he commanded his workmen to fasten sheets of gold to the cross from top to bottom, reconstructing the "shining cross" he had seen in the heavens. At the top of the gold cross, he had his workmen fasten a round victory wreath made out of gems and gold, encircling two Greek letters, also made of gold: an x (or *Chi*), intersected by a P (or *Rho*), these being the first two Greek letters of "the Savior's title," CHRISTOS. Under the crossbar, he had his workmen hang a cloth tapestry consisting of a portrait of him and his sons stitched into the fabric, surrounded by "a pattern of precious stones fastened together . . . and interwoven with much gold, producing an impression of indescribable beauty on those who saw it."[17] In an aside, Eusebius proudly adds that the emperor once let him see the original "Savior's trophy."[18]

When it was finished, Constantine took his "Labarum," as he called it,[19] and placed it at the front of his army, surrounded by fifty of his best fighters. For good measure, Constantine ordered the same Chi-Rho insignia painted on his soldiers' shields.[20] Thus fortified, Constantine confidently marched toward Rome. Before he got there, he fought two quick battles in the north of Italy against Maxentius's advance guard, winning each one.

When Constantine halted north of the imperial city, a strange thing happened. Instead of staying inside the city where they were safe, Maxentius and his men suddenly rushed out of the city and hurled themselves at Constantine's army. This sudden attack proved to be a disastrous mistake. Constantine's men resisted and soon pushed Maxentius's army back to the Tiber, where they had no room to maneuver. Maxentius, scrambling across a bridge of boats in a frantic attempt to get back into the city, fell into the river and drowned.[21] Rome was stunned: this was not the outcome anyone had expected. To make things more eerie, the date was October 9, precisely the day on which Maxentius had planned to celebrate his sixth anniversary as emperor.

The following day, Constantine entered Rome in triumph. The cheering throngs saw the strange golden Labarum preceding his army and the odd insignia on the soldiers' shields. What did it all mean? Constantine's next act did nothing to reassure anyone: in a scandalous break with tradition, he did not ascend the Capitoline Hill, where victorious generals were supposed to offer sacrifices to the Roman gods in the giant Temple of Jupiter Maximus.

Why did he not sacrifice? We may be certain that the Christian clergy traveling with him had sternly warned him not to participate in any sacrifices to the Roman gods. Johannes Straub explains:

> At the very moment of his conversion Constantine was compelled to realize that from then on . . . he had to renounce, at least for his own person, pagan sacrifices, if he really intended to remain sure of the protection of the powerful God who had just rendered such miraculous aid, or if he was seriously interested in appearing to the Christians to be worshipping their God. To make a sacrifice or to

refuse to make it had been the official test of religious faith in the time of persecution. The Spanish bishop Ossius of Cordova [who may have been traveling with Constantine at the time] may have informed the Emperor of the indispensable obligation of a believer in the Christian God to renounce sacrifices. Thus Constantine, entering Rome as a triumphant liberator, abstained from ascending to the temple of Jupiter Capitolinus; he refused to make the traditional and obligatory sacrifices.[22]

Constantine went straight to the palace, where he offered private prayers to the Christian God.[23]

Constantine lost no time reinforcing his sudden victory. He sent imperial couriers to the two eastern emperors with letters suggesting they cease all persecution of Christians lest the Christian God punish them in the same way he had punished Maxentius, Galerius, and Diocletian. He also proposed a kinship bond between his family and that of Licinius, the most powerful of the eastern emperors, offering him the hand of his sister Constantia in marriage.[24] Licinius—who probably knew next to nothing of Constantine's recent switch to the Christian God but had certainly heard of his resounding victory over Maxentius—accepted the offer, and the two met in Milan the following summer to celebrate the marriage. While there, at Constantine's urging, they issued a sweeping edict proclaiming complete religious freedom for everyone and restoration of lands, goods, and church-houses to the Christians. Here is a fragment of what has come to be known as the famous Edict of Milan,[25] promulgated in the summer of 313:

> Perceiving long ago that religious liberty ought not to be denied, but that it ought to be granted to the judgment and desire of each individual to perform his religious duties according to his own choice, we had given orders that every man, . . . both Christians and all men [should have the] freedom to follow the religion which they choose, that whatever heavenly divinity exists may be propitious to us and to all that live under our government. We have determined . . . that liberty is to be denied to no one, to choose and to follow the religious observances of the Christians, but that to

each one freedom is to be given to devote his mind to that religion which he may think adapted to himself, in order that the Deity may exhibit to us in all things his accustomed care and favor. . . . And we decree still further in regard to the Christians, that their places, in which they were formerly accustomed to assemble, . . . shall be restored to the said Christians, without demanding money or any other equivalent, with no delay or hesitation. . . . In all these things, . . . you are to use the utmost diligence, to the end that our command may be speedily fulfilled, [so that] the divine favor toward us which we have already experienced in many matters will continue sure through all time.

The Emperor Raises the Status of the Catholic Christians

As he learned more about his new religion from his Christian advisors and as he felt able to make changes without arousing too much opposition,[26] tangible signs of his new religious orientation were soon forthcoming. In the fall and winter of 312 and the spring of 313, Constantine issued a number of edicts to strengthen and enhance the status of the Catholic clergy and the Catholic church generally (a preferential treatment shown to none of the other Christian factions).[27] Martyrs' families received generous grants of money from the state treasury; special gifts were given to those who had "confessed Christ."[28] Provincial governors were instructed to permit those who had gone into exile to return and to have their property restored immediately.[29] Not only was church property restored: armed with lists of approved Catholic congregations provided by his clerical advisor, the Spanish bishop Hosius, Constantine ordered provincial prefects to give particular congregations large gifts of money to rebuild their houses of worship on a grander scale.[30]

Constantine soon moved beyond merely restoring the Christian Church to its previous condition. He published an edict in 313 instructing his provincial governors and metropolitan bishops to create the mechanism for paying all Catholic clergy out of the state treasury, making them salaried officials of the Roman government, the way pagan priests had been.[31] Thus, at one stroke, Constantine did away with one of the oldest and most meaningful customs in the Church of the Apostles, voluntary contributions for support of clergy (cf. 1 Cor 9:4-18 where St. Paul defends the practice, based on the teaching of the Lord in Matt 10:10 and Luke 10:7). Here is an excerpt from the edict Constantine sent to his North African prefect, Anulinus, explaining the new policy. Note the reason Constantine gives for being so generous.

> Greeting to thee, our most esteemed Anulinus. Since it appears from many circumstances that when that religion is despised in which is preserved the chief reverence for the most holy celestial Power, great dangers are brought upon public affairs; but that when [it is] legally adopted and observed, it affords the most signal prosperity to the Roman name and remarkable felicity to all the affairs of men. Hence, it has seemed good to me, most esteemed Anulinus, that those men who give their services with due sanctity and with constant observance of this . . . divine religion, should receive recompense for their labors. Wherefore it is also my will that those within the province [of Africa] entrusted to thee, in the Catholic Churches over which [Bishop] Caecilianus presides, who give their services to this holy religion, and who are commonly called "clergymen," . . . [should] not by any error or sacrilegious negligence be drawn away from the service due to the Deity. . . . For it seems that when they show greatest reverence to the Deity, the greatest benefits accrue to the state. Farewell, most esteemed and beloved Anulinus.[32]

With the Catholic clergy elevated to the status of state officials, Constantine decided that Miltiades, the bishop of Rome and nominal head of the entire Catholic cultus, should have a much grander residence corresponding to his exalted status. Accordingly he gave the bishop a sumptuous villa from his wife's family estates on the eastern edge of the city, known as the Lateran Villa.[33] We might wonder whether Miltiades felt some initial obligation to refuse this gift as not befitting one "taking the place of Peter and Paul" (*vicarius Petri et Pauli*), and to choose to live in relative poverty, the way Christ and his apostles had. But no: at length Miltiades accepted the gift.

Constantine had even grander plans up his sleeve. He ordered his workmen to begin building a huge new temple to the Christian God, next door to the new bishop's residence, outfitting it with dazzling gold and silver ornaments provided from the imperial treasury. This magnificent edifice, later known as St. John Lateran Cathedral, was the first imperial-style basilica in Christian history and became the model for all later basilica-style cathedrals.[34]

In the meantime, Constantine was being drawn into internal Catholic politics. When he sent money to the "approved" Catholic churches in North Africa, he accidentally stepped into a long-simmering controversy caused by the Great Persecution.[35] A number of North African and Libyan bishops, led by a presbyter named Donatus, had remained true to the Christian God and "confessed Christ" during the Great Persecution, even though it meant torture and exile or death. Other priests and bishops had caved in and performed sacrifices to the Roman gods, thus—in the eyes of the confessors—betraying Christ and the Christian God. Caecilian, the bishop of Carthage, favored letting the *traditores* ("betrayers") back into communion with the church after they had done appropriate penance, while the followers of Donatus demanded a hard line against the traitors, saying that they deserved to be cast out of office and that all of the baptisms, marriages, and ordinations they had performed ought to be annulled on the grounds that these had been performed by apostates. When Caecilian and the moderates received Constantine's funds, the Donatists were outraged and demanded that the money should be given to them on the grounds that they alone were the "true church."

Constantine personally intervened in an attempt to resolve the dispute. At first, he appointed Bishop Miltiades to convene a typical Roman-style judicial inquiry to hear the disputants and decide the issue. That came to naught, however, when the Donatists disregarded the negative verdict. Constantine must have decided he could not force them to obey the verdict, since he had just passed an edict forbidding the use of force against Christians. At the same time, however, he was terribly anxious what the Christian God would do to him if he allowed his Catholic clergy to fight and excommunicate each other. So he—not one of the bishops—convened a Catholic synod, inviting a large number of bishops to come to a neutral venue in Arles, southern Gaul, at public expense, where they might receive a fair hearing and settle the dispute. His letter to Aelafius, the secular vicar of Africa in charge of financial affairs, instructing him to make arrangements for the bishops to come to this synod at public expense, clearly reveals Constantine's reason for trying to bring about peace and concord in the Catholic Church:

> For since I am sure that you too are a worshiper of the Highest God, I confess to you that I think that it is not at all right that con-tentions and altercations of this kind be ignored by us, by which perhaps the Highest Divinity may be moved to wrath not only against the human race, but even against me myself, to whose care by his celestial will he has committed the management of all earthly affairs, and, having been angered, might determine things other than heretofore. For then truly and most fully shall I be able to be secure and always to hope for the most prosperous and best things from the very prompt benevolence of the Most Powerful God, when I shall have perceived that all people are venerating the Most Holy God by means of the proper cult of the Catholic religion with harmonious brotherhood of worship.[36]

As it turned out, the Synod of Arles did not resolve the dispute either, and the Donatist Controversy dragged on for years.

Meanwhile, the bond of concord between Constantine and Licinius was beginning to fray. Licinius's envy at Constantine's popularity, the latter's resentment at Licinius's provocations, and the inevitable political scheming on both sides now that there were only two emperors soon led to outright hostilities. The first clash came in October of 316 near Cibalae in Pannonia: Constantine's forces won a resounding victory. Licinius fled eastward with his family into Thrace. Constantine followed and confronted him again, just outside Hadrianopolis, in January 317. Licinius lost a second battle and sued for terms. Constantine demanded that he hand over all of the provinces along the Danube, which Licinius did. Constantine now controlled eight of the twelve Roman dioceses. A period of increasing tension ensued, lasting from 317 until 320.

When Constantine proclaimed Sunday as the universal day of rest in July of 321, Licinius refused to recognize the edict in his provinces.[37] For his part, Licinius became more openly anti-Christian, adopting Jupiter as his "friend" on his coins and choosing a well-known neo-Pythagorean philosopher named Iamblichus and his disciples as his court advisors.[38] When he began openly persecuting Christians and closing churches, Constantine vowed to get rid of him.[39]

By winter of 323, both sides were actively preparing for war. Licinius announced that this contest would decide who was right, he or Constantine, as to the true God. Constantine came to the battlefield outside Hadrianopolis, in July 324, ostentatiously parading the Labarum in front of his army. It was tended by a cadre of bishops in full regalia, who recited prayers to the Christian God on behalf of Constantine's army. They met for daily prayer in a cross-shaped tent set up outside the camp, openly imitating Moses and his Ark of the Covenant. Determined not to lose this time, Licinius entered the field with a huge army, much bigger than Constantine's, with a backup fleet in the Hellespont to protect his line of retreat if necessary.

On the day of battle, even though Licinius had an advantageous position, a much larger force, and statues of the Roman gods strategically placed among his men, by dint of superb maneuvering Constantine gained the upper hand. His bodyguard rushed the Labarum hither and yon to the points where his men seemed hardest pressed. This seemed to encourage his men and to frighten the enemy. At the end of the day, with his forces holding down both wings of the enemy, Constantine led a mass cavalry charge straight at the center of Licinius's lines and smashed it to pieces. Mass slaughter ensued. Licinius fled, leaving behind tens of thousands of dead and dying men on the field.[40]

Licinius headed east toward Byzantium, where he intended to make another stand, but when he heard that Constantine was right behind him and that his son Crispus was coming up the Bosporus with a large fleet that would annihilate his navy, Licinius decided to cross over to the other side and make his last stand at Chrysopolis, just across the water. In the final battle, the Labarum was more effective than ever before. Licinius had ordered his men not even to look at the Labarum or attack it directly, but to no avail. Constantine's army slaughtered what was left of Licinius's forces.[41] He let Licinius's wife—Constantine's half-sister—plead with him for favorable terms, and she gained him a stay of execution. It didn't last long: Licinius was executed a year later.[42]

Constantine and Catholic Christianity were now the undisputed masters of the Roman empire. Signaling the new situation, Constantine sent a long victory letter to all of the eastern provinces.[43] It clearly expresses Constantine's sense of being at a great juncture in human history:

VICTOR CONSTANTINUS MAXIMUS AUGUSTUS to the inhabitants of the province of Palestine. To all who entertain just and sound sentiments respecting the character of the Supreme Being, it has long been most clearly evident, . . . how vast a difference there has ever been between those who maintain a careful observance of the hallowed duties of the Christian religion, and those who treat this religion with hostility or contempt. But at this present time, we may see by still more manifest proofs, . . . both how unreasonable it is to question this truth, and how mighty is the power of the Supreme God: since it appears that they who faithfully observe His holy laws, and shrink from the transgression of His commandments, are rewarded with abundant blessings, and are endued with well-grounded hope as well as ample power for the accomplishment of their undertakings. . . . [But those] who have been bold in the practice of oppression or injustice; who have either directed their senseless fury against God himself, or have conceived no kindly feelings towards their fellow-men, but have dared to afflict them with exile, disgrace, confiscation, massacre, or other miseries of the like kind, . . . have found that they received a recompense proportioned to their crimes. . . . Many a time have their armies been slaughtered, many a time have they been put to flight; and their warlike preparations have ended in total ruin and defeat.

But now, with such a mass of impiety oppressing the human race, and the commonwealth [of Rome] in danger of being utterly destroyed as if by the agency of some pestilential disease and therefore needing powerful and effectual aid; what was the relief, and what the remedy which the Divinity devised for these evils? . . . I myself, then, was the instrument whose services He chose, and esteemed suited for the accomplishment of his will. Accordingly, beginning at the remote Britannic ocean, and the regions where, according to the law of nature, the sun sinks beneath the horizon, through the aid of divine power I banished and utterly removed every form of evil which prevailed, in the hope that the human race, enlightened through my instrumentality, might be recalled to a due observance of the holy laws of God, and at the same time our most blessed faith might prosper under the guidance of his almighty hand. . . . Believing, therefore, that this most excellent service had been confided to me as a special gift, I proceeded as far as the regions of the East, which, being under the pressure of severer calamities, seemed to demand still more effectual remedies at my hands. At the same time I am most certainly persuaded that I myself owe my life, my every breath, in short, my very inmost and secret thoughts, entirely to the favor of the Supreme God. . . . [Hence] I deem it incumbent on me to remove at once and most completely from all persons the hard necessities laid upon them for a season, and the unjust inflictions under which they have suffered, though free from any guilt or just liability.[44]

In the rest of the "letter," Constantine goes on to issue a mass of regulations intended to deal with the injuries suffered by Christians during the persecutions of the previous twenty years: permission for exiles[45] as well as those sent to work in the mines or public construction projects[46] to return; restitution of those who had been ejected from the military because they confessed Christ;[47] and return of all lands, gardens, and houses to exiles, prisoners, confessors, and churches.[48] He concluded with an appeal to all inhabitants of the eastern provinces to reverence and honor "that Divine law" taught in the Catholic Christian churches.[49]

Constantine and the Catholic Bishops
Create a New Imperial Christian Cult

Before Constantine, Christians—whether Montanists, Gnostics, Marcionites, or Catholics—had somehow assumed that they were responsible for everything that happened in their religion until the Day of Judgment, when Christ their Savior, the Son of God, the master of the whole universe, would return. He, they expected, would destroy the Romans and all others who did not confess Christ. Now, however, it seemed that the Christian God was doing something radically different. He had apparently chosen Constantine to be his champion and was using this weapon to destroy every vestige of the old pagan order and all those who opposed Christianity. It didn't take long for the orthodox leadership, led by Lactantius, Eusebius, Hosius, and Miltiades, to grasp the main outlines of this new divine plan. They expressed deep gratitude to their God for Constantine's edicts in support of Catholic Christianity.

They may not have been prepared, however, for the way Constantine as the new Christian emperor continued to act according to the traditional Roman imperial principle whereby the emperor's responsibilities included the state religion—which was now Catholic Christianity. For his part, despite a close working relationship with these bishops and theologians, Constantine soon learned that it would be more difficult than he had expected to get the Catholic bishops to conform to Roman standards of harmony and unity.

After his defeat of Licinius, for example, Constantine was in sole control of the entire Roman empire. He thought he would be free to implement his agenda of building up and unifying the Christian church everywhere. Instead, he discovered a violent controversy raging, under the surface of the shattered and ravaged churches, among the bishops of the eastern provinces, a controversy that threatened the peace of the whole empire. The bishops could not agree on the proper definition of the nature of Christ as the second person of the Trinity.[50]

As soon as he learned of this conflict, later known as the Arian Controversy after one of the disputants, Constantine was filled with anger and dismay. He wrote a long letter to Alexander, Bishop of Alexandria, sending it by his top Christian advisor, Bishop Hosius, with the charge that he learn first-hand what was going on. Here are some excerpts that give a clear idea of Constantine's wounded feelings and reason for intervening in the dispute. Once again, notice the emperor's rationale:

> It is my design to bring the diverse judgments formed by all nations respecting the Deity to *a condition . . . of settled uniformity*. . . . For I am aware that if I can succeed in establishing a common harmony of sentiment among all the servants of God, the general course of affairs would also experience a change [for the better] corresponding to the pious desires of everyone.

Constantine went on to express the intense pain he felt at the news of their dispute. It was obvious, he declared, that the bishop of Alexandria was not doing his job properly, letting subordinate clerics wrangle over trivial doctrinal matters like this.

> How deep a wound did my heart receive in the report that divisions exist among yourselves! . . . And yet, having made a careful enquiry into the origin and foundation of these differences, I find the cause to be of a truly insignificant character and quite unworthy of such fierce contention. Thus I feel myself compelled to address you in this letter and to appeal at the same time to your unanimity and sagacity, . . . I call on Divine Providence to assist me in the task while I interrupt your dissension in the character of a minister of peace.

Constantine scolded the two parties at length (his letters and speeches are notable for their long-windedness) on how wrong it is for "holy people to be rent into diverse parties." He adds:

> Is it right that, because of some trifling and foolish verbal difference, brethren should assume towards each other the attitude of enemies, and . . . the Synod be rent by profane disunion because of you who wrangle on points so trivial and altogether unessential? This is vulgar and characteristic of childish ignorance rather than consistent with the wisdom of priests and men of good sense.[51]

To his amazement, the imperial chiding and personal arm-twisting by Hosius had no effect whatever. Constantine may have realized that downplaying the importance of this theological dispute had been a tactical blunder. Such a disagreement—"is the person of Christ equal to God or slightly secondary to God?"—could have seemed to a layman like a semantic squabble over a nebulous and abstract issue. But to the professional theologians and biblical scholars involved in it, it was a dispute of the utmost importance, with implications on many levels: biblical interpretation, fundamental theology, and liturgical practice. At any rate, Constantine abruptly switched tactics and sent a letter to all bishops throughout Christendom ordering them to come to a General Council[52]—the first in the history of the church—to be held at Nicaea in Bithynia, within a year.

So it was, in June of 325, that more than two thousand bishops, presbyters, and deacons, with their servants and attendants, descended upon Nicaea, a pleasant hill town northeast of Constantinople, where Constantine owned a spacious summer palace overlooking a beautiful lake. Of the approximately three hundred bishops that came, only a few were prominent western bishops (the controversy was not their problem), but the eastern bishops were out in force.[53]

Once they were gathered, the emperor, with skillful help from Bishop Hosius, assumed direct control of the conference. On opening day, the bishops entered the great hall and sat on long benches down the length of the hall. There must have been great excitement: many of them had never actually seen their God's invincible champion. After everyone was seated, Constantine entered with his entourage, dressed modestly in purple and wearing a small gold crown. He went to the front and sat on a small golden stool. Eusebius, the bishop of Nicomedia, their nominal host, rose and gave a short welcoming speech. After that, Constantine rose and spoke, in Latin, urging them all to work in harmony and to remember forgiveness in their deliberations. It was all very dramatic and beautifully staged.

Then the business at hand began. Immediately several petitions were handed to Constantine alleging complaints against various brethren. Without saying a word, he rose and placed them in a little brazier where they burned up. Everyone got the message. As debate heated up, Constantine intervened and led the discussion himself, speaking in Greek. As Eusebius later remembered it, Constantine gave a brilliant demonstration in leadership:

> appearing in a truly attractive and amiable light, persuading some, convincing others by his reasoning, praising those who spoke well, and urging all to unity of sentiment, [he] at last succeeded in bringing them all to one mind and judgment respecting every disputed question.[54]

At a critical juncture, Eusebius—a leader of the Arian party and thus under suspicion of hersy, but also one of the three most influential bishops present—was asked to validate his orthodoxy by giving his confession of faith. He rose and repeated the creed he had said all his life, based on the creed in use in his congregation at Caesarea. Constantine immediately indicated his approval, and went on to ask Eusebius point blank whether he could accept the term *homoousios,* "of one substance," to explain the relationship between the Son and the Father within the divine Trinity. Thus put on the spot, Eusebius reluctantly agreed. With his acquiescence, the position of the Arian party, which had been holding out for some sort of subordinate position for the Son, collapsed.[55] The theological dispute over the nature of the second person of the Trinity was over—for the time being at least—and the bishops turned their attention to other matters.

When the council broke up a month later, the bishops had been asked to put their signatures to a new creedal formulation including the term *homoousios.* This was later called the Nicene Creed. They all knew that if they didn't they would be thrown out of office, or worse.[56] Two bishops, close friends of Arius, refused to sign the new creed and were immediately sent into exile so that they could no longer infect their congregations with their deviant thinking. The bishops also agreed on a uniform method for calculating the date of Easter, possibly also proposed by Constantine, and passed a number of canons or laws dealing with church order that set up regulations for promotion through the church hierarchy.[57]

When they were finished, the bishops sent letters to all other bishops throughout Christendom conveying the Council's decisions. In addition, Constantine sent his own letter to the same recipients, conveying the council's decisions, and making them the law of the realm. His letter is noteworthy for another reason: the rationale put forward in it for rejecting the original Jewish method for deciding the date of Passover/Easter included harsh statements about Jews:

> It appeared unworthy that in the celebration of this most holy feast we should follow the practice of the Jews, who have impiously defiled their hands with enormous sin, and are, therefore, deservedly afflicted with blindness of soul. . . . Let us then have nothing in common with the detestable Jewish crowd, for we have received from our Savior a different way.[58]

We might ask whether Eusebius or any of the other bishops ever objected to the emperor's deep involvement in the internal affairs of the Christian Church. But there is no evidence that they did. Occasionally Eusebius seems to reveal some discomfort, however. For example, at one point in his *Life of Constantine,* after several pages lauding the emperor's extensive activities on behalf of the church, Eusebius makes this striking comment:

> To the Church of God Constantine paid particular personal attention. When some were at variance with each other in various places, like a universal bishop [*koinos episkopos*] appointed by God, he convoked councils of the ministers of God. [Nor] did he disdain to be present and attend during their proceedings, and he participated in the subjects reviewed, by arbitration promoting the peace of God among all.[59]

The striking expression "universal bishop" speaks volumes. It shows that Eusebius well knew how strange it was for the Roman emperor to be intruding himself so deeply into every aspect of the church's life and doctrine. Eusebius seeks both to illustrate, and to justify this intrusion, by inventing a new office in the Catholic Church: "universal bishop."

What were some of the other things this "universal bishop" did?

- In 321, Constantine decided to standardize Christian worship by making the Roman Sun Day (*dies Solis*) a legal day of rest so that Christians across the empire would not have to work and could attend worship. Naturally, pagans were not pleased with this regulation. Again, Eusebius tries to justify the imperial decree: "This observance was recommended by this blessed prince to all classes of his subjects, his earnest desire being gradually to lead all mankind to the worship of God."[60]

- That same year, Constantine issued an edict making it legal to free slaves using Catholic Churches as the place of manumission (instead of the courts)—a major public-relations boon. He also legalized the bequeathing of estates, lands, and other legacies to Catholic churches, an act that had the immediate effect of providing individual churches with considerable long-term financial security. (There were many who wished to give such gifts to God out of gratitude for healing, forgiveness of sins, or simply for church use.)[61] Thus the Catholic church began to acquire property on an unprecedented scale.

- From the very beginning, in 312, Constantine promoted and encouraged an unprecedented building campaign in magnificent large buildings. In addition to repeated legislation providing for the rebuilding and improvement of house-churches[62] that had been destroyed during the Great Persecution, Constantine provided government funds and valuable space for large, beautifully appointed basilicas in Rome, Nicomedia, and elsewhere.[63]

- In the summer of 326, his mother, Helena, made an extended pilgrimage to the Holy Land, where she eventually commissioned the building of two huge basilicas (each was over 100 meters long), the first over Christ's supposed tomb in Jerusalem (the Church of the Holy Sepulchre) and the second over his birthplace in Bethlehem (the Church of the Nativity).[64]

- Far surpassing all previous building activities on behalf of the Christian religion was Constantine's decision to abandon ancient polytheistic Rome, the old pagan capital of the empire, and to build a new Christian capital at Byzantium on the peninsula overlooking the straits of the Bosporus. It would have glorious new build-ings, many of them intended solely for Christian worship.[65] He called it "new Rome," but his subjects called it Constantinople—"Constantine's *polis*." He did not object.

• As part of his relentless campaign to bring everyone into the Christian religion (since that would please the Christian God and cause him to look favorably on Constantine and the empire), Eusebius reports that Constantine used the army as a guinea pig in the methods of mass conversion. Having ordained Sun Day as the universal day of rest, he gave orders that Christian soldiers should be permitted to leave their bases on that day to attend church. For the other soldiers who stubbornly clung to heir pagan beliefs, he composed a little monotheistic prayer and ordered them to recite it every Sunday:

> We acknowledge thee the only God: we acknowledge thee as our King and implore thy help. By thy favor have we gotten the victory: through thee are we mightier than our enemies. We render thanks for thy past benefits, and trust thee for future blessings. Together we pray to thee, and beseech thee long to preserve to us, safe and triumphant, our emperor Constantine and his pious sons.[66]

But pagans did not convert to the new religion fast enough for the Christian emperor. He decided to increase the pressure on them and passed an edict outlawing pagan rituals.[67] He sent govern-ment agents out to remove from pagan temples all of their gold and silver (greatly increasing the contents of the state treasury), and transported the statues and notable relics to adorn his new Christian capital city, Constantinople.[68] This confidently aggressive attitude even found its way into Constantine's foreign policy as he sent letters and ambassadors to "barbarian countries," urging them to accept the Christian God, or at least commending the Christians living within their domains to their care—in effect serving notice that he was watching to see how Christian subjects were treated.[69]

Toward the end of his life, Constantine completely abandoned his original moderate approach and adopted a far more severe attitude toward all types of Christianity not in compliance with

Catholic orthodoxy. Eusebius proudly relates that after he "reduced
the Church of God to a state of uniform harmony" by means of the
councils just discussed, Constantine

> ... next proceeded to a different duty, feeling it incumbent on him
> to extirpate another sort of impious persons as pernicious enemies
> of the human race. These were the pests of society who ruined
> whole cities [by their false teachings]. . . . Hear, then, in what man-
> ner he addressed [the heretics] in this letter:[70] "VICTOR CONSTAN-
> TINUS, MAXIMUS AUGUSTUS, to the heretics. Understand now,
> by this present statute, ye Novatians, Valentinians, Marcionites,
> Paulians, ye who are called Cataphrygians, and all ye who devise
> and support heresies by means of your private assemblies, with
> what a tissue of falsehood and vanity, with what destructive and
> venomous errors, your doctrines are inseparably interwoven, so
> that through you the healthy soul is stricken with disease and the
> living becomes the prey of everlasting death. Ye haters and enemies
> of truth and life, in league with destruction! . . . Ever trespassing
> under the mask of godliness, ye fill all things with defilement. . . . [71]
> We have directed, accordingly, that you be deprived of all the
> houses in which you are accustomed to hold your assemblies . . .
> and that you should enter the Catholic Church and unite with it
> in holy fellowship . . . [and your houses] made over without delay
> to the Catholic Church."[72]

Eusebius adds with grim satisfaction:

> Thus were the lurking-places of the heretics broken up by the
> emperor's command and the savage beasts they harbored. I mean
> the chief authors of their impious doctrines driven to flight. . . .
> Some, intimidated by the emperor's threats, disguising their real
> sentiments, crept secretly into the Church. For the law directed
> that search should be made for their books [which they had to
> give up]. . . . Thus the members of the entire [church] became
> united and compacted in one harmonious whole; and the one
> Catholic Church, at unity with itself, shone with full luster, while
> no heretical or schismatic body anywhere continued to exist. And
> the credit for having achieved this mighty work our Heaven-pro-
> tected Emperor alone, of all who had gone before him, was able to
> attribute to himself.[73]

At this point in his *Life of Constantine,* Eusebius pauses and tells a little story about something the emperor once said, the audacity of which seems to have shocked even Eusebius. He has prepared the way for this anecdote by describing all of the things the emperor did to abolish paganism, stamp out heresy, and get everyone to go to church and believe in the correct religion, thus pleasing the Christian God who would thereby grant further blessings to the empire. Then Eusebius describes this fascinating dinner table vignette:

> Hence it is not surprising that on one occasion, when entertaining bishops to dinner, he let slip the remark that he was perhaps himself a bishop too, using some such words as these in our hearing: "You are bishops of those within the church, but I am perhaps a bishop appointed by God over those outside."[74]

Eusebius does not reveal his or the bishops' reaction to Constantine's statement. The phrase "bishop over those outside" clearly rankled Eusebius, however, as is evident from his somewhat defensive introduction, "hence it is not surprising. . . ." It certainly *was* a surprising turn of phrase, but not out of character. After all, Constantine was constantly trying to figure out just how he fit into the Catholic hierarchy. As emperor, he was clearly in charge; but insofar as he was neither ordained nor officially installed into any church office, he repeatedly invented his own ad hoc offices: "common bishop" (*koinos episkopos*) or "bishop of all those outside" the church (*episkopos tōn ektos*). As far as we can tell, the other bishops were well pleased with his attempts.

But Constantine had far loftier ambitions. During the last ten years of his life, he ordered his workmen to begin work on a magnificent new church on the highest hill in Constantinople, to be dedicated to the Holy Apostles. The central building would be structured in the Greek cross fashion, with two equal arms, nave and transept, crossing under a high dome.[75] Around the base of the dome would be twelve ornate coffins with their lids carved to represent each of the twelve apostles. In the center, under the dome, there would be a space for one more coffin: his own, for when the time came.

Constantine didn't have long to wait. In February 337, while en route to give battle to the Persians, he became ill near the coastal city of Drepanum. As his condition worsened, he realized he was dying and requested baptism and full admission to the Catholic church. Eusebius of Nicomedia and the other clergy who were traveling with him on the expedition conducted the ritual, and a few weeks later, on May 22, 337, he died at age 65. His son Constantius II came to escort the body back to Constantinople, where it was placed inside a magnificent porphyry sarcophagus directly under the dome of the Church of the Holy Apostles, surrounded by the coffins of the twelve apostles. Eastern orthodoxy would bestow the title "Equal to the Apostles" (*Isapostolos*) upon Constantine, but he was best known as the "Thirteenth Apostle."[76]

Eusebius lived on a few years longer before he, too, died in 339, at the age of 81. His unbounded admiration for Constantine and his profound gratitude to the God of the Christians for giving the world and the church this great champion never dimmed. His rapturous exclamation celebrating Constantine's entry as victor into Rome, penned years earlier, sums up the perspective on the emperor that shaped Eusebius's career:

> Thus the pious Emperor, glorying in the confession of the victorious cross, proclaimed the Son of God to the Romans with great boldness of testimony.... All the nations, as far as the limit of the western ocean, being set free from the calamities which had heretofore beset them, and gladdened by joyous festivals, ceased not to praise him as the victorious, the pious, the common benefactor; all indeed, with one voice and one mouth declared that Constantine had appeared by the grace of God as a general blessing to mankind.[77]

Constantine's Influence on the Selection of Scripture

The account given above can only suggest the scope and depth of the transformation, under Constantine, of the Christian faith, which had had its origins in the life and teachings of Jesus Christ and the heroic example of the apostles. The Church had long been fiercely loyal to its traditions. After the Edict of Milan in 313, and as a result of Constantine's bountiful gifts and numerous direct interventions and the eager cooperation of the Catholic bishops, virtually all of Catholic Christianity's most important elements—traditions, staff, institutions, regulations, customs, rituals, calendar, places of worship—were replaced by the elaborate customs, values, prerogatives, rituals, calendar, places of worship and governmental machinery of imperial Rome. The most important change, of course, was the acceptance of the Christian emperor's aspiring to act as master and director of the church of Jesus Christ and the apostles, with all of the changes in value, outlook, and theology that that entailed.[78] That transformation included a dramatic turn in the ongoing scripture selection process described in the two preceding chapters, as documented by Eusebius in Books 1–7 of his *Ecclesiastical History.*

A thorough assessment of the legacy of this period is not the concern of this book. We may simultaneously recognize the tremendous benefit accorded the church when Constantine halted the terrible persecution and restored church property and personnel, *and* the fateful consequences of the Roman government's intrusion into the church's theological disputes and its relentless press for uniformity of thought throughout the empire. We may observe the simultaneous chilling and inflammatory effect over all theological disputes, including what had been an open, vigorous debate about scripture.

After the Council of Nicaea, Constantine issued an Edict against the Heretics, quoted above. We have seen how Eusebius quoted the Edict with obvious relish as it forbade heretics, the "pests of society," from ever meeting again, ordered their houses of worship to be confiscated, and their books to be destroyed.

What books were these?

Eusebius did not list them. How would the authorities know which were proscribed books and which were not, especially if, as was often the case, the heretical books had apostles' names on them and were written in a kind of arcane jargon that no one could understand?

Were orthodox bishops or scholars available to imperial officials who could help them decide? Might such an auxiliary body provide a list of books containing "the fictions of heretical men," based on Eusebius's list (in *Hist. eccl.* 3.25.7). If we are correct that Eusebius published the final edition of the *History* (Books 1–10) before the Council of Nicaea in 325,[79] by 330 its fame would surely have reached Constantine's ears. It is possible he had a list drawn up and sent to various authorities to aid in the search for heretical books. As a matter of fact, banning books had already begun before the Council of Nicaea, just after the founding of Constantinople, when Constantine initiated an Index of banned books. The first book he put on it was the hated writing of Porphyry, *Against the Christians.* The writings of Arius were added not much later.[80]

By this edict, Constantine (and the Catholic bishops who cooperated with him) closed down what had been a thriving, sometimes heated, and fundamentally beneficial controversy over the authentic writings of the apostles and the correct interpretation of them. If Marcion, Montanus, Valentinus, and the others had not freely and vociferously challenged the orthodox Catholics, compelling Irenaeus, Tertullian, Origen, and Eusebius to respond to their accusations about the true apostolic writings and their correct interpretation—and thus goading the forces of orthodoxy into sustained efforts to prove the validity of the orthodox use and interpretation of scripture—we would not have the many attempts to defend and explain the selection of Christian scripture eventually known as the New Testament, nor the Creed, nor above all the invaluable history of the scripture selection process written by Eusebius. All of the competing collections of scripture—Marcion's tiny scripture comes immediately to mind—forced the orthodox scholars to justify their rejection of selections like his. The same goes for their interpretation of these writings. Precisely because the "heretics" were free to argue, challenge, and pursue their own agendas, the rationale for each and every book in the scripture we have today was more strongly established.

When the Roman government, in the person of the emperor, powerfully intruded into the church's activities, it irrevocably skewed the whole debate by transplanting it into the state's legal framework, where coercive enforcement of the outcome was routine. After the

Edict against the Heretics came out, what nonorthodox Christian would dare publicly to use a non-accepted writing or attack the orthodox collection and propose an alternative selection of scripture? It is true that the Edict did not cause the "heretics" simply to disappear or to convert en masse to Catholic Christianity; rather they mostly went underground, where their traditions survived for centuries. But the surface, public debate over scripture within the Christian Church withered away.

As part of his campaign to properly equip his new church buildings in Constantinople, Constantine sent an order to Eusebius, as the leading scholar of his day, for fifty new Bibles. Eusebius proudly records the letter in its entirety:

> VICTOR CONSTANTINUS, MAXIMUS AUGUSTUS, to Eusebius. It happens through the favoring providence of God our Savior, that great numbers have united themselves to the most holy church in the city which is called by my name. It seems, therefore, highly requisite, since that city is rapidly advancing in prosperity in all other respects, that the number of churches should also be increased. Do you therefore receive with all readiness my determination on this behalf. *I have thought it expedient to instruct you to order fifty copies of the sacred scriptures . . . to be written on prepared parchment in a legible manner, . . . by professional transcribers thoroughly practiced in their art, . . . [and that they] be completed with as little delay as possible.* You have authority, also, in virtue of this letter, to use two of the public carriages for their conveyance, by which arrangement the copies, when fairly written, will most easily be forwarded to me for my personal inspection. One of the deacons of your church may be instructed with this service, who, upon his arrival here, shall experience my liberality. God preserve you, beloved brother![81]

Eusebius does not explain why Constantine chose him. There were other scriptoria that could have handled the request; why Caesarea, and why Eusebius? I think two factors must have convinced Constantine's advisors that Eusebius was the obvious choice. First, Caesarea was the authoritative center for Old Testament textual studies, thanks to Origen's Hexapla, which was still in the library there. They had been making copies of books at the library in Caesarea for decades, and with the right funding (which Constantine said he would provide), skilled copyists could be procured. Secondly, Eusebius had just published his *Ecclesiastical History,* a most impressive demonstration of which books belonged in the Catholic New Testament and which did not.

The effect of this order—and of the resulting imperially authorized copies of the Bible—was significant. I think M. Odahl states the effect precisely: "By patronizing the production of Bibles for his new capital, the emperor hastened the closing of the Christian canon of scriptures and helped preserve a New Testament of twenty-seven books."[82] After Constantine's Bible had been produced, and in the tense atmosphere that followed the Council of Nicaea, what bishop would dare use a Bible in his cathedral that differed in content from one used by the bishops in Constantinople? He would likely be informed upon and investigated. He could lose his office or worse!

Eusebius' masterful analysis of the intricacies of the scripture selection process was widely regarded as the "last word" on the subject. But after Constantine ordered his Bibles and Eusebius proudly filled the order, the evidence shows that the debate over "true" and authentic scripture simply withered up and practically disappeared. The number of scholars after Eusebius who had anything to say about which writings to use in worship were few and far-between—and they just repeated Eusebius' findings. Compared to the earlier centuries' tumultuous debates, this remarkable conformity cannot have been a coincidence.

Most strikingly, for the basic theme of this book, Catholic bishops and scholars stopped using the old terminology as well, and, for the first time, began using a new legal term in their discussions of scripture: *canon* = law, as we can see in the example of Athanasius' Festal Letter of 367.[83] Where before scholars had spoken of "authentic," "spurious," "genuine," and "disputed" writings, now the terminology is dominated by two opposed terms: "canonical" (legal) and "non-canonical" (illegal). Instead of scholarly discussion and debate, now Church synods met and voted on which writings were legal = "canonical."[84]

What I have called the chilling and inflammatory effect can also be seen in Constantine's intrusion into the debate over the proper way to interpret the Gospels, in the question of Jesus Christ's relation to God the Father. When Constantine discovered the raging debate among eastern bishops and theologians about the proper way to interpret the Gospels and Paul on this question, his impulse was to step in and stop the debate. T. D. Barnes rightly asks, "When a Christian emperor believed and affirmed that councils of bishops spoke with divine authority, how then could any individual bishop challenge the definition of the faith adopted by the fathers at Nicaea?"[85] Constantine's heavy-handed intervention "invested the Nicene Creed with a unique, inviolable status," writes Barnes. Constantine's goal may have been to calm the dispute and arrive at consensus. What he accomplished, instead, was to make it likely that the Council of Nicaea would not only "fail to bring harmony to the eastern church but instead sharpen the divisions and inaugurate a whole new phase of ecclesiastical politics."[86]

The fundamental issue at stake at Nicaea went to the heart of the Christian religion, and there differing points of view had long been appropriate. The willingness of Constantine and the bishops to resolve theological disputes by means of banishment, begun at Nicaea, grew more violent with subsequent emperors and bishops, forever poisoning theological debates. When Ambrose, the eminent theologian and bishop of Milan and Augustine's teacher (340–97), said something that offended the emperor Valentinian II and his mother, suddenly, as Augustine later remembered, the church was ringed around with soldiers bearing arms.[87] By the end of the fourth century, bishops and emperors were relying on violence to subdue, coerce, and marginalize dissident thinkers—a trend that continued on into the bloody Middle Ages and beyond.[88]

In short, the former vibrant, active, free atmosphere has disappeared.[89] Gone, as well, is any flexibility to understand the person of Christ in different ways and still remain within the broader Christian movement. Gone is the sense that these issues are profound mysteries and that the human mind is in the end incapable of comprehending them—so that many different approaches are needed. Gone is the spirit of theologians like Origen, who once gave a classic justification for the spirit of diversity and openness within Christianity: When the pagan critic Celsus complained that there were so many different kinds of Christians that all they had in common was the name, Origen replied, in so many words, what's so bad about that? He pointed out that a variety of schools of thought is often desirable, using the Greek word *haireseis* (from which the derogatory term *heresies* would later derive):

> *Haireseis* [i.e., schools of thought] of different kinds have [always] originated from any matter in which the principle involved was . . . important and beneficial to human life. The science of medicine is useful and necessary to the human race and many are the points of dispute in it respecting the manner of curing bodies. There are found, for this reason, numerous *haireseis* . . . among the Greeks, and . . . [other] nations who . . . employ medicine. Likewise, since philosophy makes a profession of the truth, and promises a knowledge of existing things with a view to the regulation of life, and endeavors to teach what is advantageous to our race, and since the investigation of these matters is attended with great differences of opinion, innumerable *haireseis* have consequently sprung up in philosophy, some of which are more celebrated than others. [By the same token] Christianity appeared an object of veneration to men, and not [just] to the . . . servile class but to many among the Greeks who were devoted to literary pursuits, there necessarily originated *haireseis* [here as well], not as the result of faction and strife, but through the earnest desire of many literary men to become acquainted with the doctrines of Christianity. . . . And yet [who would avoid] medicine because of its *haireseis*; . . . [or hate] philosophy because of its many *haireseis*? . . . Now, if these arguments hold good, why should we not defend, in the same way, the existence of *haireseis* in Christianity? For example, St. Paul . . . says, "There must be *haireseis* among you, that they who are approved may be made manifest" (1 Cor 11:19). For as that man is "approved" in medicine who, on account of his experience in various [medical] *haireseis,* and out of his honest examination of the majority of them has selected the preferable system, — and as the [one] proficient in philosophy is he who, after acquainting himself experimentally with

the various views, has given his adherence to the best,—so I would say that the wisest Christian was he who had carefully studied the *haireseis* both of Judaism and Christianity. [Whoever] finds fault with Christianity because of its *haireseis* would find fault also with the teaching of Socrates, from whose school have issued many others of discordant views. For the opinions of Plato might be chargeable with error, on account of Aristotle's having separated from his school and founded a new one.[90]

At the beginning of the fourth century, the Catholic Church faced a great temptation. The church of Jesus Christ, hailed as the "Prince of Peace," was offered recourse to the imperial sword—and took it, gladly. No longer would it have to give reasoned, honest replies to difficult questions from critics and fellow theologians; now it could simply compel agreement and punish disagreement. When it began to use the sword against its enemies, the "heresies" (*haireseis*), the church thus became deeply twisted and lost its way.[91] Power-hungry, greedy politicians began to take over positions of leadership. In this alien atmosphere, how could Jesus of Nazareth or the Apostle Paul or Amos, Isaiah, Jeremiah, and the prophets speak? Were not their voices almost snuffed out, encased in heavy leather bindings of the lavishly illustrated codexes, lying on cold stone altars in giant stone buildings? How could those voices speak and be heard?

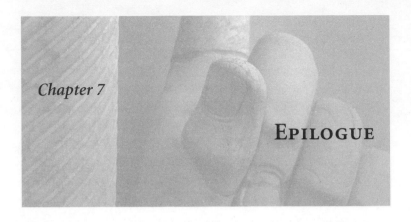

Chapter 7

EPILOGUE

In this Epilogue, I return to the discussion of canon and scripture in formative Judaism and early Islam begun in Chapter One and comment briefly on some of the main developments pertaining to the New Testament canon after Constantine and Eusebius, down to the present.

Eusebius's *Ecclesiastical History* (325 C.E.) turned out to be the last attempt at a critical assessment of the writings considered for Christian scripture until the Enlightenment in the eighteenth century, when Eusebius's history came to be largely discredited as unreliable and incomplete, necessitating a fresh examination of the ancient records.

But this was not the case for the rest of the fourth century through the seventh century. Eusebius's achievement was considered so impressive that subsequent church historians imitated his writing, including its novel title, contenting themselves with filling in gaps in his narratives and carrying the historical record down to their own times.[1] Meanwhile, numerous church councils passed resolutions officially approving of the writings in his "acknowledged" list and occasionally adding a few other writings from the "disputed" list—though without any stated rationale.[2] Typical of these brusque conciliar statements is the "24th Canon respecting Holy Scripture" from the Third Synod of Carthage (397), which lists 27 books:

> Canon 24. Besides the *canonical Scriptures,* nothing shall be read in church under the name of divine Scriptures. Moreover, the *canonical Scriptures* are these: [OT books are listed]. The New Testament [books are]: the Gospels, four books; the Acts of the apostles, one book; the Epistles of Paul, thirteen; of the same to Hebrews, one Epistle; of Peter, two; of John, apostle, three; of James, one; of Jude, one; the Revelation of John. Concerning the confirmation of this *canon,* the transmarine Church shall be consulted. On the anniversaries of martyrs, their acts shall also be read.[3]

In 383, Roman Catholic pope Damasus (366–384) commissioned a brilliant young scholar and linguist named Sophronius Eusebius Hieronymus (in English, Jerome) to bring out an accurate Latin version of the Greek Old Testament and New Testament.[4] Jerome did not make a fresh translation from the Greek; instead, he sifted through the best Latin manuscripts and tried to compile the most accurate text. It was a task similar in difficulty and monumental impact to Origen's stabilization of the text of the Greek Old Testament, the Hexapla.[5] But Jerome seems to have not spent much effort on deciding which books to include in the New Testament, beyond translating Eusebius's *Ecclesiastical History* into Latin. Otherwise he "was content to acquiesce to the list of those that were then in general use."[6] Jerome created the official Latin version of Holy Scripture that would be used in western Christianity for the next one thousand years.

Islam Follows the Example of Fourth- and Fifth-Century Christianity

In the first chapter, I suggested that *canonization* of scripture was a relatively rare event in the history of the world's religions.[7] I said that it had occurred only in those areas where Greek *polis* structures and institutions, and the values, customs, and goals of Greek "philosophy," prepared the way by focusing attention on using authentic scriptures accompanied by accurate interpretation. *Canonization,* properly speaking, did not occur until official governmental intervention in the Christian scripture selection process. Correct doctrine became the purview of the state's legal machinery and obedience was compelled under threat of armed force. The only religions that exhibited all of these features were second- to fourth-century Christianity, first- to third-century rabbinic Judaism (to some extent), and seventh-century Islam. In the previous three chapters, I showed in detail how fourth-century Christianity suddenly, and without intending to do so, acquired a *canon* of holy scripture. I will now consider parallel developments in early Islam and late Second-Temple Judaism.

In the early decades following the death of Muhammad, we can see an official canonizing process that resembles the canonizing activity of Catholic Christianity during the previous two centuries. Shortly after Muhammad's death, in 632, Muslim officials in Mecca (the '*ulamā*) met at the order of the Caliph 'Uthman (644–656)[8] to create a standard edition of the Qur'an. These officials wanted to put a decisive end to the confusion arising from the many differing and overlapping fragments and pieces of revelation that had been given to different individuals by the Prophet over the twenty-year period when he was in Medina and then Mecca. Caliph 'Uthman called together a commission of specialists from different regions, and this group created a single standard edition, called the Qur'an ("Recitation"). This edition—the first book written in Arabic— was officially promulgated in the early 650s at Mecca and then sent to Kufa, Basra, and Damascus, where it was readily accepted. There is evidence that the Caliph aroused considerable opposition when he tried to destroy all existing variants, but the new official version gradually drove other recensions out of circulation in the general desire for uniformity.

In addition to creating a single consistent text of God's revelation to the Prophet, Muslim scholars also encouraged the use of a creed of sorts, the *shahāda:* "There is no God but Allah, and Muhammad is His Prophet." The Greek-school type of three-fold structure: *official succession,* responsible for preserving and maintaining the *sacred scripture,* and its officially accepted *summary interpretation* (or creed), did not extend in Islam's case to the *sunna* (the example) of Muhammad, which became the basis, along with the Qur'an, of all Muslim law. The *sunna* is made up of numerous *hadith*—narrative anecdotes about the Prophet. These have proliferated broadly in the diverse ethnic regions to which Islam has spread.[9] It would be intriguing to speculate as to why the *hadith* literature was not drawn into Islam's powerful "canonizing" tendency but instead allowed to remain more or less free from it, following a more traditional, boundless model of scripture accumulation.

The Canonization of Halakah in Third-Century Rabbinic Judaism

It used to be the custom to point to the "Council of Jamnia" as the occasion when the Hebrew Bible was "canonized." No longer. The scholarly consensus has gone through a sea-change in understanding, largely because of the devastating critiques of the Jamnia hypothesis brought forward by two scholars, Jack P. Lewis[10] and Sid Z. Leiman.[11] However, "shedding the Jamnia mentality has not been easy."[12] I suggested in Chapter One that this was because biblical scholars were ignorant of the comparative religions evidence concerning the enormous difference between *scripture* and a *canon* of scripture. As far as Judaism is concerned, there is no evidence that the Hebrew *scriptures* were ever *canonized.* Christian scholars invented the canonization event called "the Council of Jamnia" and described it in terms resembling a Christian council. The evidence from Qumran vindicated Lewis and Leiman, so that today scholars like J. VanderKam can categorically assert: "As nearly as we can tell, there was *no canon* of scripture in Second Temple Judaism."[13] C. A. Evans agrees: "From the sources we possess, it is not possible to deduce the precise boundaries of the 'canon' of Jesus . . . or of anyone else in the early first century."[14]

With the illusion of a "Council of Jamnia" out of the way, the question remains: did *any* scripture selection process take place in formative rabbinic Judaism?[15] As we saw in Chapters Two and

Three, to answer that question we must first ask: are there any signs of the influence of Greek philosophy and Greek *polis* ideology upon early rabbinic Judaism? The answer given in those chapters was *Yes*: each Jewish community had a synagogue with a president and a ruling council. The rabbis carefully preserved their successions of teachers. There were two prominent "schools of thought," Beth Hillel and Beth Shammai, in which the rabbis argued according to Greek-style rules of logic. Why did they need logical arguments? Because the rabbis believed that "prophecy had ceased" in Israel and that God's will was now to be discerned by majority vote.[16]

So did they vote on the scripture? There is no evidence that they did. But the story doesn't end there. In the early third century C.E., under the leadership of Judah the Prince, the rabbis said, "There are too many torahs in Israel," and set about condensing and pruning all existing *halakoth* until there was one authoritative collection: the Mishnah. It was organized into topics ("seeds," "women," "sabbath," and so on) and became the official basis for all rabbinic legal decisions, or, if you will, a Jewish version of canon law. To me, this is a close parallel to the church councils canonizing the scriptures in the Christian Church. Both are efforts to put a boundary around what had threatened to become boundless. The observations of J. N. Lightstone are suggestive:[17]

> Both in substance and in literary form Mishnah gives the impression of completeness, exhaustiveness, and closure. . . . [It contains a historical perspective that] defines the limits of the rabbis' canon. In their view, no books authored outside of this frame are scriptural, and, therefore, scripture is closed by definition. It is a perfect whole, . . . just as Mishnah, in its subject matter and literary traits, . . . is exhaustive and complete.[18]

Was there ever an express attempt to canonize the Hebrew Bible? The evidence is meager at best. Within the Mishnah we find the earliest datable rabbinic discussion of which scriptures "defile the hands."[19] Is this a reference to a scripture selection process such as we see in Eusebius's careful discussions, or is it more similar to a conciliar canonization of Hebrew scripture? For a variety of reasons, scholars don't think so—although *some sort of sifting process* is clearly going on. Whatever it was, the first reference to an explicit *approved list of scripture* does not appear until the sixth century, in the Babylonian Talmud, *Baba Batra* 14b–15a.[20]

The codification of the Mishnah by Judah the Prince around 220 C.E. resembles the intense and creative halakic activity at Qumran in some ways, but differs in others. The influence of Greek culture on the rabbis may be one reason for the difference. Judah the Prince was well versed in the Greek language and may have known elements of Greek philosophy. For a much clearer illustration of the influence of Greek philosophy and Greek culture upon first century C.E. Judaism, consider this passage from *Against Apion*, by Josephus. He is telling his enemy, the Egyptian philosopher Apion, that the records of the Greeks, Chaldeans, and Egyptians are full of confusion, inconsistency, and inaccuracy (all Greek-style insults), but not so those of the Hebrews. Israel's histories, Josephus assured Apion, were all written by Israel's prophets:

> It therefore naturally, or rather necessarily, follows—seeing that with us it is not open to everybody to write the records, and that there is no discrepancy in what is written; seeing that, on the contrary, the prophets alone had this privilege, obtaining their knowledge of the most remote and ancient history through the inspiration which they owed to God, and committing to writing a clear account of the events of their own time just as they occurred—it follows, I say, that we do not possess myriads of inconsistent books, conflicting with each other. Our books, those which are justly accredited, are but two and twenty, and contain the record of all time. . . . [Thus] we have given practical proof of our reverence for our own Scriptures. For, although such long ages have now passed, no one has ventured either to add, or to remove, or to alter a syllable.[21]

This paragraph has raised many questions.[22] For the purposes of this discussion, however, I merely note that in this passage Josephus exhibits all of the basic elements that appear later in second- and

third-century philosophical Christianity, when it began to imitate
the Greek schools: a strong emphasis upon accuracy, consistency,
and clarity; an explicit reference to *a small, fixed number of completely harmonious scriptures* that have been "justly accredited"
or *approved* (implying that this is a unanimous opinion, though
Josephus does not say among which authorities); and that all this
is possible because of the dedication and fidelity of *an unbroken
succession of Israel's priests.* This clear illustration of the influence
of the Greek philosophical schools' values and goals[23] should not
be overemphasized. *Against Apion* was an apologetic writing that
was intended to be read by outsiders (Greeks and Romans). In it,
Josephus defended the honor and dignity of his nation and its sacred
writings in ways he hoped would be effective with his Greek-speaking audience, but there is no evidence that his statement describes
the actual situation in late Second-Temple Judaism.[24]

After Judah the Prince and the promulgation of the Mishnah,
the somewhat Greek-influenced schools of rabbinic Judaism continued to standardize, clarify, control, regulate, and, most important
of all, dispute matters of halakah. This effort came to fruition in the
fifth-century Babylonian Talmud, where each page is a visual monu-
ment to freedom of thought and interpretation. In the center of
each page, a small portion of the Mishnah is quoted. Ranged around
it are the interpretive and explanatory comments of subsequent rabbis (the Tannaim and Amoraim—the Gemara), sometimes from
different countries and rarely agreeing with each other. At the bottom of the page are quotations of anonymous rabbis of unknown
date and provenance, usually disagreeing with the authoritative
statements above. As the halakic tradition continued to expand and
develop, Jack Lightstone observes, by the fifth century "the core rabbinic curriculum" included much additional traditional material:
"Scripture, Mishnah, midrash, halakah, and aggadah."[25] All of these
components "were perceived as constituent elements of the 'whole
Torah' and they all rested on the authority of Moses."[26]

This huge mass of growing, evolving, traditional material illustrates my contention in Chapter One that *scripture* is a boundless,

living mass of heterogeneous sacred texts found in many religions of the world.[27] These *scriptures* are very different from *canons of scripture,* which are brought into being by government officials legalizing the choice of a particular collection of scripture. Comparisons with other scriptures and other canons allow us to recognize that the Christian *canonization* process involved a governmental intrusion into what had been a *scripture selection* process, which grew naturally out of the Greek schools, and the Greek philosophical quest for authentic writings of a school's founder and accurate interpretations of them. Judah the Prince and Josephus represent partial parallel variants caused by the same Greek influence in the early Judaism of the Common Era. It is noteworthy that Josephus, who otherwise represents a clear example of the influence of the Greek philosophical school model in this as in other respects, does not use the word *canon* when referring to the normative list of twenty-two sacred writings in the Hebrew Bible. He did not speak of a canon because explicit "canonization" of Jewish scripture never happened. Indeed, my second contention in this book is that the creation of a *canon of scripture* was a unique development in the world's religions, found for the first time in fourth- and fifth-century Romanized Catholic Christianity and imitated three centuries later by the Caliph 'Uthman's official canonization of the official text of the Qur'an.

Developments in Christianity during the Middle Ages Down to the Reformation

In two ways, Augustine created a path that would be followed by subsequent bishops and theologians in the west for the next thousand years. First, he established a conception of the Christian faith that, in practice, had little need for the scriptures which had been laboriously selected and preserved by his predecessors over hundreds of years. Second, he pioneered a harmonizing method of Gospel interpretation that permitted the church to overlook the embarrassing presence of four rather disparate narratives (the Gospels) by treating them as a single, monolithic block.

As a recent convert (386) and more recently installed bishop of Hippo (395), Augustine took part in a number of church councils that fixed the number of what were—by his time—the conventionally accepted[28] twenty-seven writings for the New Testament: the Council of Hippo (ca. 393), the First Synod of Carthage, and the Third Council of Carthage (397). When Augustine heard that one of his former Manichaean associates was circulating a list containing criticisms and objections to the Gospels, like the criticisms raised by Porphyry a century earlier, he dropped what he was doing and wrote a defense of the Gospels entitled *On the Harmony of the Evangelists* (ca. 405–410). During this same period, Augustine was also writing a guide to biblical interpretation, eventually misleadingly titled *On Christian Doctrine* (begun in 397 and completed about 426). Without detracting from the skillful and important discussion of the science of hermeneutics contained in the *De doctrina christiana,* I wish to mention two points. First of all, it is in this writing that Augustine closed the door, as far as western Christianity was concerned, on any further discussion regarding which books should be in the Bible:[29]

> The most skillful interpreter of the sacred writings, then, will be he who in the first place has read them all and retained them in his knowledge, if not yet with full understanding, still with such knowledge as reading gives,—those of them, at least, that are called canonical. . . . *Now, in regard to the canonical Scriptures, he must follow the judgment of the greater number of catholic churches.*[30]

In short, Augustine recommended that everyone should abide by what the majority of Catholic Churches—meeting in church councils—had decided. Then, having established what he took to be a secure basis for the canon of the Bible, he went on to argue that while much of the Bible could be taken literally, much of it needed to be interpreted allegorically. Once that is done, he said, Christian interpreters were left with three central theological and moral truths to guide them, and had little further need for the Bible.

Thus a man who is resting upon [these three truths:] faith, hope and love, and who keeps a firm hold upon these, *does not need the Scriptures except for the purpose of instructing others.* Many live without copies of the Scriptures . . . [because they possess] these three graces.[31]

Secondly, Augustine decided to quell once and for all the sniping and mockery of generations of learned critics of the faith about the alleged inconsistencies among the Gospel accounts. The problem arose in the first place because the "philosophically" oriented church of the second and third centuries vigorously claimed to use, only the very earliest, authentic, and true narratives about the Lord and his apostles. As the conviction grew that the four Gospels now in the New Testament were genuine and authentic, church leaders were increasingly nonplussed to discover that each Gospel was considerably different from the others. Periodic attempts to dismiss or paper over the differences (especially between the two diverse genealogies in Matthew and Luke) were made, but these stopgap measures crumbled before the serious and sustained objections and critiques of philosophical scholars such as Celsus and Porphyry. So Augustine devised an ingenious, indeed unique theory of Gospel composition that made it possible for him to remove all inconsistencies, all differences in time references, and all basic incongruities in narrative structure—even the great theological divergences between the Synoptic Gospels and John—by harmonizing them.[32] This approach immediately became popular and remained the preferred way to "make the Gospels agree with one another" through the Middle Ages, the Reformation (think of John Calvin's *Harmony of the Synoptic Gospels*), and on down to modern times.

Martin Luther Breaks Free of the Canonical Straitjacket

When Luther stood before the emperor Charles V and his advisors and dignitaries on April 17, 1521, and claimed that "popes and councils have erred and contradicted each other," he cancelled at one stroke the primary justification for accepting the Christian canon that had been provided by Augustine and Catholic bishops all the way back to Nicaea. In the tumult that followed his appearance at Worms, the elector Fredrick hid Luther, who was now an outlaw, in the Wartburg Castle. During this period of enforced seclusion, he took up the task of translating the Bible into German with the help of Philipp Melanchthon and some trusted friends.

What books did Luther include in his Scripture? For the Old Testament, everyone knew that Jerome had designated the writings in the Greek Old Testament (the Septuagint), but not in the Hebrew Old Testament, as "apocrypha" (meaning uncanonical). Luther followed the same procedure. As for the New Testament, he had read or heard of the *Ecclesiastical History* of Eusebius, with its precise list of "disputed" writings: 2 Peter, 2 and 3 John, James, Epistle to the Hebrews, Revelation of John. He had serious theological objections to statements in the Epistle of James, with its claim that "faith without works is dead" (Jas 2:17) and that "if a man says he has faith but has not works, can his faith save him?" (Jas 2:14). He also objected to the basic idea in the Epistle to the Hebrews that there was only one repentance (Heb 6:4): Luther asserted that "our whole life must consist of repentance!" Again, he felt that the Revelation of John was not a revelation at all but a confusing and dangerous document. Accordingly, he put these writings in a separate group at the end of his German translation of the New Testament, with the warning not to found any doctrines upon them.

In so doing, Luther contributed to the rumblings that had been going on for more than one hundred years in France, Spain, England, Hungary, Czechoslovakia, Italy, Holland, and the Scandinavian countries. These rumblings eventually erupted in a massive series of explosions that dislodged the huge logjam that had accumulated in western civilization for over a millennium. Along with the enormous upheaval in Christian doctrine, the straitjacket of canon was torn off Christian scripture, and a prodigious religious vitality began to flow through Europe once again. As always, enormous religious vitality was not a harbinger of peace.

Enlightenment Scholars Reject the Christian (and Jewish) Canon of Scriptures

The Roman Catholic Church launched numerous attempts to thwart, or to co-opt, the Protestant revolution of Martin Luther and the other reformers in efforts collectively known as the Counter-Reformation. One signal event affecting the history of the biblical canon was the Council of Trent (1545–1563). From the perspective of the Council, it might have been bad enough for Luther to follow Jerome's lead and relegate certain writings in the Old Testament to second-class status; it was another matter altogether for him to demote a number of well-known New Testament writings to "non-canonical" status. True, no other reformer followed Luther in this, even his own colleagues in Germany. Nevertheless, the Council of Trent was concerned enough to declare officially that no writings could be removed from the Bible and none added.

The Protestant Reformation, following on the heels of the Italian Renaissance and coinciding with new currents of popular nationalism, unlocked passions and aspirations of peoples and nations across Europe. Before long, sixteenth-century Europe was embroiled in a series of wars and revolutions—religious, political, and economic—as nation fought nation, class fought class, and Protestant fought Catholic. The period between 1555 (the Peace of Augsburg) and 1648 (the Peace of Westphalia) was one of the bloodiest in Europe's history, causing men and women everywhere to cry out, "There must be a better way!" Consequently, in the latter part of the 17th century and throughout the 18th, vocal critics denounced Christianity in all its forms, including Christian monarchy. Not Christianity alone, but all religious enthusiasm, obedience to tradition, and blind acceptance of religious authority were vehemently rejected.

In the eyes of many, Christianity had failed the test of living up to its own moral standards. When "Christian" princes and bishops used torture and death to coerce obedience, and when "Christian" theologians retreated behind authority and subterfuge to coerce dissidents into obeying orthodox Christian doctrine, people might well have asked: "But doesn't the Bible say, 'Thou shalt not kill'? And didn't Jesus teach, 'Turn the other cheek'?" Whole generations of Christians, Roman Catholic as well as Protestant, had failed the most important test of all: "Let your works shine before men so that people will see them and give God glory."

Grief in the wake of a century of bloody strife welled up in rage at religion and all that it stood for. No longer were people willing to vest authority in any religion—Christianity, Judaism or Islam. All religions were seen as potential breeding grounds for tyranny, hypocrisy, and ignorance. In country after country, intellectuals and common people alike turned against all religion in favor of the scientific preference for objective fact and tangible evidence. *Sapere aude,* "Dare to think for yourselves," became the motto of the Enlightenment, and the spirit of modern science, with its inherent suspicion of religion, was born.

We in America have inherited the legacy of that repudiation of religious tyranny and preference for scientific truth. We received from our European ancestors our belief in the fundamental rightness of "freedom of thought." We have heeded the advice of John Locke and established in our Constitution what we now regard as a great wall of separation between Church and State (though not between God and Country) so as never again to ruin the purity of religious exploration and belief by mixing it with political power and armed coercion.

It is no accident that it is primarily in modern America that the most persistent, creative, and important proposals for alternatives to traditional Christian and Jewish and Muslim belief, practice, *and scripture* have appeared. Many scholars and laypeople strongly agree that "the Christian [and Jewish] canon is obsolete."[33]

Unfortunately, this repudiation is so broad and sweeping that it also takes in the entire structure of orthodoxy, as expressed in authentic early writings and doctrines, and formulated by figures like Origen and Eusebius. I would propose this correction to our modern rejection of the scriptural canon: freedom from having a *canon,* i.e., from restriction to a specific set of writings compelled by the use of force, need not and should not extend to jettisoning, at the same time, the valuable results of the original orthodox Christian *scripture selection process* as described by Eusebius in his *Ecclesiastical History.* Although our modern grasp of what the early Catholic authorities accomplished may go hand-in-hand with a number of disagreements as to specific books they included in the New Testament, their objectivity, honesty, and dedication are nevertheless worthy of our sincere admiration and respect.

Appendix A

REFERENCES IN EUSEBIUS'S ECCLESIASTICAL HISTORY TO EARLY CHRISTIAN WRITINGS

Early Christian Writing	Reference in Eusebius's Ecclesiastical History (X.X.X = Book, Chapter, and Verse)	Page number in Cruse's translation
Acts of the Apostles by Luke	1.5.3	16
	1.12.1	28
	2.8.1	43–44
	2.8.2–2.9.1	44
	2.10.1	45
	2.11.1	46
	2.12.2	47
	2.17.6, quoting Philo	51
	2.18.9	56
	2.21.3	57
	2.22.1	58
	2.22.6	58
	3.4.1	68–69
	3.4.4	69
	3.4.6	69
	3.4.10	69
	3.25.1–3	91
	3.31.5	96
	3.39.10	105

Early Christian Writing	Reference in Eusebius's Ecclesiastical History (X.X.X = Book, Chapter, and Verse)	Page number in Cruse's translation
	4.23.3, quoting Dionysius of Corinth	135
	4.29.5	142
	6.14.2, quoting Clement of Alexandria	204
	7.25.15, quoting Dionysius	262
Acts of Andrew	3.25.6	91
Acts of John	3.25.6	91
Acts of Paul	3.3.5	68
	3.25.6	91
Agbar, Jesus' letter to	1:13.9–10, quoting public records of Edessa	30–32
Apostles, epistles of	7.24.5, quoting Dionysius	259
Apostles, writings of	2.17.12, quoting Philo	52
Barnabas, Epistle of	3.25.4	91
	6.14.1, quoting Clement of Alexandria	204
	6.13.6, quoting Clement of Alexandria	203
1 Clement	3.16.1	82
	3.38.1	103
	4.22.1	134
	4.23.11	137
	5.6.3, quoting Irenaeus	162
	6.13.6, quoting Clement of Alexandria	203
2 Clement	3.38.4	103
1 Corinthians	1.12.1	28
Dialogues of Peter and Apion	3.38.5	103
Diatessaron	4.29.6	142
Galatians, Epistle to	1.12.1	28

Early Christian Writing	Reference in Eusebius's Ecclesiastical History (X.X.X = Book, Chapter, and Verse)	Page number in Cruse's translation
Gospels (Matthew and Luke)	1.7.1, quoting Africanus	19
	1.7.3, quoting Africanus	19
	1.11.3	27
	1.12.1	28
	2.17.12	52
	3.25.1–3	91
	3.37.2	102
	6.14.5, quoting Clement of Alexandria	205
	6.25.4, quoting Origen	215
	7.15.4	252
	7.24.5, quoting Dionysius	259
Hebrews, Epistle to	2.17.12, quoting Philo	52
	3.3.5	68
	3.4.2	69
	3.38.1–3	103
	5.26.1, quoting Irenaeus	185
	6.13.6, quoting Clement of Alexandria	203
	6.14.2, quoting Clement of Alexandria	204
	6.20.3, quoting Caius	211
	6.25.11–14, quoting Origen	215–16
Hebrews, Gospel according to the	3.25.5	91
	3.27.4	93
	3.39.17, quoting Papias	106
	4.22.8, quoting Hegesippus	135
Hermas; see Pastor [The Shepherd, by Hermas]		
Institutions of the Apostles	3.25.4	91
James, Epistle of	2.23.25, quoting Josephus	62
	3.25.3	91

Early Christian Writing	Reference in Eusebius's Ecclesiastical History (X.X.X = Book, Chapter, and Verse)	Page number in Cruse's translation
1 John	3.24.17	90
	3.25.2–3	91
	3.39.17, quoting Papias	106
	5.8.7, quoting Irenaeus	164
	6.25.10, quoting Origen	215
	7.25.7, quoting Dionysius	261
	7.25.8, quoting Dionysius	261
	7.25.9–10, quoting Dionysius	262
	7.25.17, quoting Dionysius	263
	7.25.24, quoting Dionysius	264
2 John	3.24.18	90
	3.25.3	91
	6.25.10, quoting Origen	215
	7.25.11, quoting Dionysius	262
3 John	3.24.18	90
	3.25.3	91
	6.25.10, quoting Origen	215
	7.25.11, quoting Dionysius	262
John, Gospel of	3.24.2	88
	3.24.5	89
	3.24.7	89
	3.24.11	90
	3.24.13	90
	3.24.14	90
	3.24.17	90
	5.8.4, quoting Irenaeus	164
	6.14.7, quoting Clement of Alexandria	205
	6.24.1	213
	6.25.6, quoting Origen	215
	6.25.9; quoting Origen	215
	7.25.7, quoting Dionysius	261
	7.25.8, quoting Dionysius	262
	7.25.12, quoting Dionysius	262
	7.25.17, quoting Dionysius	263
	7.25.24, quoting Dionysius	264

Early Christian Writing	Reference in Eusebius's Ecclesiastical History (X.X.X = Book, Chapter, and Verse)	Page number in Cruse's translation
John, Revelation (Apocalypse) of	3.18.2, quoting Irenaeus	83
	3.24.18	90
	3.25.2–3	91
	3.25.4	91
	3.28.2, quoting Caius	93–94
	3.29.1	94
	3.39.6	104
	4.18.8, quoting Justin Martyr	132
	4.26.2, quoting Melito of Sardis	138
	5.1.58	156–57
	5.8.5, quoting Irenaeus	164
	5:18.14, quoting Apollonius	177
	6.25.10, quoting Origen	215
	7.24.2–3	259
	7.24.3, quoting Dionysius	259
	7.25.1, quoting Dionysius	260
	7.25.6, quoting Dionysius	261
	7.25.9, quoting Dionysius	261
	7.25.15, quoting Dionysius	262
	7.25.24, quoting Dionysius	264
Jude, Epistle of	2.23.25	62
	3.25.3	91
	6.13.6, quoting Clement of Alexandria	203
	6.14.1, quoting Clement of Alexandria	204
Luke, Gospel of	1.7.1	19
	1.7.3, quoting Africanus	3
	1.7.10, quoting Africanus	20
	3.4.6	69
	3.24.7	89
	3.24.10	89
	3.24.13	90
	3.24.15	90
	5.8.3, quoting Irenaeus	164

Early Christian Writing	Reference in Eusebius's Ecclesiastical History (X.X.X = Book, Chapter, and Verse)	Page number in Cruse's translation
	6.25.6, quoting Origen	215
	6.31.3	219
Mark, Gospel of	2.15.1, quoting Clement of Alexandria	50
	2.15.2, quoting Clement of Alexandria and Papias	50
	2.16.1	50
	3.24.7	89
	3.24.10	89
	3.24.14	90
	3.39.14	105
	3.39.15–16, quoting John the Presbyter (as quoted by Papias)	106
	5.8.3, quoting Irenaeus	164
	6.14.6–7, quoting Clement of Alexandria	205
	6.25.5, quoting Origen	215
Matthew, Gospel of	1.7.5, quoting Africanus	19
	1.7.10, quoting Africanus	20
	3.10.3	166
	3.24.5	89
	3.24.6	89
	3.24.9	89
	3.24.13	90
	3.29.3–4, quoting Clement of Alexandria	94–5
	3.39.16, quoting Papias	106
	5.8.2, quoting Irenaeus	164
	6.17.1	207
	6.25.3–4, quoting Origen	215
	6.31.3	219
	6.36.2	221
Matthew, Gospel of (pseudo)	3.25.6	91
Pastor [The Shepherd by Hermas]	3.3.6	68
	3.25.4	91

Early Christian Writing	Reference in Eusebius's Ecclesiastical History (X.X.X = Book, Chapter, and Verse)	Page number in Cruse's translation
	5.8.7, quoting Irenaeus	164
Paul, Epistles of	2.17.12, quoting Philo	52
	3.3.5	68
	3.15.1	82
	3.24.4	89
	3.25.2–3	91
	3.30.1, quoting Clement of Alexandria	95
	4.29.5	142
	7.25.23, quoting Dionysius	263–64
1 Timothy	5.6.1, quoting Irenaeus	162
2 Timothy	2.22.2	58
	2.22.6	58
	3.4.8	69
1 Peter	2.15.2	50
	3.3.1	67
	3.25.2–3	91
	3.39.17, quoting Papias	106
	4.14.9	121
	5.8.7, quoting Irenaeus	164
	6.25.5, quoting Origen	215
	6.25.8, quoting Origen	215
2 Peter	3.3.1	67
	3.25.3	91
	6.25.8, quoting Origen	215
Peter, Acts of	3.3.2	67–68
Peter, Gospel of	3.3.2	67–68
	3.25.6	91
	6.12.2, quoting Serapion	202
	6.12.4, quoting Serapion	202
Peter, Preaching of	3.3.2	67–68
Peter, Revelation of	3.3.2	67–68
	6.14.1, quoting Clement of Alexandria	204
Thomas, Gospel of	3.25.6	91

Appendix B

WRITINGS CONSIDERED "SCRIPTURE" BY ONE OR ANOTHER CHRISTIAN GROUP

GOSPELS

Tatian, Diatessaron
Gospel of the Ebionites
Gospel of the Egyptians
Gospel of the Hebrews
Gospel of the Hebrews
Gospel of James (Protevangelium Jacobi)
Gospel according to John
Gospel of Judas
According to Luke
Gospel of Mary
Marcion's "Gospel"
Gospel according to Mark
Gospel according to Matthew
Gospel of the Nazarenes
Gospel of Nicodemus
Gospel of Philip
Gospel of Peter
The Preaching of Peter (Kerygma Petri)
Gospel of Thomas
Infancy Gospel of Thomas
Gospel of Truth

ACTS

Acts of Andrew
Acts of the Apostles
Acts of Paul and Thecla
Acts of Peter
Acts of Pilate
Acts of Thomas

LETTERS OF PAUL

Colossians
1, 2, and 3 Corinthians
Ephesians
Galatians
To the Hebrews
To the Laodiceans
Correspondence of Paul and Seneca
Philemon
Philippians
Romans
1 & 2 Thessalonians
1 & 2 Timothy
Titus

OTHER EPISTLES

Jesus' Correspondence with King Agbar
Epistle of the Apostles
Epistle of Barnabas
1 & 2 Clement
Epistle of James
1, 2 & 3 Epistles of John
Epistle of Jude
1 & 2 Epistles of Peter

APOCALYPSES, SECRET TEACHINGS

Apocalypse of John
Greater Questions of Mary

Lesser Questions of Mary
Apocalypse of Paul
Apocalypse of Peter
Kerygma Petri
Pistis Sophia
Sibylline Oracles
Apocalypse of Thomas

DIDACTIC WRITINGS

The Pastor (The Shepherd of Hermas)
Didache or Teachings of the Lord

WISDOM, HYMNS

Odes of Solomon
Wisdom of Solomon

Based on the lists of New Testament Apocrypha in M. R. James, *The Apocryphal New Testament* (Oxford: Oxford University Press, 1960), and Edgar Hennecke, *New Testament Apocrypha* (ed. W. Schnee-melcher; trans. R. McL. Wilson; 2 vols.; Philadelphia: Westminster, 1965). This list attempts to be complete, but there are lesser-known writings not included, particularly from the Nag Hammadi Library, because they were so little known to Christians elsewhere and never mentioned by Eusebius. (Writings in the Nag Hammadi Library are listed in Appendix C.)

THE LIBRARY FROM NAG HAMMADI

The following writings were contained in thirteen codexes buried in the fourth century outside a Pachomian monastery near Chenoboskion, Egypt, probably in the wake of Athanasius's Festal Letter of 362, which proscribed a number of writings, including the *Gospel of Philip* and the *Gospel of Thomas*, which appear on this list. The wide range of materials included here—some clearly arising from Christian Gnosticism, some not clearly Christian, others (like Plato's *Republic*) predating both Gnosticism or Christianity—gives some indication of the eclecticism and tolerance for diversity embraced by some, at least, in the fourth-century church. From *The Nag Hammadi Library*, revised edition by James M. Robinson (1988).

Writings mentioned by Eusebius are shown in italics.

The Prayer of the Apostle Paul
The Apocryphon of James
The Gospel of Truth
The Treatise on the Resurrection
The Tripartite Tractate
The Apocryphon of John

The Gospel of Thomas
The Gospel of Philip
The Hypostasis of the Archons
On the Origin of the World
The Exegesis on the Soul
The Book of Thomas the Contender
The Gospel of the Egyptians (also titled *The Holy Book of*
    the Great Invisible Spirit, probably *not* the Gospel of the
    Egyptians discussed by Eusebius)
Eugnostos the Blessed and The Sophia of Jesus Christ
The Dialogue of the Savior
The Apocalypse of Paul
The (First) Apocalypse of James
The (Second) Apocalypse of James
The Apocalypse of Adam
The Acts of Peter and the Twelve Apostles (probably *not* the
    Acts of Peter discussed by Eusebius)
The Thunder, Perfect Mind
Authoritative Teaching
The Concept of Our Great Power
Plato, *Republic* 588A–589B
The Discourse on the Eighth and Ninth
The Prayer of Thanksgiving (and Scribal Note)
Asclepius 21–29
The Paraphrase of Shem
The Second Treatise of the Great Seth
Apocalypse of Peter (probably *not* the Apocalypse of Peter
    discussed by Eusebius)
The Teachings of Silvanus
The Three Steles of Seth
Zostrianos
The Letter of Peter to Philip
Melchizedek
The Thought of Norea
The Testimony of Truth
Marsanes

The Interpretation of Knowledge
A Valentinian Exposition (with *On the Anointing, On Baptism* A
and B, *On the Eucharist* A and B)
Allogenes
Hypsiphrone
The Sentences of Sextus
Fragments
Trimorphic Protennoia
The Gospel of Mary
The Act of Peter (probably *not* related to the Acts of Peter
discussed by Eusebius)

Timeline of Figures and Events Discussed in the Text

B.C.E.

Earlier *Upanishads* (Hinduism), 7th century
First stirrings of Athenian Democracy: **Solon** (*ca.* 640–560),
    Cleisthenes (*ca.* 570–508), **Peisistratus** (560–527)
Emphasis on precision in philosophical thinking: **Pythagoras** (*ca.*
    569–*ca.* 475); **Plato** (427–347); **Aristophanes'** parody in *The*
    Frogs (*ca.* 405); in political thinking, **Aristotle** (384–322);
    Aeschines (*ca.* 390–314)
Earliest Taoist writings, 4th century
Conquests of **Alexander the Great** and institution of the *polis*
    (336–23)
Callimachus of Cyrene, librarian at Alexandria (305–240)
Dionysius of Halicarnassus, historian and rhetorician, 1st
    century

C.E.
First century

Philo of Alexandria (*ca.* 20 B.C.E.–50 C.E.)
Jesus of Nazareth crucified, 30
Didache, mid to late first century

James, brother of Jesus, killed in Jerusalem (62); **Peter** and **Paul,** killed in Rome (64)

Jewish revolt against Rome (66–73); **Titus** destroys the Temple (70)

At the end of the 1st century: Early Christian writings *1 Clement, Epistle of Barnabas, Shepherd of Hermas*

Rise of Pharisaism; "Council of Jamnia" (*ca.* 90)?

Apollonios of Tyana, pagan teacher and savior figure

Second century

Cerinthus, millennialist Christian (*fl.* 100)

Early Christian bishops and apologists **Ignatius of Antioch** (lived *ca.* 50–*ca.*107) and **Polycarp of Smyrna** (69–155)

Jewish Revolts in the eastern Roman Empire and Palestine (113–115 and 132–135)

Gnostic teachers **Marcion** in Rome (*ca.* 140–160); **Basilides** in Alexandria (120–130); **Valentinus** in both cities (*fl.* 136–160)

Lucian of Samosata, pagan philosopher (*ca.* 115–200)

Age of the Christian apologists: **Justin Martyr** (*fl.* 130–165); **Melito of Sardis, Miltiades, Theophilus of Antioch, Athenagoras of Athens; Irenaeus of Lyons,** author of *Against the Heresies* (*ca.* 185)

Montanus, with companions Prisca and Maximilla, inaugurates the "New Prophecy" in Phrygia (172)

Clement of Alexandria, theologian and apologist (*fl.* 190–215)

Galen of Pergamum, physician and critic (*ca.* 130–200); **Celsus of Alexandria,** philosopher and critic (*fl.* 178)

Third century

Tertullian of Carthage, Christian apologist and theologian (*fl.* 197–230)

Hippolytus, bishop of Rome, writes *Refutation of All Heretics* (*ca.* 210)

Judah "the Prince" compiles the *Mishnah* (220)

Diogenes Laertius writes *Lives and Opinions of Eminent Philosophers* (*ca.* 230)

Origen of Alexandria, Christian theologian and biblical scholar
 (185–254)
Persecution of Christians under the emperor **Decius** (249–51);
 under the emperor **Valerian** (258–60)
Mani, founder of Manicheism (*ca.* 210–275)
Plotinus, pagan philosopher (*ca.* 205–269); **Porphyry of Tyre**,
 pagan philosopher (*ca.* 233–304)

Fourth century

The "Great Persecution" under Galerius and Diocletian (303–
 313); **Pamphilius of Caesarea** is martyred
Constantine defeats **Maxentius** at the Milvian Bridge (311); pro-
 mulgates the "Edict of Milan" (313); defeats Licinius (324) to
 become sole emperor; convenes the Council of Nicaea (325);
 dies, 337
Eusebius (*ca.* 260–339), with **Lactantius, Hosius,** and **Miltiades,**
 bishop of Rome, provide orthodox leadership of the Catho-
 lic church under Constantine; writes Books 1–7 of the *Ecclesiastical History* (315); Books 8–10 (by 325)
Pope Damasus commissions **Jerome** to translate the Greek Bible
 into Latin (383)
Third Synod of Carthage (397)
Ambrose, theologian and bishop of Milan (340–97); **Augustine,**
 converted to Christianity (386), installed bishop of Hippo
 (395); writes *On the Harmony of the Evangelists* (*ca.* 405–10),
 On Christian Doctrine (completed 426)

Fifth and sixth centuries

Compilation of the Jerusalem and Babylonian Talmuds

Seventh century

After the death of **Muhammad** (632), the caliph **'Uthman** convenes Muslim officials (the *'ulamā*) in Mecca to create a standard edition of the Qur'an (644–656)

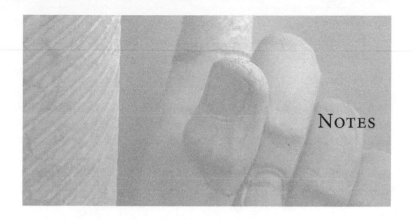

Chapter 1. What a "Canon" of Scripture Is—and Is Not

1. Lee Martin McDonald and James A. Sanders, eds., *The Canon Debate* (Peabody, Mass.: Hendrickson, 2002), 14 (emphasis added). See also Lee M. McDonald, *The Formation of the Christian Biblical Canon* (2nd ed.; Peabody, Mass.: Hendrickson, 1995).

2. For general comparative religions discussions of the term *scripture*, see Gustav Mensching, *Das heilige Wort: Eine religionsphänomenologische Untersuchung* (Bonn: Rohrscheid Verlag, 1937); Leo Koep, *Das himmlische Buch in Antike und Christentum* (Bonn: P. Hanstein, 1952); Johannes Leipoldt and Siegfried Morenz, *Heilige Schriften* (Leipzig: Harrassowitz, 1953); Frederick F. Bruce and Ernest G. Rupp, *Holy Book and Holy Tradition* (Grand Rapids, Mich.: Eerdmans, 1968); Jacob Neusner et al., eds., *Religious Writings and Religious Systems: Systemic Analysis of Holy Books in Christianity, Islam, Buddhism, Greco-Roman Religions, Ancient Israel and Judaism* (2 vols.; Brown Studies in Religion 2; Atlanta: Scholars Press, 1989); Frederick M. Denny and Rodney L. Taylor, eds., *The Holy Book in Comparative Perspective* (Columbia: University of South Carolina Press, 1985); and Miriam Levering, ed., *Rethinking Scripture: Essays from a Comparative Perspective* (Albany: State University of New York Press, 1989). The reports by Levering and her contributors reveal a number of ways in which automatic Western assumptions have skewed our perceptions of other religious traditions. For instance, William Graham protests against

the common Western assumption that *scriptures* necessarily mean written texts ("Scripture as Spoken Word," 129–69). Here the very term *scripture* is the culprit, since it literally means something written. But Wilfred Cantwell Smith, in "Scripture as Form and Concept: Their Emergence for the Western World," in Levering, *Rethinking Scripture,* 34–35, notes that the Hindu sacred texts were primarily oral for millennia, indeed, at least until the European Max Müller's printed edition of the Rig Veda in 1854. Smith continues: "[Müller's] turning of the Hindu Veda into *a book* is an instance of 19th century Western cultural imperialism" (35), not any the less dangerous for being totally unself-conscious. Moreover, Thomas Coburn writes that "the Western notion of a *critical edition* of an *'original text'* represents a startling intrusion upon Hindu reality with consequences that are complex and ill-understood" ("'Scripture' in India," in Levering, *Rethinking Scripture,* 122; italics added).

3. Levering, *Rethinking Scripture,* 12n3; italics added.

4. See Coburn, "Scripture in India," in ibid., 102–28.

5. L. Thompson, "Taoism: Classic and Canon," in Denny and Taylor, *The Holy Book in Comparative Perspective,* 204–23.

6. Ibid., 204.

7. Ibid. Thompson goes on to state that various attempts were made from time to time "to bring them all together in a rational system," with no success. Even the mid-fifteenth-century printed woodblock edition did not really stabilize the whole collection (205). However, despite Thompson's obvious awareness of the unbounded heterogeneity of the *Tao Tsang,* he can still say that "there is a recent abridgment of the Ming *Tao Tsang* that . . . attempts to prune the canon [*sic*] to manageable size" (207).

8. Consider this comment of Hartmut Stegemann in *The Library of Qumran* (Grand Rapids, Mich.: Eerdmans and Brill, 1998), 92: "Ten of the sixteen scrolls of Jubilees came from Cave 4. [In addition, six more were found in Caves 1, 2, 3, and 11.] This [large number of copies] unambiguously shows that, to the very end, the Qumran settlers considered Jubilees one of the most important works of their traditional literature." Cf. Eugene Ulrich's comment in *The Dead Sea Scrolls and the Origins of the Bible* (Grand Rapids, Mich.: Eerdmans and Brill, 1999), 16: "Beyond those books we now consider scripture, [the Sons of Israel] were composing a wide library of religious literature, some of which was considered as serious, as holy, [as later canonical texts including] Enoch and Jubilees, Sirach and Tobit."

9. Stegemann, *The Library of Qumran*, 96, writes: "The text of the Temple Scroll is conceived by its author as the sixth book of the Torah. The entire work was joined to the five books of Moses as of equal rank.... In particular, [putting] the many declarations of God in the first person singular is intended to document the fact that this book had the same authority as the other books of the Torah." J. VanderKam ("Questions of Canon Viewed through the Dead Sea Scrolls," in McDonald and Sanders, *The Canon Debate*, 100–104) declares: "The Temple Scroll includes material from approximately Exod 24 through much of Deuteronomy, but Deuteronomy appears to be the central scriptural foundation. As [Michael] Wise writes, the Temple Scroll 'mixes and matches portions from the latter four books with no real regard to the order of books in the Torah. The real basis for the scroll's redactional plan is quite different. Put simply, the redactor had in mind the production of a new Deut.'"

10. A. C. Sundberg, in "The Septuagint: The Bible of Hellenistic Judaism," in McDonald and Sanders, *The Canon Debate*, 86, cites B. J. Roberts's comment: "We can visualize the Biblical literature of the New Covenanters as covering a far wider range than either the Hebrew or the Alexandrian canon." He adds that, in Jean Carmignac's analysis of the War Scroll, "one cannot differentiate between the use of the books of the Hebrew canon and the extracanonical writings."

11. See E. Tov, "The Status of the Masoretic Text in Modern Text Editions of the Hebrew Bible: The Relevance of the Canon," in McDonald and Sanders, *The Canon Debate*, 240: "When the Qumran scrolls were written at Qumran and elsewhere, scribes created and consulted without distinction different texts of the Bible; all ... reflected the 'Bible' [to them] and all were authoritative, though not to the same extent.... The goal of [striving for] textual uniformity [did not appear until] later in the Judaism of the first century C.E. onward."

12. Ulrich, *Dead Sea Scrolls and the Origins of the Bible*, 25–31, 36–41; for a discussion of the views of F. M. Cross, E. Tov, and S. Talmon, see "Pluriformity in the Biblical Text," 79–98.

13. Cited in VanderKam, "Questions of Canon Viewed through the Dead Sea Scrolls," 94.

14. See Tov, "The Status of the Masoretic Text in Modern Text Editions of the Hebrew Bible," 234–51: "All of these literary stages were equally original, or alternatively, none of these stages should be thought to constitute 'the original text'" (248). See also Vanderkam, "Questions

of Canon Viewed through the Dead Sea Scrolls," 95: "It is clear that at Qumran, even for the pentateuchal books, there was some textual fluidity, not a single fixed text."

15. Ulrich, *The Dead Sea Scrolls and the Origins of the Bible*, 23.

16. McDonald and Sanders, *The Canon Debate*.

17. Vanderkam, "Questions of Canon Viewed through the Dead Sea Scrolls," in ibid., 91 (italics added); cf. 92.

18. J. N. Lightstone, "The Rabbis' Bible: The Canon of the Hebrew Bible and the Early Rabbinic Guild," in ibid., 174.

19. G. M. Hahneman, "The Muratorian Fragment and the Origins of the New Testament Canon," in ibid., 415: "If the earliest churches intended their successors to have a canon of scripture, either Old Testament or New Testament, we have no clear tradition to that effect."

20. See Sanders's discussion of the "stability and adaptability" of scripture, in "The Issue of Closure in the Canonical Process," in ibid., 256ff., 262–63.

21. Ibid., 253.

22. Ibid., 258–59.

23. Ibid., 262.

24. See Smith, "Scripture as Form and Concept: Their Emergence for the Western World," in Levering, *Rethinking Scripture*, 29–57, esp. 38–43; quote from p. 39.

25. Ibid., 43; italics added.

26. One looks in vain for any evidence that biblical scholars are conversant with other major religious traditions and their scriptures in the recent, full-scale discussion, in McDonald and Sanders, *The Canon Debate*. The same lack of any world religions perspective is also typical of the most recent full-scale monographs on the subject. These include McDonald, *The Formation of the Christian Biblical Canon*; R. Beckwith, *The Old Testament Canon of the New Testament Church and Its Background in Early Judaism* (Grand Rapids, Mich.: Eerdmans, 1985); and the influential study guide by H. Y. Gamble, Jr., *The New Testament Canon: Its Making and Meaning* (Minneapolis: Fortress Press, 1985). Although this last writing is now dated, Gamble's latest discussion of the topic is no different in this respect; see his otherwise magisterial treatment of the whole subject, "The New Testament Canon: Recent Research and the Status Quaestionis," in McDonald and Sanders, *The Canon Debate*, 267–94. For a classic survey and discussion of the older literature on the Christian canonization process, see Bruce M. Metzger, *The Canon of the New Testament: Its Origin, Development and*

Significance (Oxford: Clarendon, 1989), 24–36. One encounters a nadir in canon discussion in James Kugel's essay, "The Rise of Scripture in Israel," in *Early Biblical Interpretation* (ed. James L. Kugel and Rowan A. Greer; Philadelphia: Westminster, 1986). It is characterized by unhelpful statements. An example: "It may be appropriate here to say something about the 'canonization' of the Bible. This term has long been used by scholars to designate a moment in history when the final content of the Hebrew Bible was fixed, an act of sorting between the 'ins'. . . and the 'outs'" (57). After this simplistic description, Kugel goes on to say that perhaps it did not really happen "in a moment" nor was it a single act—indeed, that canonization was probably a "process that went on for some time." Then the issue is further confused when Kugel writes that it wasn't really a canon that was produced but "a group of basic texts . . . or at least it was a curriculum, or different curricula studied [!] by various groups [?]."

27. Gamble, "Christianity: Scripture and Canon," in Denny and Taylor, *The Holy Book in Comparative Perspective*, 47n3. For the three-year course of seminars and reports sponsored by the Canada Council on the Humanities and McMaster University in 1980–82, entitled "Normative Self-Definition of Judaism and Early Christianity," see *Jewish and Christian Self-Definition, Vol. 1: The Shaping of Christianity in the Second and Third Centuries* (Philadelphia: Fortress Press, 1980); *Vol. 2: Aspects of Judaism in the Graeco-Roman World* (Philadelphia: Fortress Press, 1981); and *Vol. 3: Self-Definition in the Greco-Roman World* (Philadelphia: Fortress Press, 1982).

28. The same complaint applies to Kendall W. Folkert's essay "'Canons' of 'Scripture,'" in Levering's anthology, *Rethinking Scripture*, 170–79), that might have shed light on the uniqueness of canonizing scripture. Unfortunately, his discussion of "vectoring" succumbs to all of the pitfalls of novel terminology. Levering's own four categories in the "reception of scripture" are much more illuminating and useful; see "Scripture and Its Reception," in *Rethinking Scripture*, 58–101.

29. See H. Beyer, "κανών," in G. Kittel, ed., *Theological Dictionary of the New Testament* (trans. G. Bromiley; 10 vols.; Grand Rapids, Mich.: Eerdmans, 1965), 3:597. The discussion of κανών in Wilhelm Schmid und Otto Stählin's revised edition of Wilhelm von Christ, *Geschichte der griechischen Literatur* (6th German ed.; Munich: C. H. Beck, 1961), Part II: "Die nachklassische Period der griechischen Literatur," 1122ff., boringly and misleadingly rehashes the usual material on the canonization of the Old Testament and the New Testament.

30. For the most extensive recent discussion, see McDonald, "Factors Limiting the Scope of the New Testament Canon," in *The Formation of the Christian Biblical Canon,* 170–90, which gives more or less the same alleged "factors" found already in H. von Campenhausen, *The Formation of the Christian Bible* (Philadelphia: Fortress Press, 1972). E. Ferguson, "Factors Leading to the Selection and Closure of the New Testament Canon: A Survey of Some Recent Studies," in McDonald and Sanders, *The Canon Debate,* 295–320, makes the unfortunate decision to split the "factors" into "internal" and "external," as if the canonization process took place within some sort of protective shell. The scheme comes to grief immediately when he lists Marcion, Valentinus, and Montanus as "external" influences on Christianity! (309–16). H. Y. Gamble, "The New Testament Canon," in McDonald and Sanders, *The Canon Debate,* 293, gives a quick survey of the usually cited "influences" from the major heretical groups but then dismisses them all by saying, "None of the heterodox movements of the second century can be shown to have had any strong, let alone decisive, effect on the history of the canon." Instead, writes Gamble, "it was the liturgical life of the ancient church which was the primary context of the use and interpretation of scripture." I doubt that the variety of liturgical practices found in the second- and third-century orthodox branch of Christianity was so standardized or uniform that it produced a single standard set of writings.

Chapter 2. The Greek *Polis* and the Demand for Accuracy

1. For the classic discussion, see Karl Jaspers, "The Axial Period," in *Basic Philosophical Writings* (ed. E. Ehrlich et al.; Grand Rapids: Zondervan Reprint, 1994), 381–90. Jaspers defined the Axial Age as the period from 600 to 200 B.C.E., during which lived Socrates of Greece, Isaiah of Israel, Zoroaster of Persia, Buddha of India, and Confucius of China—each one a revolutionary figure. In Greece, the main Axial Age figures were Parmenides (ca. 515 B.C.E.), Heraclitus (ca. 540–480 B.C.E.), Socrates (ca. 469–399 B.C.E.), Plato (428–348/7 B.C.E.), Aristotle (384–322 B.C.E.), Thucydides (460–404 B.C.E.), and Archimedes (ca. 287–212 B.C.E.).

2. For a still useful overview of the evolution of urban types, see Lewis Mumford, *The City in History: Its Origins, Its Transformations, and Its Prospects* (New York: Harcourt Brace and World, 1961).

3. For the main characteristics of the Neolithic village culture, see ibid., ch. 1, "Sanctuary, Village, and Stronghold," esp. 21–28.

4. This is similar to the kind of society we see reflected in the Code of Hammurabi (ca. early eighteenth century B.C.E.).

5. See Mumford, *The City in History,* ch. 2, "The Crystallization of the City," 29–118, i.e., what I am calling the "archaic" city type. See also Paul Wheatley, *The Pivot of the Four Quarters: A Preliminary Inquiry into the Origins and Character of the Ancient Chinese City* (Chicago: Aldine, 1971), 477–82, for a superb profile of the first "archaic" Chinese cities.

6. Gilbert Murray, *Five Stages of Greek Religion* (New York: Doubleday, 1955), 38.

7. Ibid., 41.

8. Aristotle *Pol.* 1275b.17–22.

9. The same term was used for both; see Aristotle *Ath. pol.* 42.1. Cf. Cicero *Rep.* 25.39: "A commonwealth is the property of a people [*res publica res populi*] . . . [namely] an assemblage of people in large numbers associated in an agreement with respect to justice and a partnership for the common good" (C. W. Keyes trans.; Loeb ed.).

10. Aristotle *Pol.* 1297b16–1298a4.

11. For these terms, see Aristotle *Ath. pol.* 42–50. For a historical discussion, see A. H. M. Jones, *The Greek City from Alexander to Justinian* (New York: Oxford, 1940), especially "The Hellenistic Age," 162–69. More recently, see Raphael Sealey, *A History of the Greek City States, ca. 700–338 B.C.* (Berkeley: University of California Press, 1976); and O. Murray and S. Price, *The Greek City from Homer to Alexander* (New York: Oxford, 1990).

12. Aeschines *Tim.* 4–5 (trans. C. D. Adams; Loeb ed., p. 7); for this and the next reference, see Herbert Oppel, *KANΩN: Zur Bedeutungsgeschichte des Wortes und seiner lateinischen Entsprechungen (regula-norma)* (in *Philologus* suppl.; Bd. 30, Heft 4; Leipzig: Dieterichsche Verlagsbuchhandlung, 1933), 52n68.

13. Aeschines *Ctes.* 199–200 (trans. C. D. Adams; Loeb ed., p. 465).

14. In the discussion that follows, I am particularly indebted to the monograph by Oppel, *KANΩN.* Oppel's superbly documented discussion of the whole range of κανών meanings, from early Indo-European cognates down to the fifth century C.E., still is the definitive analysis. In particular, Oppel documents the close connection between the widespread use of the κανών metaphor and the quest for ἀκρίβεια and ὅροι during the creation of democracy at Athens (see pp. 51–57) and the influence of the revolutionary new *polis* ideology on Second Temple Judaism (use this part with caution) and early Christianity. Few biblical scholars seem aware

of Oppel's study. For a still useful survey of the term κανών, see Appendix I of Bruce Metzger, *The Canon of the New Testament: Its Origin, Development and Significance* (New York: Oxford: Clarendon, 1989), 289–94.

15. Oppel, *KANΩN*, 14f, esp. 48f, with quotations from Galen, Lucian, and Plutarch. Polykleitos's original text no longer exists. Oppel suggests (15) that Albrecht Dürer's *Vier Büchern von menschlicher Proportion* (1525) could be based on a medieval version of it.

16. Ibid., 18–19.

17. Ibid., p. 15.

18. Ibid., p. 21.

19. Aristophanes *Ran.* 799; discussed by Oppel, *KANΩN*, 22.

20. For an illuminating discussion of the primary sources in each of these fields, see Oppel, *KANΩN*, 28–39.

21. Cited and discussed in Oppel, *KANΩN*, 26.

22. This term can be translated "distinct, unmixed, clear" (Latin: *sincerus*). See Liddell-Scott, *Greek-English Lexicon* (rev. supplement; ed. P. G. W. Glare; New York: Oxford, 1996).

23. See the discussion in Oppel, *KANΩN*, 26f.

24. For a broad description of this phenomenon, see F. E. Peters, *Harvest of Hellenism: The Impact of Alexander the Great upon Eastern Mediterranean Culture and Civilization* (New York: Simon and Schuster, 1970); see also A. Kuhrt and S. Sherwin-White, eds., *Hellenism in the East: The Interaction of Greek and Non-Greek Civilizations from Syria to Central Asia after Alexander* (Hellenistic Culture and Society No. 2; Berkeley: University of California Press, 1987).

25. This is the actual beginning of the radically new idea of "conversion" in the ancient world and a far cry from the statements of A. D. Nock in *Conversion: The Old and the New in Religion from Alexander the Great to Augustine of Hippo* (New York: Oxford University Press, 1933). The campaign of Alexander to "Greekize" or "Hellenize" the barbarian nations was history's first "conversion" campaign (in western Asia, at any rate). It is difficult for us to gain a sense of the love for and fascination with things Greek, in the wake of Alexander's campaigns, or his stirring vision of international harmony based on a revolutionary new common culture. Suffice it to say that Paul's ringing declaration seems not too distantly related to Alexander's powerful vision of the ideal of human community: "For in Christ Jesus you are all sons of God, through faith. For as many of you as were baptized into Christ have put on Christ. There is neither Jew nor Greek, there is neither slave nor free, there is neither male nor female; for

you are all one in Christ Jesus" (Gal 3:26–28). Cf. Col 3:11: "Here there cannot be Greek and Jew, circumcised and uncircumcised, barbarian, Scythian, slave, free man, but Christ is all, and in all." Becoming a (Pauline-type) Christian was one way to accept this ancient ideal for oneself.

Chapter 3. Greek *Polis* Ideology within Second Temple Judaism and Early Christianity

1. Recent European and English biographies of Alexander say nothing about this episode, so formative for the subsequent history of Second Temple Judaism. For a balanced analysis of the evidence, see Victor Tcherikover, *Hellenistic Civilization and the Jews* (trans. S. Applebaum; New York: JPS, 1961), 41–49.

2. Older treatments of this broad topic include Elias Bickerman, *From Ezra to the Last of the Maccabees: Foundations of Postbiblical Judaism* (New York: Schocken, 1962); Saul Lieberman, *Greek in Jewish Palestine* (New York: Jewish Theological Seminary, 1942); Saul Lieberman, *Hellenism in Jewish Palestine* (New York: Jewish Theological Seminary, 1961), Tcherikover, *Hellenistic Civilization and the Jews*; Abraham Schalit, ed., *The Hellenistic Age: Political History of Jewish Palestine from 332 B.C.E. to 67 B.C.E.* (New Brunswick, N.J.: Rutgers University Press, 1972); Martin Hengel, *Judaism and Hellenism: Studies in Their Encounter in Palestine during the Early Hellenistic Period* (trans. John Bowden; Minneapolis: Fortress Press, 1974); S. Applebaum, *Judaea in Hellenistic and Roman Times: Historical and Archeological Essays* (Leiden: Brill, 1989).

3. See especially Ellis Rivkin, "Pharisaism and the Crisis of the Individual in the Greco-Roman World," *JQR* 61 (1970–71): 27–53; Ellis Rivkin, "The Pharisaic Revolution: A Decisive Mutation," in *The Shaping of Jewish History* (New York: Scribner's, 1971); and Ellis Rivkin, *A Hidden Revolution* (Nashville: Abingdon, 1978), especially 242–43. More recently, see Anthony J. Saldarini, *Pharisees, Scribes and Sadducees in Palestinian Society: A Sociological Approach* (Wilmington, Del.: Glazier, 1988). See also two essays in the symposium comparing Hillel and Jesus: J. Sievers, "Who Were the Pharisees?" 137–55; and B. Pixner, "Jesus and His Community: Between Essenes and Pharisees," 193–224, in *Hillel and Jesus: Comparative Studies of Two Major Religious Leaders* (ed. J. Charlesworth et al.; Minneapolis: Fortress Press, 1997).

4. See the famous introduction to *Pirke Aboth,* in *Mishnah Nezikin* 1.1: "Moses received the Law from Sinai and committed to Joshua and

Joshua to the Elders and the Elders to the Prophets and the Prophets to the Men of the Great Synagogue. They said three things: Be deliberate in judgment, raise up many disciples, and make a fence around the Torah." See also E. J. Bickerman, "La chaîne de la tradition pharisienne," in *Studies in Jewish and Christian History* (3 vols.; Leiden: Brill, 1979), 2:256–69, and most recently Daniel Boyarin, *Border Lines: The Partition of Judaeo-Christianity* (Philadelphia: University of Pennsylvania Press, 2004), chap. 3, "Naturalizing the Border: Apostolic Succesion in the Mishna," pp. 74–86. I wish to thank Jimmy Barker for bringing Boyarin's important book to my attention.

5. For a thorough discussion of the origins of the synagogue institution, see most recently Birger Olsson and Magnus Zetterholm, eds., *The Ancient Synagogue from Its Origins until 200 C.E.* (Stockholm: Almqvist and Wiksell, 2003). This question is hotly contested at present: "There is no consensus any longer" (30). Of the different hypotheses presented in this volume, I tend to agree with Peter Richardson, who argues that the archeological and literary evidence points to origins of the synagogue in the Jewish Diaspora, where it was a Jewish adaptation of the Hellenistic association (*thiasos*). See "An Architectural Case for Synagogues as Associations," 90–117; cf. the similar view of P. V. M. Flesher, in ibid., 33.

6. For the most complete examination of the ancient accounts, together with secondary literature, see Jacob Neusner, *A Life of Rabban Yohanan ben Zakkai Studia, Post-Biblica* (Leiden: Brill, 1962), 104–28.

7. In the past, scholars have looked in the wrong place for evidence of Jewish "canonization" when they focus on rabbinic activities at Jamnia. J. N. Lightstone suggests that the real locus of "canonization"-like activity took place in the third century when Judah the Prince standardized Israel's halakah and produced the *Mishnah*; see Lightstone, "The Rabbis' Bible: The Canon of the Hebrew Bible and the Early Rabbinic Guild," in *The Canon Debate* (ed. Lee Martin McDonald and James A. Sanders; Peabody, Mass.: Hendrickson, 2002), 181–84. See also chapter seven.

8. See Neusner, *A Life of Rabban Yohanan ben Zakkai Studia, Post-Biblica,* 18: "Tradition claims that Hillel . . . had come from Babylon about the last third of the first century B.C.E. . . . [and] taught a methodology of interpreting scripture which revolutionized . . . the intellectual life of Pharisaism. These principles, known to exegetes of Greek classic texts as well, included the following: (1) Inference *a minori ad maius*; (2) Inference by analogy; (3) Extending an inference from one scripture passage to others." See also Lieberman, *Hellenism in Jewish Palestine,* 47–82.

9. This term is customarily translated as *church* in English, a word that goes back through the German word *Kirche* to the ancient Greek κυριακὸς οἶκος, "the Lord's house." As such, it connotes the church building and loses altogether the original political sense of the popular council of citizens "called out to vote or take action" from the larger urban population approximately once a week.

10. K. L. Schmidt, "ἐκκλησία," in *TDNT* 3:530: "The NT *ekklēsia* is the fulfillment of the OT *qahal* assembly." *Ekklēsia-qahal* indicates many different kinds of assembly, including 'assembly of the people of God' (Jg 2:20). Such assemblies are clearly 'called out' for some action from the larger ethnic collective: *qol Israel,* 'all Israel.'"

11. In Hellenistic Judaism, πολίτευμα is a synonym for the term πολιτεία, which, as we have seen, can mean citizenship or citizens, as well as the city constitution. On this use of πολίτευμα, see Philo *Ios.* 14.69: "I am not a slave but as highly-born as anyone, I who claim enrolment among the citizens of that best and greatest state: the world [μεγίστῳ καὶ ἀρίστῳ πολιτεύματι τοῦδε τοῦ κόσμου]" (Loeb ed.). Being a citizen of the world was a favorite Stoic maxim. For the use of the term as referring to the citizen body, see 2 Macc 12:7: "The whole community of Joppa [τὸ σύμπαν τῶν ' Ιοππιτῶν πολίτευμα]." I am indebted for these references to J. B. Lightfoot, *St. Paul's Epistle to the Philippians: Lightfoot's Commentaries on the Epistles of St. Paul* (Peabody, Mass.: Hendrickson, 1995), 156n20.

12. On σωτήρ as a conventional political/religious title, see D. R. Cartlidge and D. L. Dungan, "Savior Gods of the Mediterranean World," *Documents for the Study of the Gospels* (ed. D. R. Cartlidge and D. L. Dungan; 2nd ed.; Philadelphia: Fortress Press, 1994), 5–16.

13. Much recent work has been done on the *Didachē*; see especially H. van den Sandt and D. Flusser, *The Didache: Its Jewish Sources and Its Place in Early Judaism and Christianity* (CRINT 3.5; Minneapolis: Fortress Press, 2002). For this date of *Didachē,* see the literature cited on 48n28. The *Apostolic Tradition* has traditionally been ascribed to Hippolytos. This important text has recently been given a detailed commentary by Paul F. Bradshaw, Maxwell E. Johnson, and L. Edward Philips, *The Apostolic Tradition,* ed. Harold W. Attridge (Hermeneia; Minneapolis: Fortress, 2002).

14. The literature on *1 Clement* has not made this connection. The classical older studies by A.von Harnack and Werner Jaeger have been republished in Cilliers Breytenbach and Laurence L. Welborn, *Encounters with Hellenism: Studies on the First Letter of Clement* (Leiden: Brill, 2004),

along with an article by W. C. van Unnik that discusses the genre of *1 Clement* under συμβουλῇ, "advice, counsel"; see 153. Other recent monographs focus on *1 Clement* as evidence for rising ecclesiastical bureaucracy (e.g., Karlmann Beyschlag, *Clemens Romanus und der Frühkatholizismus* [BHT 13; Tübingen: J. C. B. Mohr, 1966]); and the disappearing eschatogical horizon in the church (e.g., Otto Knoch, *Eigenart und Bedeutung der Eschatologie im theologischen Aufriß des ersten Clemensbriefes: Eine auslegungsgeschichtliche Untersuchung* [Bonn: Peter Haanstein Verlag, 1964]); or evidence of the increasing assumption of authority of Rome over other congregations (e.g., Adolf W. Ziegler, *Neue Studien zum ersten Klemensbrief* [Munich: Manz Verlag, 1958]). The detailed commentary by Andreas Lindemann, *Die Klemensbriefe* (HNT 17; Tübingen: J. C. B. Mohr/Siebeck, 1992), says nothing of the legal nature of *1 Clement* brought out here. Indeed, the strictly legal brief character of the whole letter does not fully emerge until the very end. The peroration begins with a striking use of the ancient Hebrew oath of binding: "As the Lord lives" (Judg 8:19; 1 Sam 14:39, 14:45, 19:6 et passim; 2 Sam 2:2; cf. 2 Sam 11:11, 12:5; 1 Kg 1:29; Hos 45:15 (frequently here given an unusual three-fold Christian structure [58:2]). The author passes immediately to a dire threat: "If there are some [among you] who fail to obey what God has told them through us" (59:1) they will answer to God on the Day of Judgment. Not only that, the author informs the Corinthian rebels that the Roman congregation will not be responsible for the punishment God will certainly inflict on them on that Day: "They [the rebels] will find themselves in no insignificant danger [because] we, for our part [having previously warned them by this letter] will not be held responsible [for their fate]" (59:2). Meanwhile, the church at Rome will "pray that the Creator of the Universe will keep intact the precise number of his Elect" (another veiled threat), and the author launches into direct prayer to God, the Judge, in the text of this legal brief, asking God mercifully to accept the Corinthian rebels' repentance (59:3–4). In closing, the author says that he has "touched on every topic" (62:2) to impress upon the rebellious Corinthians that they do not have any argument to defend their continuing schism, which explains the compendious character of *1 Clement*. Then comes the proof that what is happening is some sort of legal action: Rome is sending a two-man delegation (men of high standing in the Roman congregation), by name, Claudius Ephebus and Valerius Bito, with their manservant Fortunatus ("Lucky," 65), and they will function as "witnesses to mediate between us" (63:3). In Jewish law, the concurrent testimony of two witnesses was necessary to convict in cases involving capital crimes (Deut 17:6), which is the accusation brought against them now. Earlier, the author(s) had accused the Corinthian church of "Blaspheming the Name" (*1 Clem* 47.7), a crime requiring death by stoning (Lev 24:16; cf. Deut 5:11; cf. Rom 2:24). The two Roman delegates must have planned to read the letter aloud to the whole Corinthian congregation in the presence of the illegal officeholders and probably hoped to return to the Roman congregation with a report of the complete acquiescence of the rebels to the advice of the Roman church, including an immediate restoration of the original officeholders to their positions.

15. The crime being alleged here is stated in Greek in *1 Clement*, but the underlying Hebrew term for the crime committed is *hillul hashem*, "blaspheming the Name." In Jewish law, causing the Lord's Name (reputation, honor) to be blasphemed (*hll*, defile, profane, violate), was a capital offense and was punishable by stoning (Lev 24:16). We will see that *1 Clement* concludes with a threat of equivalent eschatological punishment.

16. *1 Clem* 7:2: διὸ ἀπολίπωμεν τὰς κενὰς καὶ ματαίας φροντίδας, καὶ ἔλθωμεν ἐπὶ τὸν εὐκλεῆ καὶ σεμνὸν τῆς παραδόσεως ἡμῶν κανόνα.

17. Eusebius *Hist. eccl.* 4.23.11.

18. Ignatius of Antioch *Trall* 2.2: ἄνευ τοῦ ἐπισκόπου μηδὲν πράσσειν καὶ ὑποτάσσεσθε τῷ πρεσβυτερίῳ ὡς τοῖς ἀποστόλοις Ἰησοῦ Χριστου.

19. Ignatius of Antioch *Mag* 6.1: προκαθημένου τοῦ ἐπισκόπου εἰς τόπον θεοῦ καὶ τῶν πρεσβυτέρων εἰς τόπον συνεδρίου τῶν ἀποστόλων.

20. Gal 6:16: καὶ ὅσοι τῷ κανόνι τούτῳ στοιχήσουσιν, εἰρήνη ἐπὶ αὐτοὺς καὶ ἔλεος καὶ ἐπὶ τὸν Ἰσραὴλ τοῦ θεοῦ.

21. 4 Macc 7:21: ὅλων τῆς φιλοσοφίας κανόνα. I am indebted for these examples to Herbert Oppel, *ΚΑΝΩΝ*. This reference was cited in ibid., 59n2. On this date of 4 Maccabees, see Hugh Anderson, "Fourth Maccabees," in *ABD* (6 vols.; ed. David Noel Freedman et al.; New York: Doubleday, 1992), 4:452ff.: "We may think of *4 Maccabees* as roughly contemporaneous with the mission and letters of the Apostle Paul."

22. *1 Clem* 7.2: τήν εὐκλεῆ καὶ σεμνὸν τῆς παραδόσεως ἡμῶν κανόνα. The same kind of "basic guideline" thought is expressed in *1 Clem* 1.3: "You [the Corinthian church] instructed your women to do everything with a blameless and pure conscience, and to give their husbands the affection they should. You taught them, too, to abide by the rule of obedience

[ἐν τῷ κανόνι τῆς ὑποταγῆς] and to run their homes with dignity and discretion."

23. Irenaeus *Haer.* 1.22.1: κανὼν τῆς ἀληθείας (*ANF* 1.347). The same creed is referred to again as "the ancient tradition" and paraphrased at 3.4.2.

24. Tertullian *Praescr.* 13; *ANF* 3.249.

25. Clement of Alexandria *Strom.* 4.15: ἐκκλησιαστικὸς κανών; cited in Oppel, *KANΩN*, 61.

26. Clement of Alexandria *Strom.* 4.15: κανὼν τοῦ εὐαγγελίου; cited in Oppel, *KANΩN*, 61. I have modified the quote slightly.

27. Origen *Comm. Jo.* bk. 13, sec. 13, v. 98; τὸν δὲ κανόνα τὸν κατὰ τοὺς πολλοὺς τῆς ἐκκλησίας (Greek text: SC 222 [Paris: Éditions du Cerf, 1975]). R. E. Heine translates the final phrase "the church's rule of faith according to most people," even though the Greek is obvious (*Commentary on the Gospel According to John,* vol. 80; FC; Washington, D.C.: Catholic University of America Press, [1990]), 88. In the text I use the translation of R. P. C. Hanson, *Origen's Doctrine of Tradition* (London: SPCK, 1954), 91.

28. Origen *Princ.* 4.2.2; Greek: ἐχομένοις τοῦ κανόνος τῆς ᾽Ιησοῦ Χριστοῦ κατὰ διαδοχὴν τῶν ἀποστόλων. Greek text and translation from Hanson, *Origen's Doctrine of Tradition*, 92 (emphasis added).

29. See Hanson, *Origen's Doctrine of Tradition*, 91: "Canon for Origen stands for the whole gospel or content of the Christian faith." And on 95: "κανὼν and κανὼν ἐκκλησια σπκός never refer to any list of articles of belief or creed in Origen. . . . Whatever his canon was, it was very closely linked with the Scriptures though not identical with them."

30. See ibid., 93: "Neither Clement nor Origen has a conception entirely equivalent to an official list of inspired Scripture guaranteed by the Church as authentic." And, further: "The evidence should surely be enough to convince anyone that Clement of Alexandria has almost no conception of what we mean by a Canon of Scripture" (133). "In other words, the conception of an official list [*sic*], which is what the word Canon suggests to us, is as entirely absent from Origen as it is from Clement" (138).

31. Philo *Virt.* 219; see also Philo *Mos.* 1.76: "Each of them the exemplar of the wisdom [κανὼν σοφίας] they have gained—Abraham by teaching, Isaac by nature, and Jacob by practice"; references in Oppel, *KANΩN*, 42.

32. Lucian *Scyth.* 7; reference in Oppel, *KANΩN*, 42.

33. *1 Clem* 41.1: μὴ παρεκβαίνων τὸν ὡρισμένον τῆς λειτουργίας αὐτοῦ *κανόνα*, ἐν σεμνότητι.

34. 2 Cor 10:15ff.: οὐκ εἰς τὰ ἄμετρα καυχώμενοι ἐν ἀλλοτρίοις κόποις, ἐλπίδα δὲ ἔχοντες αὐξανομένης τῆς πίστεως ὑμῶν ἐν ὑμῖν μεγαλυνθῆναι κατὰ τὸν *κανόνα* ἡμῶν εἰς περισσείαν εἰς τὰ ὑπερέκεινα ὑμῶν εὐαγγελίσασθαι, οὐκ ἐν ἀλλοτρίως *κανόνι* εἰς τὰ ἕτοιμα καυχήσασθαι. Cf. 2 Cor 10:13: "We will not boast beyond measure but will keep to the limits [κατὰ τὸ μέτρον τοῦ κανόνος] God has apportioned us" (RSV).

35. For the examples listed here, see Oppel, *KANΩN*, 66ff.

36. Hanson, *Origen's Doctrine of Tradition*, 133: "The most we can say is that [Origen] assumes that the Canon of the Gospels is closed, though even here he apparently is ready on occasion to admit exceptions. He shows no sign at all of wanting to call in the judgment of the Church to decide the genuineness of any work which may be Scripture." Hanson does admit that Origen and Clement may reflect the somewhat more relaxed attitude in Alexandria and that Irenaeus did seem to have "a much more definite conception of the finality of the Canon of the Gospels at least" (133).

37. Oppel, *KANΩN*, 67.

38. See H. H. Oliver, "The Epistle of Eusebius to Carpianus: Textual Tradition and Translation," in *NovT* 3 (1959): 138–45.

39. The full text of the *Epistula ad Carpianum* and the Eusebian canons can be found after the introductory matter in all recent editions of the Nestle-Aland *Greek New Testament* (Stuttgart: Deutsche Bibelgesellschaft).

40. See B. M. Metzger, *The Canon of the New Testament* (Oxford: Clarendon, 1989), 291.

Chapter 4. The Influence of Greek Philosophy upon Early Christianity

1. For surveys of the influence of aspects of Greek philosophy on first-century Christianity, see D. E. Aune, *The New Testament in Its Literary Environment* (Louisville, Ky.: Westminster/John Knox Press, 1988); J. J. Collins and Gregory Sterling, *Hellenism in the Land of Israel* (Notre Dame, Ind.: University of Notre Dame Press, 2001); and A. J. Malherbe, *Social Aspects of Early Christianity* (Baton Rouge: Louisiana State University Press, 1977). See also John T. Fitzgerald, *Early Christianity and Classical*

Culture: Comparative Studies in Honor of Abraham J. Malherbe (NovTSup 110; Leiden: Brill, 2003).

2. In ancient times, the term *philosopher* could refer to any of a whole spectrum of roles: teacher, healer, political consultant, public conscience, scientist, musician, and wandering street-corner preacher. Applied in Christian contexts, it could refer to what we would now call a *theologian*.

3. The first such defense of Christianity was probably written around the year 140 c.e. by Aristo of Pella and was entitled "Dialogue between Jason and Papiscus Concerning Christ." Possibly composed in the Greek-speaking region of the Decapolis, it was a philosophical defense of Christianity against Judaism. The early third-century Christian theologian Origen later noted that the pagan philosopher Celsus wrote a reply to it entitled *The True Doctrine* (Origen *Cels.* 4.52).

4. Eusebius *Hist. eccl.* 4.26.7 (trans. *NPNF²*, 1.205). The Greek of the last part of the quotation is φυλάσσων τῆς βασιλείας τὴν σύντροφον καὶ συναρξαμένην Αὐγούστῳ φιλοσοφίαν, ἣν καὶ οἱ πρόγονοί σου πρὸς ταῖς ἄλλαις θρησκείαις ἐτίμησαν.

5. Cf. Justin *Dial.* 2–8; and 35, where he explicitly compares the many Christian "schools of thought" named after their founders with the similar custom among the Greek philosophical schools. One is reminded of Josephus's attempt to explain to Gentiles the characteristics of various factions within first-century Palestinian Judaism by comparing them to the same Greek schools: the Epicureans, the Stoics, and the Pythagoreans; see Josephus *Ant.* 18.11–25; cf. *Ant.* 13.111–73; *B. J.* 2.119–66.

6. See the account of Justin's martyrdom in Eusebius *Hist. eccl.* 4.16.

7. See my discussion of Justin's novel manner of referring to the gospels and its possible missionary purpose, in *A History of the Synoptic Problem* (New York: Doubleday, 1999), 30ff.

8. See the discussion of the reason for the quest for accuracy, ἀκρίβεια, in chapter two.

9. The preface to any study edition of Sirach/Ecclesiasticus will explain that this is a rare case of a writing giving the author's actual name (see Sir 50.27). For a study of the Christian church's struggle with pseudonymous and anonymous authorship in the scripture selection process, see David G. Meade, *Pseudonymity and Canon: An Investigation into the Relationship of Authorship and Authority in Jewish and Early Christian Tradition* (Grand Rapids, Mich.: Eerdmans, 1986).

10. See Armin D. Baum, "Der neutestamentlichen Kanon bei Eusebios

(*Hist. Eccl.* III, 25, 1–7) im Kontext seiner literaturgeschichtlichen Arbeit," *ETL* 73 (1997): 309.

11. Ibid., 309f.

12. Ibid., 310f.

13. Diogenes Laertius *de vit. phil.* 3.57: γνήσιοι διάλογοι.

14. Ibid., 3.62: νοθεύονται δὲ τῶν διαλόγων ὁμολογουμένως.

15. Ibid., 2.64: τοὺς δε ἄλλους ἀναιρεῖ πάντας. Laertius mentions a similar three-fold division in the dialogues of Phaedo, the disciple of Socrates: "Of the dialogues which bear his name the Zopyrus and Simon are genuine [γνήσιους]; the Nicias is doubtful [δισταζόμενον], while the Medius is said by some to be the work of Aeschines" (2.105).

16. See ibid., 3.66: "Since certain critical marks [σημεῖα τίνα] are affixed to [copies of] his works, let us now say a word about these. The cross (X) is used to indicate Plato's peculiar genuine expressions and figures of speech; ... the diple (>) calls attention to doctrines and opinions characteristic of Plato; ... the dotted diple (⩳), editors' corrections of the text; the dotted obelus (÷) suspect passages, the antisigma (Ɔ) repetitions and proposals for transpositions; and the ... obelus (—) a spurious passage. Antigonus of Carystus says ... that when the writings were first edited with these critical marks, their possessors charged a fee to anyone who wished to consult them."

17. Ibid., 3.65: "The right interpretation of Plato's dialogues includes three things" (ἔστι δὲ ἡ ἐξήγησις αὐτους τῶν λόγων τριπλῆ).

18. Ibid., 5.22–27.

19. Ibid., 5.34; Greek: τὰ ὅσα γε ἀναμφίλεκτα.

20. Ibid.: "Many other works ... are attributed to him"; Greek: πολλὰ γὰρ καὶ ἄλλα εἰς αὐτὸν ἀναφέρεται συγγράμνατ' αὐτοῦ....

21. Ibid., 5.35. The list included an Athenian statesman named Aristotle, an Aristotle who wrote a commentary on the *Iliad*, a Sicilian Aristotle who taught rhetoric, and an Aristotle who was a disciple of Aeschines, among others.

22. Ibid., 5.28–34; Greek: βούλεται δὲ ἐν αὐτοῖς τάδε.... Summarizing Aristotle's ideas in three pages would be difficult for anyone. Laertius abruptly ends his summary with this explanation: "He held many other opinions on a variety of subjects which it would be tedious to enumerate."

23. I should say that the modern opinion of Laertius is not high. He tends to be viewed as something of a hack, assembling and summarizing opinions the import of which he barely understands. Examples of this

include his brief summary of the ideas of Aristotle and his "three handy rules for correctly interpreting Plato." This negative assessment is partly caused by the fact that it is not clear which philosopher he favors person-ally, and some say he is so dull he does not even have an opinion of his own—although judging by the way the book is organized, it may have been the view of the last school he discussed, that of Epicurus. I do not share this condescending viewpoint. I much prefer the balanced and more sophisticated analysis of scholars such as Jørgen Mejer, *Diogenes Laertius and His Hellenistic Background* (Stuttgart: Steiner Verlag, 1978).

24. The classic collection is A. Hilgard, A. Lentz, R. Schneider, G. Uhlig, eds., *Grammatici Graeci* (4 vols.; Leipzig, 1867–1910; repr., New York: Hildesheim, 1965).

25. Tertullian *Marc.* 1.1: "His disciples will not deny that his first faith he held along with ourselves; a letter of his own proves this" (*ANF* 3.272).

26. For this detail, see Tertullian *Marc.* 1.15.

27. See my more complete discussion of Marcion and his teachings in *A History of the Synoptic Problem* (ABRL; New York: Doubleday, 1999), 44–58. The recent discussion by John Barton, "Marcion Revisited," in *The Canon Debate* (ed. Lee Martin McDonald and James A. Sanders; Peabody, Mass.: Hendrickson, 2002), 341–54, contains the usual methodological mistakes found in Marcion research, beginning with uncritical reliance upon Harnack's reconstruction of Marcion's "Gospel," the claim that Marcion avoided allegorical interpretation, and others.

28. See J. J. Clabeaux, "Marcion," *ABD* 4.515b: "Scholars conjecture that . . . Marcionites may have nearly surpassed non-Marcionites in the decades of the 160s and 170s."

29. According to Tertullian, at one point Valentinus was so well received that he thought he could be elected bishop of the orthodox con-gregation at Rome. As it turned out, he was passed over in favor of another candidate, but it was a close race; see Tertullian *Val.* 4.

30. Valentinus had received this secret instruction directly from Paul's disciple Theudas; see Elaine Pagels, *The Gnostic Paul* (Harrisburg, Pa.: Trinity Press International, 1992), 54.

31. Irenaeus *Haer.* 3.4.1.

32. Ibid., 3.3.1 (emphasis added).

33. Ibid., 3.3.4. See D. M. Farkasfalvy, "The Synthesis of St. Irenaeus," in *The Formation of the New Testament Canon* (ed. W. R. Farmer and Dennis Farkasfalvy; New York: Paulist Press, 1983). Supporting the thesis of Farmer

and Farkasfalvy that the church's tradition goes back to Jesus' own actual teaching methods, see B. Gerhardsson, *Memory and Manuscript: Oral Tradition and Written Transmission in Rabbinic Judaism and Early Christianity* (2nd printing, with foreword by J. Neusner; Grand Rapids, Mich.: Eerdmans, 1998); see also R. Riesner, *Jesus als Lehrer: Eine Untersuchung zum Ursprung der Evangelien-Überlieferung* (Tübingen: J. C. B. Mohr, 1981).

34. Irenaeus *Haer.* 3.3.3. He prefaced his list of the succession at Rome with the statement that he would not try to give the names of all of the successions: "It would be tedious . . . to reckon up the successions of all the churches" (3.3.2). This was precisely the challenge that Eusebius, who knew the writings of Irenaeus well, took upon himself a century later. Daniel Boyarin's comment is appropriate here: "The rabbinic movement should essentially be considered on the model of a Hellenistic philosophical school: the Rabbis, as they articulated their self-understanding in Avot, so perceived and portrayed themselves. At about he time that Christianity began to transform itself from a 'collection of philosophical schools'. . . into an orthodoxy, the Rabbis were making the same attempt. . . . The invention of rabbinic orthodoxy is the Jewish parallel to the [invention of orthodoxy by] Justin, Irenaeus, and their successors at the same time" (*Border Lines: The Partition of Judaeo-Christianity* [Philadelphia: University of Pennsylvania Press, 2004], 85). I am indebted for this reference to Jimmy Barker.

35. Ibid., 1.22.2; 23.1; 2. Pref.

36. Ibid., 3.2.1.

37. Ibid., 3.11.9.

38. Ibid., 1.20.1.

39. Ibid., 3.1.1.

40. At this point, Irenaeus supports the idea of four Gospels with the famous allegorical justification as to why there had to be precisely four apostolic narratives making up the Gospel (ibid., 3.11.8). It is noteworthy that no later orthodox theologian used this justification.

41. Ibid., 1.22.1: κανὼν ἀληθείας.

42. Ibid., 1.10.1.

43. Ibid., 1.30.15; 2.pref.; *ANF* 1.358–59. The original Greek for these two passages no longer exists.

44. Tertullian *Val.* 1.25.6.

45. Ibid., 1.7.1.

46. Eusebius *Hist. eccl.* 2.2.3: "Tertullian . . . made himself accurately acquainted with the laws of the Romans, and, besides his eminence in other respects, was particularly distinguished among the eminent men of Rome."

For his part, Tertullian was very impressed by Irenaeus, calling him "that very exact inquirer into all doctrines" (*Val.* 5).

47. Tertullian *Praescr.* 18.

48. Ibid., 4.4. Latin: *Ego meum dico verum Marcion suum; ego affirmo adulteratum Marcion meum. Quis inter nos determinabit?*

49. Ibid., 4.2. Latin: *Lucam videtur Marcion elegisse, quem caederet.*

50. Ibid., 38. There is a long analysis of Marcion's adulteration of Luke in *Marc.* 4.6–8.

51. Tertullian *Marc.* 4.5.

52. Ibid., 4.2.

53. Ibid., 28. Latin: *Nullus inter multos eventus unus est exitus. . . . Caeterum, quod apud multos unum invenitur, non est erratum sed traditum.* Cf. ibid., 20–21.

54. Ibid., 20.

55. Ibid., 32 (emphasis added).

56. Ibid., 36.

57. Ibid., 3, 19. Latin: *regula fidei*; Greek: κανὼν πίστεως.

58. Ibid., 9.

59. Ibid., 13; cf. 14.

60. Particularly revealing, in my estimation, of the depth to which Greek philosophy had permeated Hippolytus's version of Christianity is his account of his conflict with another orthodox Christian leader in Rome, the "other bishop," Callistus. It is striking that the entity over which Callistus presided was not only called an ἐκκλησία (by Callistus) but also a διδασκάλεια, a "school," including the sense of a school building; see Hippolytus *Haer.* 9.2 and this remarkable formulation: "[Callistus] dares to establish a school against the church" (διδασκάλειον κατὰ τῆς ἐκκλησίας, 9.7). This "school" had all the functions of entities otherwise called assemblies (ἐκκλησίαι): it could accept or reject new members, had its succession of bishops (9.2; 9.6), its own martyrs (9.6), and its own worship services (9.7), and it referred to itself by the preferred self-designation of the orthodox Christians, "general assembly" (ἐκκλησία καθολικῇ).

61. See ibid., 9.1. Basilides' teachings go back to Aristotle, not Christ (ibid., 7.2); Marcion imported Empedocles into the Gospel narratives (ibid., 7.18); Noetianism was really an offshoot from Heracleitus (ibid., 9.3); other teachers were not Christian but Pythagorean or Platonist (ibid., 6.24). These heretics mixed in other deities with Christ: Justinus worshipped Elohim, Edem, Hercules, Omphale, Christ, and others (ibid., 5.21); Simon had statues made depicting himself as Jupiter and his con-

sort Helen as Minerva (ibid., 6.15). Hippolytus also referred to the various false successions: the Ophite succession (ibid., 6.1), the Noetian succession (ibid., 9.3), the Valentinian succession (ibid., 6.50), and so on. He also described how each heretical Christian school had its own false sacraments. For example, the Sethians staged orgies similar to the Great Mother rituals (ibid., 5.15); Justinus required his initiates to swear a strange and unique oath before being admitted to his mysteries (ibid., 5.22); Simon Magus demanded promiscuous intercourse as a religious ritual (ibid., 6.14); and a certain Marcus had a magically overflowing cup of wine, similar to the mysteries of Dionysius (ibid., 6.35). Hippolytus also described how each heretical Christian school relied on spurious writings, etc.

62. See ibid., bk. 1 proem. Later Hippolytus insisted that, in contrast to all rival Christian and pagan schools everywhere in the world, his Catholic church (ἐκκλησία καθολικῇ) alone possessed the pure Divine Truth: "Therefore ye Greeks, Egyptians, Chaldeans, and the entire race of men, become adepts in our doctrine and learn from us, who are the friends of God (τῶν φιλῶν τοῦ θεοῦ), what the nature of God is and what His well-arranged creation." And further, "We have cultivated this system not expressing ourselves in mere pompous language but executing our treatises (λόγοι) in terms that prove our knowledge of truth and our practice of good sense, our object being the demonstration of His Truth" (ἀποδείξις τοῦ λόγου) (ibid., 10.27; *ANF* 5.150). The Wendland edition of the *GCS*, vol. 26, has this passage at the end of 10.31.

63. According to R. P. C. Hanson, *Origen's Doctrine of Tradition* (London: SPCK, 1954), 128f., Clement acknowledged "the four Gospels handed down to us" but also quoted, without questioning their legitimacy, the Gospel to the Hebrews (once) and the Gospel to the Egyptians (four times). He quoted the *Sybilline Oracles* as scripture ("to know the truth you must consult the prophets: the Sibyl, Jeremiah, and Isaiah," *Protrep.* 8), as well as the *Epistle of Barnabas* (eight times). He quoted as scripture all of the writings later found in the New Testament but in addition the *Preaching of Peter* (six times), the *Shepherd of Hermas* (four times), the *Apocalypse of Peter* (three times), the *Traditions of Matthew* (once), *Enoch* (once), and the *Didache* (once).

64. See D. C. Parker, "Hexapla," *ABD* 3:188ff.

65. See Chapter Six below.

66. Origen *Comm. Matt.* pref. This is no longer extant but is preserved by Eusebius in *Hist. eccl.* 6.25.4 (Cruse trans., emphasis added).

67. See the discussion above.

68. The Greek for this phrase is περὶ τῶν τεσσάρων εὐαγγελίων, ἃ καὶ μόνα ἀναντίρρητά ἐστιν ἐν τῇ ὑπὸ τὸν οὐρανὸν ἐκκλησίᾳ τοῦ θεοῦ. The same term, ἀναντίρρητα ("undisputed"), occurs four times in Eusebius *Hist. eccl.* The formulation "the church of God under heaven" did not arise with Origen but became popular in the later third century, as, for example, when Eusebius wanted to stress the whole, international, orthodox organization: "Finally [in the days of Constantine] a bright and splendid day... illuminated with beams of heavenly light the *churches of Christ throughout the entire world*" (*Hist. eccl.* 10.1.8). As if in conscious echo of Origen, Eusebius wrote, concerning the Gospel of John, "His Gospel is known to all the churches under heaven, [and] must be reckoned as genuine" (*Hist. eccl.* 3.24.2). The longer formulation, found already in the late second century (see below), meant precisely the same thing as the older formulation, καθολικῇ ἐκκλησία, a term that is first attested at the beginning of the second century in Ignatius *Smyrn.* 8: "Where Jesus Christ is, there is the *Catholic church*" (emphasis added). Contemporary with him is Polycarp's *To the Philippians*, which also refers to the *Catholic church* (it is quoted in Eusebius *Hist. eccl.* 4.15.15). *Catholic church* became the preferred self-designation of the orthodox faction in the second and third centuries (Tertullian, Clement of Alexandria, Origen). Additional adjectives were added toward the end of the third century to stress breadth. For example, in the time of Aurelian (270–275), the bishops of the eastern provinces excommunicated Paul of Samosata, and Eusebius described it thus: "He was excommunicated from *the Catholic church under heaven*" (*Hist. eccl.* 7.29.1, italics added). The bishops, in their letter to Dionysius of Rome, Maximus of Alexandria, and "all the [bishops in the eastern] provinces," addressed their letter thus: "To Dionysius and Maximus and to all our fellow-ministers throughout the world: bishops, presbyters, and deacons, and to *the whole Catholic church under heaven* [πάσῃ τῇ ὑπὸ τῶν οὐρανῶν καθολικῇ ἐκκλησίᾳ]." Then comes a list of sixteen bishops' names. And then "to the churches of God" (*Hist. eccl.* 7.30.2). Note the parallelism with "churches of God" indicating the latter's specific meaning. For the use of the term *Catholic* by Constantine in his edicts and letters, see chapter six below. There were other all-encompassing formulations available in the early days. Serapion could refer to "all the brotherhood throughout the world" (*Hist. eccl.* 5.19.2), Greek παρὰ πάσῃ τῇ ἐν κόσμῳ ἀδελφότητι, a usage that also occurs in the writings of his contemporary, Irenaeus, in tandem with "church": "Often times in the brotherhood... our entire church [ἐκκλησίας πασῆς] has besought with fasting" (Eusebius *Hist. eccl.* 5.7.2: καὶ ἐν τῇ ἀδελφότητι πολλάκις διὰ τὸ

ἀναγκαῖον καὶ τῆς κατὰ τόπον ἐκκλησίας πάσης). This term had roots backward in the Semitic term *haberim* found in the Qumran literature and elsewhere and in later Islam's "Muslim Brotherhood." Eusebius could also use the more secular phrase "the whole race of Christians" (*Hist. eccl.* 4.7.11) and even the somewhat shocking "our θίασος" (*Hist. eccl.* 10.1.8).

69. My translation departs slightly from the Cruse translation of C. F. Cruse, *Eusebius's Ecclesiastical History,* new ed. (Peabody, Mass.: Hendrickson, 1998), in order to more closely follow the Greek: μίαν ἐπιστολὴν ὁμολογουμένην καταλέλοιπεν. Origen's use of the term "acknowledged," ὁμολογουμένος, is found in many places in Laertius and is used eleven times by Eusebius; see Chapter Five.

70. Greek: ἔστω δὲ καὶ δευτέραν· ἀμφιβάλλεται γάρ. The Greek term ἀμφιβάλλεται, "disputed," is not used by Eusebius; he prefers some form of ἀντιλεγόμενος, "disputed."

71. See below, Chapter Five.

72. Origen *Comm. Jo.* 5.3 = *Hist. eccl.* 6.25.8 (Cruse trans., with modifications). Greek: ἔστω δὲ καὶ δευτέραν καὶ τρίτην, ἐπεὶ οὐ πάντες φασὶ *γνησίους* εἶναι ταύτας.

73. Greek: Ἐγὼ δὲ ἀποφαινόμενος εἴποιμ' ἄν, ὅτι τὰ μὲν νοήματα τοῦ ἀποστόλου ἐστίν, ἡ δὲ φράσις, καὶ ἡ σύνθεσις, ἀπομνημονε-ύσαντός τινος τὰ ἀποστολικά, καὶ ὡσπερεὶ σχολιογραφήσαντος τὰ εἰρημένα ὑπὸ τοῦ διδασκάλου. Εἴ τις οὖν ἐκκλησία ἔχει ταύτην τὴν ἐπιστολὴν ὡς Παύλου, αὕτη εὐδοκιμείτω καὶ ἐπὶ τούτῳ, οὐ γὰρ εἰκῇ οἱ ἀρχαῖοι ἄνδρες ὡς Παύλου αὐτὴν παραδεδώκασι. Τίς δὲ ὁ γράψας τὴν ἐπιστολήν, τὸ μὲν ἀληθὲς Θεὸς οἶδεν.

74. Eusebius *Hist. eccl.* 6.25.11–14 (Cruse trans.).

Chapter 5. Against Pagans and Heretics

1. At the level of Roman imperial affairs, however, things were not so tranquil; see Charles M. Odahl, "The Imperial Crisis and the Illyrian Emperors," in *Constantine and the Christian Empire* (New York: Routledge, 2004), 15–41.

2. A "quotation" from Porphyry's *Against the Christians,* cited by W. H. C. Frend, *The Rise of Christianity* (Philadelphia: Fortress Press, 1984), 443, 467n24. On the difficulty of coming up with an accurate reconstruction of anything Porphyry said, see note 6 below. For a succinct description of the "advance of Christianity" during the latter part of the third century, with bibliography, see Frend, *The Rise of Christianity,* 444–52.

3. We are deeply indebted to Henry Chadwick, author of *Origen: Contra Celsum* (Cambridge: Harvard University Press, 1965), for taking the trouble to put Origen's quotations from and allusions to Celsus's tract in italics in his English translation and thus facilitating enormously the tasks of ascertaining what Celsus actually said; see my attempt in "Celsus Attacks Christianity in True Doctrine," in *A History of the Synoptic Problem: The Canon, the Text, the Composition, and the Interpretation of the Gospels* (New York: Doubleday, 1999), 59–64.

4. *Adv. Cel.* 3.10, Chadwick edition, p. 134.

5. *Adv. Cel.* 5.61–63, Chadwick edition, pp. 311–13.

6. Amos B. Hulen estimates that it compared in length to a volume in the *Ante-Nicene Fathers* library (average length of 500 pages); see *Porphyry's Work, Against the Christians: An Interpretation* (Yale Studies in Religion #1; Scottdale, Pa.: Mennonite Press, 1933), 4. For a list of earlier attacks possibly drawn on by Porphyry, see ibid., 31–43. For an older list of attempts to collect the fragments and arrange them, see ibid., 56. The most famous reconstruction was by Adolf von Harnack, *Porphyrius "Gegen die Christen" 15 Bücher: Zeugnisse, Fragmente, und Referate* (Berlin: Königliche Akademie der Wissenschaften, 1916). For a devastating critique of Harnack's reconstruction, see T. W. Crafer, "The Work of Porphyry, *Against the Christians,* and Its Reconstruction," *JTS* 15 (1913–14): 360–74. T. D. Barnes (*Constantine and Eusebius* [Cambridge: Harvard University Press, 1981], 363n87), also objects that Harnack's reconstruction "contains more than fifty 'fragments' culled from Macarious Magnes which it is not legitimate to regard as direct quotations." For a more reliable collection of all known fragments, see Crafer, "The Work of Porphyry, *Against the Christians,*" 483–99. For a recent English translation of the fragments using Harnack's dubious reconstruction, see R. Joseph Hoffmann, *Porphyry's Against the Christians: The Literary Remains* (Amherst, Mass.: Prometheus Books, 1994).

7. See Eusebius's comment on Porphyry in *Hist. Eccl.* 6.14.2–9; for examples of Origen's frank Gospel criticism later used by Porphyry, see my chapter on Origen in *A History of the Synoptic Problem,* 65–88.

8. For a longer discussion with bibliography, see my chapter, "Porphyry: The Deadliest Foe—Has Read the Gospels, Carefully," in *A History of the Synoptic Problem,* 89–97.

9. For discussions of Porphyry's evolution as a philosophical critic of Christianity, see Frend, *The Rise of Christianity,* 441–44; and Barnes, *Constantine and Eusebius,* 174–81.

10. Barnes, *Constantine and Eusebius*, 364n71.

11. For the "war of words" that preceded the outbreak of persecution under Diocletian in 303, see Frend, *The Rise of Christianity*, 477. For pagan officials and writers urging Galerius and Diocletian to adopt a policy of extermination of the Christians, see Odahl, *Constantine and the Christian Empire*, 303n24.

12. For an abbreviated English translation of Philostratus' *Life of Apollonios of Tyana*, with introduction and notes, see D. R. Cartlidge and David Dungan, *Documents for the Study of the Gospels* (2nd ed., Minneapolis: Fortress Press, 1994) 203–238. The full text is available in LCL.

13. Odahl, *Constantine and the Christian Empire*, 67.

14. Ibid.

15. Ibid., 69.

16. Eusebius, *Mart. Pal.* 1.1.

17. Ibid., 7.5.

18. See H. A. Drake, *Eusebius and the Bishops: The Politics of Intolerance* (Baltimore: John Hopkins University Press, 2000), 356; and Frend, *The Rise of Christianity*, 477–79. The question of the relative dates of Eusebius's many writings (and Porphyry's and Hierocles' for that matter) is exceedingly debatable. Part of the problem lies in the fact that it has been only in the last ten years that scholars have begun to recognize the coherent pattern of the *Chronological Canons,* the *Ecclesiastical History,* the *Preparation for the Gospel,* and the *Demonstration of the Gospel* as systematic refutations of each of the four main contentions of Porphyry described in the text above. On this whole question, see R. W. Burgess, "The Dates and Editions of Eusebius' *Chrononici canones* and *historia ecclesiastica*," in *JTS* NS 48 (1997): 471–504, especially the masterly summary, 497. Drake, *Eusebius and the Bishops*, 523n3, endorses Burgess's reconstruction. For the date of 300 for the appearance of Porphyry's *Against the Christians* instead of ca. 270 (the usual view), see Burgess, "The Dates and Editions of Eusebius' *Chrononici canones* and *historia ecclesiastica*," 489 and n45. For further discussion and bibliography, see my chapter, "Eusebius of Caesarea's Four-Part Response to Porphyry," in *History of the Synoptic Problem*, 98–111.

19. For the full text of Eusebius's reply to Hierocles, see F. C. Conybeare, *Philostratus, Life of Apollonios* (LCL; Cambridge: Harvard University Press, 1960), where one finds "The Treatise of Eusebius, the son of Pamphilus, against the *Life of Apollonios of Tyana* written by Philostratus, occasioned by the parallel drawn by Hierocles between him and Christ," 2:484–605. For an abbreviated version of Philostratus's biography of Apollonios with

introduction and explanatory notes, see Cartlidge and Dungan, *Documents for the Study of the Gospels*. For a brief analysis of Eusebius's remarkable argument in his reply to Hierocles that everyone naturally looks to the goodness of God for those "rays of light sent from God called Saviors," see ibid., Introduction, "Savior Gods of the Mediterranean World," 12–14.

20. Burgess, "The Dates and Editions of Eusebius' *Chrononici canones* and *historia ecclesiastica*," 488. Burgess observes that "the importance of Porphyry's chronology for the date of Moses is emphasized again in Eusebius's discussion in the *Praeparatio Evangelica*, where he quotes Porphyry first" and discusses the question at length (*Praep. ev.* 10.9.11–25).

21. Eusebius refers to it in *Hist. eccl.* 1.1.6; in *Praep. ev.* 10.9; and in *Ecl. proph.* 1.1.

22. For this conjecture, see Frend, *The Rise of Christianity*, 478; Burgess, "The Dates and Editions of Eusebius' *Chrononici canones* and *historia ecclesiastica*," 494 (quoting Frend, *The Rise of Christianity*); Johannes Quasten, *Patrology* (3 vols.; Westminster, Md.: Newman, 1950), 3:331ff.

23. Both are now available in inexpensive reprints of good English translations: Edwin Hamilton Gifford, *Preparation for the Gospel* (2 vols.; Clarendon Press, 1903; repr. Grand Rapids, Mich.: Baker Book House, 1981); and W. J. Ferrar, ed. and trans., *The Proof of the Gospel* (London: SPCK, 1920; repr. Grand Rapids, Mich.: Baker Book House, 1981).

24. This is a hotly contested question; for an early date of Eusebius's *Ecclesiastical History*, see Barnes, *Constantine and Eusebius*, 128ff., 178ff., and the literature cited there; see also Glenn Chesnut, *The First Christian Histories: Eusebius, Socrates, Sozomen, Theodoret, and Evagrius* (2nd ed.; Macon, Ga.: Mercer University Press, 1986),113–25. For a date of composition during the Great Persecution, see Frend, *The Rise of Christianity*, 477ff. For the view adopted here, see Drake, *Eusebius and the Bishops*, 345; Burgess, "Dates and Editions," 498–502.

25. On the interrelated character of these publications as a coordinated response specifically aimed at the four main criticisms of Porphyry, see my chapter on Eusebius, in *A History of the Synoptic Problem*, 98–111.

26. Greek: προϊούσης δὲ τῆς ἱστορίας προύργου ποιήσομαι σὺν ταῖς διαδοχαῖς ὑποσημήνασθαι τίνες τῶν κατὰ χρόνους ἐκκλησιαστικῶν συγγραφέων ὁποίαις κέχρηνται τῶν ἀντιλεγομένων, τίνα τε περὶ τῶν ἐνδιαθήκων* καὶ ὁμολογουμένων γραφῶν καὶ ὅσα περὶ τῶν μὴ τοιούτων αὐτοῖς εἴρηται. McGiffert's translation (Arthur

Cushman McGiffert, "The Church History of Eusebius," in *A Select Library of Nicene and Post-Nicene Fathers,* second series [*NPNF²*], vol. 1 [Grand Rapids: Eerdmans, 1952], 134) is quite similar: "But in the course of my history I shall be careful to show, in addition to the official succession, what ecclesiastical writers have from time to time made use of any of the disputed works, and what they have said in regard to the *canonical* * and accepted writings, as well as in regard to those which are not of this class." The curious word with the asterisk is ἐνδιαθήκων, which is translated differently in every translation I have examined—suggesting that no one knows quite what to do with it (including Cruse, who actually leaves it in Greek in his English translation). Literally, it means "en-testamented," i.e., widely regarded as definitely included in the New Testament. You can see why no one translates it literally; in English it is meaningless. Where did Eusebius get this word? He uses it five times in the *Hist. eccl.* (3.3.1; 3.3.3; 3.9.5; 5.8.1; 6.14.1). It appears that Origen coined it, using it once in *Or.* 4. (The other occasion is Eusebius quoting Origen, so it could be Eusebius's word.) In any case this neologism did not catch on (see references in Bruce Metzger, *The Canon of the New Testament: Its Origin, Development, and Significance* [New York: Oxford University Press, 1987], 292), being supplanted in the course of the fourth century by the word *canonical* (κανονικός).

27. One is reminded of Irenaeus's boast that he could give the succession of every orthodox congregation, but he shrank at the daunting prospect, giving just the succession for Rome—without the dates of each bishop, which Eusebius provided; see Irenaeus *Haer.* 3.3.1–2.

28. As we learn from Justin *1 Apol.* 67: "And on the day called Sunday, there is a meeting in one place of those who live in cities or the country, and the memoirs of the apostles or the writings of the prophets are read as long as time permits. [Then] the president in a discourse urges and invites us to the imitation of these noble things. [Then we say prayers, etc.]."

29. For references to passing down actual copies of the apostles' writings see *Hist. eccl.* 3.3.2; 3.37.2; 6.12.3.

30. I am indebted for this chronological outline of the *Hist. eccl.* to H. Attridge, *Introduction to Eusebius, Christianity, and Judaism* (Leiden: Brill, 1992), 35ff. For evidence of the specific benefactions to the Catholic Christians, see chapter 6 below.

31. Eusebius mentions that he also drew on the archives of the library in Jerusalem (or, as he calls it, "Aelia") (*Hist. eccl.* 6.20.1).

32. Metzger, *The Canon of the New Testament,* 188, writes that "the Shepherd of Hermas was used as Scripture by Irenaeus, Tertullian (before his conversion to Montanism), Clement of Alexandria, and Origen, though according to Origen it was not generally read in church."

33. Cruse's translation is very similar to McGiffert's in *NPNF*[2] vol. 1, 134: "One epistle of Peter, that called the first, is acknowledged as genuine. And this the ancient elders used freely in their own writings as an undisputed work. But we have learned that his extant second Epistle does not *belong to the canon;** yet, as it has appeared profitable to many, it has been used with the other Scriptures." Greek: Πέτρου μὲν οὖν ἐπιστολὴ μία, ἡ λεγομένη αὐτοῦ προτέρα, ἀνωμολόγηται, ταύτῃ δὲ καὶ οἱ πάλαι πρεσβύτεροι ὡς ἀναμφιλέκτῳ ἐν τοῖς σφῶν αὐτῶν κατακέχρηνται συγγράμμασιν· τὴν δὲ φερομένην δευτέραν οὐκ ἐνδιάθηκον** μὲν εἶναι παρειλήφαμεν, ὅμως δὲ πολλοῖς χρήσιμος φανεῖσα, μετὰ τῶν ἄλλων ἐσπουδάσθη γραφῶν. On the term ἐνδιάθηκον, translated by Cruse as *embodied* and by McGiffert as *canonical,* see note 26 above.

34. I have substituted Kirsopp Lake's translation (*Eusebius: The Ecclesiastical History,* LCL [Cambridge, Mass.: Harvard University Press, 1959]) for Cruse's, who seriously mistranslates an important point here. McGiffert's translation is similar to Lake's: "It is my purpose to write an account of the successions of the holy apostles, as well as of the times which have elapsed from the days of our Saviour to our own; and to relate the many important events which are said to have occurred in the history of the church; and to mention those who have governed and presided over the church in the most prominent parishes, and those who in each generation have proclaimed the divine word either orally or in writing. It is my purpose also to give the names and number and times of those who through love of innovation have run into the greatest errors, and, proclaiming themselves discoverers of knowledge falsely so-called [cf. 1 Tim 6:20], have like fierce wolves unmercifully devastated the flock of Christ." Greek: Τὰς τῶν ἱερῶν ἀποστόλων διαδοχὰς σὺν καὶ τοῖς ἀπὸ τοῦ σωτῆρος ἡμῶν καὶ εἰς ἡμᾶς διηνυσμένοις χρόνοις, ὅσα τε καὶ πηλίκα πραγματευθῆναι κατὰ τὴν ἐκκλησιαστικὴν ἱστορίαν λέγεται, καὶ ὅσοι ταύτης διαπρεπῶς ἐν ταῖς μάλιστα ἐπισημοτάταις παροικίαις ἡγήσαντό τε καὶ προέστησαν, ὅσοι τε κατὰ γενεὰν ἑκάστην ἀγράφως ἢ καὶ διὰ συγγραμμάτων τὸν θεῖον ἐπρέσβευσαν λόγον, τίνες τε καὶ ὅσοι καὶ ὁπηνίκα νεωτεροποιίας ἱμέρῳ πλάνης εἰς ἔσχατον ἐλάσαντες, ψευδωνύμου γνώσεως εἰσηγητὰς ἑαυτοὺς ἀνακεκηρύχασιν, ἀφειδῶς οἷα λύκοι βαρεῖς τὴν Χριστοῦ ποίμνην ἐπεντρίβοντες....

35. On Eusebius's own assessment of the novel character of his *Ecclesiastical History,* see *Hist. eccl.* 5., Intro. 3–4; see further Barnes, *Constantine and Eusebius,* 128.

36. The apologetic purpose of the *Chronological Canons* is discussed more fully above.

37. See the chart of bishop's successions for a few cities in Cruse, 466; cf. also McGiffert, *NPNF* [2] vol. 1, 401ff., for Rome, Alexandria, Antioch, and Jerusalem (with dates where possible). See also Eduard Schwartz and Theodor Mommsen, *Eusebius Werke* (2nd ed.; ed. F. Winkelmann; GCS n.F. 6, no. 3; [Berlin: Akademie Verlag], 1999), Bd. 2, Teil 3, 34–40: Rome, Alexandria, Antioch, and Jerusalem.

38. Reference in the Edict of Milan to the "Corporation of the Christians" (σῶμα τῶν χριστιανῶν): *Hist. eccl.* 10.5.10, 11, 12. Distinguishing "Catholic Christians" from others: *Hist. eccl.* 10.5.15, 20. Calling the Catholics the true "school" or "heresy," αἱρέσις τῆς καθολικῆς: *Hist. eccl.* 10.5.21; cf. 10.5.1. See McGiffert, *NPNF* [2], 1: 379–81.

39. For a recent discussion of this dimension of Eusebius and his predecessors, see Harold W. Attridge and Gohei Hata, *Eusebius, Christianity, and Judaism* (StPB 42; Leiden: Brill, 1992), specifically, pt. 4, "The Fate of the Jews," in *Eusebius: Ecclesiastical History,* with articles by Kituo Matsunaga, "Christian Self-Identification and the Twelfth Benediction" (355–71); Louis H. Feldman, "Jewish Proselclytism" (372–408); and Alan J. Avery-Peck, "Judaism without the Temple: The Mishnah" (409–31).

40. The choice of Moses rather than King David may seem a bit odd; see the explanation below in chapter 6, and the discussion in A. Cameron and S. G. Hall, *Eusebius, Life of Constantine* (Oxford: Clarendon Press, 1999), 35–39; further Glenn Chesnut, *The First Christian Histories: Eusebius, Socrates, Sozomen, Theodoret, and Evagrius,* 2nd ed. (Macon, Ga.: Mercer University Press, 1986), 163.

41. Here is McGiffert's translation, which is very similar to Cruse: (1) "Since we are dealing with this subject it is proper to sum up the writings of the New Testament which have been already mentioned. First then must be put the holy quaternion of the Gospels; following them the Acts of the Apostles. (2) After this must be reckoned the epistles of Paul; next in order the extant [sic] former epistle of John, and likewise the epistle of Peter, must be maintained. After them is to be placed, if it really seem proper, the Apocalypse of John, concerning which we shall give the different opinions at the proper time. (3) These then belong among the *accepted* writings." (*NPNF* [2] vol. 1, 155ff.). Greek: (1) Εὔλογον δ' ἐνταῦθα γενομένους

ἀνακεφαλαιώσασθαι τὰς δηλωθείσας τῆς καινῆς διαθήκης γραφάς. καὶ δὴ τακτέον ἐν πρώτοις τὴν ἁγίαν τῶν εὐαγγελίων τετρακτύν, (2) οἷς ἕπεται ἡ τῶν Πράξεων τῶν ἀποστόλων γραφή· μετὰ δὲ ταύτην τὰς Παύλου καταλεκτέον ἐπιστολάς, αἷς ἑξῆς τὴν φερομένην Ἰωάννου προτέραν καὶ ὁμοίως τὴν Πέτρου κυρωτέον ἐπιστολήν· ἐπὶ τούτοις τακτέον, εἴ γε φανείη, τὴν Ἀποκάλυψιν Ἰωάννου, περὶ ἧς τὰ δόξαντα (3) κατὰ καιρὸν ἐκθησόμεθα. καὶ ταῦτα μὲν ἐν ὁμολογουμένοις.

42. See article τετρακτύς, in Liddell-Scott-Jones, *A Greek-English Lexicon* (New York: Oxford University Press, 1996); Hermann Diels, *Doxographi Graeci* (Berlin: G. Remeiri, 1879), article "The First Philosophers," trans. A. Fairbanks, and reproduced in K .S. Guthrie, *The Pythagorean Sourcebook* (Grand Rapids, Mich.: Phanes Press, 1987), 307, which contains a quotation from Aetius *Vetusta Placita* 1, 3; Dox. 280. Lake's translation, "holy tetrad," uses the accepted English translation of the Pythagorean *terminus technicus* (which means he got the point); "quaternion" (McGiffert, Cruse) and "quartet" (Williamson) destroy the allusion.

43. See the discussion on this passage above, pp. 64f.

44. See the discussion of this term as used by Origen and others in chapter 4, note 68.

45. See above, chapter 4.

46. Still the best general study of this whole question is Walter Bauer, *Orthodoxy and Heresy in Earliest Christianity* (trans. and ed. Robert Kraft and Gerhard Krodel; Minneapolis: Fortress Press, 1971).

47. Cruse consistently translates νόθοι as "spurious." Lake's "not genuine" gets the right idea; McGiffert's "rejected writings" is not a good choice. I prefer "illegitimate" or "counterfeit."

48. See above, pp. 63f.

49. Some thought Barnabas was one of Christ's "seventy" disciples (Lk 10:1; cf. *Hist. eccl.* 1.12.1). Clement of Alexandria is quoted as saying Barnabas was one of the 70 in *Hist. eccl.* 2.1.4, and he quotes his Epistle in his *Stromata* as scripture; see *Hist. eccl.* 6.13.6. Acts portrays Barnabas as an associate of Paul, *Hist. eccl.* 2.3.3.

50. The *Revelation of Peter* is listed with several rejected writings in *Hist. eccl.* 3.3.2, while the *Acts of Paul* is dismissed with the statement: "I have not found it among the *undisputed* writings" (*Hist. eccl.* 3.3.5).

51. For a complete list of all references to the Apocalypse of John in Eusebius' *Ecclesiastical History,* see Appendix A.

52. See *Eccl. hist.* 7.24 25.

53. See the record of the dispute on this topic between Bishop Dionysius and another bishop in Egypt named Nepos; *Eccl. hist* . 7.24.

54. Eusebius' records regarding Cerinthus can be found at *Eccl. hist.* 3.27; 4.14.6; 7.25.3–4.

55. This is that odd Greek term ἐνδιάθηκος that Eusebius got from Origen; McGiffert and Lake, as usual, translate it "canonical," but that is not its literal meaning.

56. McGiffert's translation is very similar to Cruse: "But we have nevertheless felt compelled to give a catalogue of these also, distinguishing those works which according to ecclesiastical tradition are *true* and *genuine* and *commonly accepted,* from those others which, although not *canonical* but *disputed,* are yet at the same time *known* to most ecclesiastical writers . . ." (*NPNF*[2] 1:157). Greek: ταῦτα δὲ πάντα τῶν ἀντιλεγομένων ἂν εἴη, ἀναγκαίως δὲ καὶ τούτων ὅμως τὸν κατάλογον πεποιήμεθα, διακρίνοντες τάς τε κατὰ τὴν ἐκκλησιαστικὴν παράδοσιν ἀληθεῖς καὶ ἀπλάστους καὶ ἀνωμολογημένας γραφὰς καὶ τὰς ἄλλως παρὰ ταύτας, οὐκ ἐνδιαθήκους* μὲν ἀλλὰ καὶ ἀντιλεγομένας, ὅμως δὲ παρὰ πλείστοις τῶν ἐκκλησιαστικῶν γινωσκομένας. . . .

57. Lake's translation gracefully handles all of Eusebius's dependent clauses: "These would all belong to the disputed books, but we have nevertheless been obliged to make a list of [all of] them [i.e., both preceding categories], distinguishing between those writings which, according to the tradition of the church, are *true, genuine,* and *recognized,* and those which differ from them in that they are not *canonical** but *disputed,* yet nevertheless are *known* to most of the writers of the church" (Eusebius, *Ecclesiastical History,* LCL, vol. 1, 258ff.).

58. Other discussions of these three criteria are Armin D. Baum, "Der neutestamentlichen Kanon bei Eusebios (*Hist. Eccl.* III, 25, 1–7) in Kontext seiner literaturgeschichtlichen Arbeit," in *Ephemerides Theologicae Lavaniesis* 73 (1997), 328–33; Harry Y. Gamble, *The New Testament Canon: Its Making and Meaning* (Philadelphia: Fortress Press, 1985), 67–72; and especially Lee Martin McDonald, *The Formation of the Christian Biblical Canon* (Peabody, Mass.: Hendrickson, 2002), 228–49; and idem, *The Canon Debate,* 423–34.

59. See *Hist. eccl.* 3.24.

60. By Eusebius' day, the category "apostle" had expanded considerably beyond Jesus' twelve disciples and Paul. Because Eusebius and the orthodox Catholics were so scrupulous about identifying all the apostles

by name, they took at face value the widespread use of the term in Acts and the letters of Paul. As a result, the precise definition of who Jesus' "apostles" were became increasingly ambiguous. Eusebius lays out the whole problem in *Hist. eccl.* 1.12. He begins with "the twelve apostles," then mentions the "seventy apostles" (cf. Luke 10:1), saying "there is no catalog of their names." Then he mentions Judas's replacement, then adds, "our Savior had more than 70" apostles, citing Paul's recitation of appearances of the risen Christ to more than 500 people, then to James, then to "all the apostles" (1 Cor. 15:5–7). Eusebius takes Paul's last reference to "all the apostles" as indicating that there were "many others who were called apostles in imitation of the Twelve, as was Paul." If we add to these references the fact that by Eusebius's day the candidates for the New Testament also included two writings from Jesus' brothers (who were never "apostles"), it is clear that the term had become quite expansive in the later church's attempt to be exhaustive.

61. This kind of vigilant response is seen in *Hist. eccl.* 4.24 and in Eusebius's many accounts of vociferous reactions to Marcion, Montanus, Cerinthus, etc. Serapion's evaluation and rejection of the *Gospel of Peter* is described in *Hist. eccl.* 6.12.

62. See Justin Martyr, *1 Apol.* 12: "We are of all men your best helpers and allies in securing good order . . ."; also *1 Apol.* 17: "More even than others we try to pay the taxes and assessments to those whom you appoint. . . ." On the Jews, *1 Apol.* 1:35: "Jesus Christ stretched out his hands when he was crucified by the Jews who contradicted him and denied that he was the Christ"; cf. 1:31.

63. This term comes from Armin D. Baum, "Der neutestamentliche Kanon bei Eusebius," *Ephemerides Theologicae Lovaniensis* 73 (1997) 331 ("ein dreifaches Sieb").

64. See Appendix B and C for a list of writings that were candidates for inclusion in the New Testament.

65. This is the Coptic *Gospel of Thomas* which today is enjoying a wide popularity. It should not be confused with another writing of the same name, the *Infancy Gospel of Thomas.* For the full text and an introduction to many of these gospels, see David Cartlidge and David Dungan, eds., *Documents for the Study of the Gospels,* 2nd ed. (Minneapolis: Fortress, 1994), pp. 19–121.

66. A gnosticizing *Gospel of Judas* surfaced in 2006, published with great fanfare by *National Geographic* after bouncing around the antiquities market for at least two decades. At this point no one can say where it came from.

67. For texts and introductions to all these writings, see Edgar Hennecke, *New Testament Apocrypha,* ed. Wilhelm Schneemelcher, 2 vols. (Louisville: Westminster/John Knox Press, 2003); also J. K. Elliott, ed., *The Apocryphal New Testament: A Collection of Apocryphal Christian Literature in an English Translation* (Oxford: Oxford University Press, 2005).

68. The *Acts of Peter* is mentioned at *Hist. eccl.* 3.3.2; the *Acts of Paul,* at 3.3.5. The full text of these Acts can be found in vol. 2 of Hennecke–Schneemelcher, op. cit. (previous note).

69. There is an error at the end of Cruse's translation; the correct text is in brackets. McGiffert's translation of this passage is as follows: "... the character of the style is at variance with apostolic usage, and both the thoughts and the purpose of the things that are related in them are so completely out of accord with true orthodoxy that they clearly show themselves to be the fictions of heretics. Wherefore they are not to be placed even among the *rejected* writings, but are all of them to be cast aside as absurd and impious" (*NPNF*[2] 1:157; Greek: ἀγαγεῖν ἠξίωσεν, πόρρω δέ που καὶ ὁ τῆς φράσεως παρὰ τὸ ἦθος τὸ ἀποστολικὸν ἐναλλάττει χαρακτήρ, ἥ τε γνώμη καὶ ἡ τῶν ἐν αὐτοῖς φερομένων προαίρεσις πλεῖστον ὅσον τῆς ἀληθοῦς | ὀρθοδοξίας ἀπᾴδουσα, ὅτι δὴ αἱρετικῶν ἀνδρῶν ἀναπλάσματα. ὅθεν οὐδ' ἐν νόθοις αὐτὰ κατατακτέον, ἀλλ' ὡς ἄτοπα πάντῃ καὶ δυθφεβῆ παραιτητέον.

70. For two examples of the application of the test of style, see Eusebius' account of Origen's discussion of the style of the Epistle to the Hebrews quoted above (from *Hist. eccl.* 6.25.11–14). There is a lengthy quotation from Dionysius of Alexandria comparing the style of the Gospel of John with that of the Apocalypse of John and the three Epistles of John, cited by Eusebius in *Hist. eccl.* 7.25.

71. McGiffert's translation is very similar: to ascertain whether "the thoughts and the purpose of the things that are related in them are ... completely out of accord with true orthodoxy" (*NPNF*[2] 1:157).

72. Yigael Yadin discusses the amazing archeological discovery at Masada of an actual lot from those used to decide which one of the ten last Zealot soldiers would kill his nine comrades. The rest of the more than 700 Zealots had already chosen death rather than fall into Roman hands and certain torture and slavery, in the fateful moments prior to the final Roman victory. One lot had the name Ben Ya'ir on it, the leader of the entire Zealot force. See Masada: *Herod's Fortress and the Zealots' Last Stand* (New York: Random House, 1966), p. 201, with a photo of Ben Ya'ir's ostracon or lot. See also the description in Josephus, *B. J.* 7.395.

73. "Casting lots," according to the usual procedure, involved writing names on small pieces of clay and putting them into a pot. The pot was shaken until one fell out. See F.J. Foakes Jackson and Kirsopp Lake, *The Acts of the Apostles*, The Beginnings of Christianity, vol. 4 (Moffatt New Testament Commentary; New York: Harper, 1931), 15.

74. Examples: Acts 11:4–18, vision of different kinds of things to eat on a sheet lowered from heaven; Acts 16:8ff., vision of a "man from Macedonia" urging Paul to come over and help them; Acts 18:7–11, the Lord appears to Paul and urges him to preach boldly.

75. See the discussion, with bibliography, in Bruce M. Metzger, *The Canon of the New Testament: Its Origin, Development, and Significance* (Oxford: Clarendon Press, 1989), pp. 254–257, "Inspiration and the Canon." See esp. E. R. Kalin, "Argument from Inspiration in the Canonization of the New Testament," unpubl. Th.D. diss, Harvard Divinity School, 1967.

76. See the discussion of this phrase in chapter 4, note 69.

77. For an examination of a similar, more or less contemporary secular historian's use of sources, see Jørgen Mejer, *Diogenes Laertius and His Hellenistic Background* (Stuttgart: Steiner Verlag, 1978), 28, followed by a lengthy "source analysis."

78. The story is found in *Hist. eccl.* 6.12, where Eusebius quotes verbatim from a work Bishop Serapion composed regarding the *Gospel of Peter*. The bishop says he borrowed a copy of the gospel from local "docetics" who were using it, and "discovered many things superadded to the sound faith of our Savior, as well as (elements) that are foreign to it." I take this to mean it failed the first test, i.e. did not contain orthodox content, and thus failed the second test, of apostolic authorship, automatically. Then Serapion sent his negative opinion in a circular letter to other bishops in his region, including the library at Caesarea, where Eusebius found it and quoted this extract.

79. See Chesnut, *First Christian Histories*.

Chapter 6. An Emperor Intervenes

1. My understanding of Constantine's conversion experience is indebted to Charles Matson Odahl, *Constantine and the Christian Empire* (London: Routledge, 2004). Part of the problem with any interpretation lies in the fact that the three most ancient descriptions of Constantine's conversion—Lactantius's writing, *On the Death of the Persecutors* 44, writ-

ten in 313 shortly after the event, possibly at Constantine's court in Trier; Eusebius's *Ecclesiastical History* 9.9.2–9, also written within a year or two afterward; and another version in his *Life of Constantine* 27–32, written some twenty-five years later, two years after Constantine had died—all differ in major respects. For the primary sources and survey of the secondary literature, see Odahl, *Constantine and the Christian Empire*, 105, 381ff. Odahl's discussion is more thorough than that of Andrew Alföldi, *The Conversion of Constantine and Pagan Rome* (trans. Harold Mattingly; Oxford: Clarendon Press, 1948), 5–24; Hans A. Pohlsander, *The Emperor Constantine* (London: Routledge, 1996), 22ff.; W. H. C. Frend, *The Rise of Christianity* (Philadelphia: Fortress, 1984), 482; and others. Odahl provides evidence for the popular solar syncretism (the worship of *Sol Invictus*) in Constantine's family, which may have paved the way for his transition to a hybrid Christianity suitable for a Roman emperor to adopt. Odahl also explains the well-documented practice of previous emperors having highly publicized divine visions before battle (see below, note 13), as well as the widespread trust in magic talismans (for example, the Labarum) shared by Christians like Lactantius, Eusebius, Hosius, and Miltiades, among others.

T. G. Elliott (*The Christianity of Constantine the Great* [Scranton, Pa.: University of Scranton Press, 1996], 68), holds the opinion that Eusebius invented Constantine's "conversion" experience, as have many skeptical scholars before him. Complete skepticism on the depth of Constantine's Christianity is not justified, in my view, since there was considerable imperial activity restoring property to Catholic churches during the winter of 312, right after the defeat of Maxentius. What was the motivation for that beneficent activity? Odahl makes a comprehensive and persuasive case that Constantine made a decisive choice to begin favoring "the god of his father," which soon became identified as "the God of the Christians" (Eusebius *Vit. Const.* 1.27).

How "Christian" was Constantine? Critics rarely give any definition of the "Christianity" being used as the standard of comparison. For instance, Alföldi is typical of many scholars: "The Christianity of Constantine was not wrapped in the glory of the true Christian spirit, but *in the darkness of superstition*" (23; emphasis added). Methodologically more sophisticated is the question put by Averil Cameron and Stuart G. Hall (*Eusebius: Life of Constantine: Introduction, Translation and Commentary* [Oxford: Oxford University Press, 1999], 4): "Doubts have been expressed about the genuineness of Constantine's Christianity. . . . Was he at heart a Christian, and if so, *of what kind?*" (emphasis added). Constantine maintained a studied ambiguity about his allegiance to Christianity so that his true allegiance only slowly became more decisive and explicit: see Alföldi, *The Conversion of Constantine and Pagan Rome,* 27ff.

2. The·term *Catholic* is used (capitalized) throughout this book in the same way that Constantine and the orthodox leadership used this term about their faction: ἐκκλησία καθολική (see chapter four, note 68). This use of the term should not be confused with the later "Roman Catholic Church." By the same token, "orthodox" was the self-designation of those whose claim to right belief eventually triumphed historically. I use it to refer to this faction among the many competing for hegemony in the Christian religion; I am not referring to later Greek Orthodoxy, or to any of the other Eastern Orthodox communions.

3. H. A. Drake (*Constantine and the Bishops: The Politics of Intolerance* [Baltimore: Johns Hopkins University Press, 2000]), makes the case that the Catholic leadership evolved in their methods and goals along with Constantine in a new, fast-moving, dialectical relationship. In short, both Constantine and the bishops constitute a "moving target" that is very tricky to assess accurately at any given time. If that is true, one of our best sources of information on Constantine's personal theological views must be the sermon he gave some ten years after his conversion, possibly just before the Council of Nicaea in 325, entitled "Speech to the Assembly of the Saints." For an excellent analysis of this important document, see especially Timothy D. Barnes, *Constantine and Eusebius* (Cambridge: Harvard University Press, 1981), 73–76.

4. Alföldi has rightly identified perhaps the most intricate problem in Constantine-Catholic relations during the period between 312 (conversion) and 337 (Constantine's death): "Modern scholars have seldom been able to understand the Janus face of this short period of transition" (*The Conversion of Constantine and Pagan Rome,* 26). It is well-known that the whole field of Constantine studies has gone through several major changes or shifts in viewpoint: see Odahl, *Constantine and the Christian Empire,* 282ff. Scholars generally credit Norman H. Baynes with opening the door to a more fruitful approach after a long period of skepticism: see his *Constantine the Great and the Christian Church* (Raleigh Lectures for 1929; printed in *Proceedings of the British Academy* 15 (1929) (later published separately: Norman H. Baynes, *Constantine the Great and the Christian Church* [2nd ed.; Oxford: Oxford University Press, 1977]).

5. See especially the apse mosaic depicting a royal Christ, enthroned in his court in the Heavenly Jerusalem and surrounded by the Twelve Apostles, in the fourth-century basilica of Santa Pudenziana, Rome. This famous mosaic can be found in numerous histories of western art: cf. the discussion in John Beckwith, *Early Christian and Byzantine Art* (Pelican History of Art; 2nd ed.; New York: Penguin, 1979), 32–35, with illustration; and Ernst Kitzinger, *Byzantine Art in the Making: Main Lines of Stylistic Development in Mediterranean Art, 3rd–7th Century* (London: Faber and Faber 1977), illus. 80, for Santa Pudenziana. From a slightly later time, there is the equally magnificent mosaic of Christ the King seated on the throne of majesty and dressed in imperial purple, with two great archangels on either side—the new Praetorian Guard—on the right wall of the sixth-century basilica of Sant' Apollinare Nuovo, in Ravenna; see Kitzinger, *Byzantine Art in the Making*, illus. 106. The scale of the radical transformation in images of Jesus from pre- to post-Constantinian Christianity is best gauged by comparing the fourth- and fifth-century mosaics of the imperial Christ with the frescoes and ivory figurines in the Christian catacombs of the second and third century. For architectural comparisons, consider the unique third-century house-church discovered at Dura Europus with the basilicas at Ravenna. On this whole subject, see André Grabar, *Early Christian Art: From the Rise of Christianity to the Death of Theodosius* (New York: Odyssey Press, 1969); see also Graydon F. Snyder, *Ante-Pacem: Archeological Evidence of Church Life before Constantine* (Macon, Ga.: Mercer University Press, 1985); Pierre du Bourguet, *Early Christian Art* (trans. T. Burton; New York: Reynal, 1971); and forthcoming, David Laird Dungan, *Images of Jesus: A History of Enculturation in Western Christianity from the First Century to the Twentieth.*

6. The most insightful discussion of the striking transformation in Eusebius is Chesnut, *First Christian Histories*, 111–140.

7. Odahl, *Constantine and the Christian Empire*, 93ff.

8. The plot is described in Lactantius *Mort.* 29–30; Eusebius *Hist. eccl.* 8.13.15; and Eusebius *Vit. Const.* 1.47.1. Cf. Odahl, *Constantine and the Christian Empire*, 93.

9. Lactantius *Mort.* 33: "In the eighteenth year of his reign, God struck [Galerius] down with an incurable plague. A malignant ulcer formed itself low down on his private parts, and spread [throughout his body]. . . . A vein burst and blood flowed in such quantity as to endanger his life. . . . Gangrene set in and spread to all the neighbouring parts. . . . His

whole seat was putrified . . . worms were generated in his body. The stench
was so foul as to pervade not only the palace but even the whole city." Cf.
Eusebius *Hist. eccl.* 8.16; and Eusebius *Vit. Const.* 1.57. Odahl (*Constantine
and the Christian Empire*, 96) suggests that Galerius may have had "penile
squamous cell carcinoma."

10. For a description of the four main criticisms of Porphyry, see
chapter five. See also T. D. Barnes, *Constantine and Eusebius* (Cambridge,
Mass.: Harvard University Press, 1981), 176ff.

11. Eusebius *Hist. eccl.* 8, Appendix 2–3; cf. Odahl, *Constantine and
the Christian Empire*, 97.

12. Odahl (*Constantine and the Roman Empire*, 105f.) gives a detailed
reconstruction of the battle between Constantine and Maxentius, based on
Eusebius (in his *Vit. Const.* 1.26–41; cf. *Hist. eccl.* 9.9; Lactantius, *de Mort.
Pers.* 44, 46). On the historical reliability of the *Life of Constantine,* see
Cameron and Hall, *Eusebius: The Life of Constantine,* 4–9; Chesnut, *First
Christian Histories,* 141n1.

13. It should be noted that this custom of employing supernatural
charms, signs, and high-profile battlefield allegiances with various gods,
accompanied by public proclamations, special coins, symbolic statues, and
temples was not unusual among Roman emperors. Odahl (*Constantine and
the Christian Empire,* 37) tells of how the emperor Aurelian (270–275) had
a blazing solar vision prior to a major battle; he dedicated the subsequent
victory to *Sol Invictus,* "the Unconquered Sun," built a huge temple to the
same divinity in downtown Rome, and promoted the same divinity on
his coins (ibid., 38, illus. 5). Diocletian and his co-Augustus Maximilian
adopted Jupiter and Hercules as their divine patrons and sought to portray
their control of the Roman Empire as a replica of Jupiter's and Hercules'
rule over the divine realm (ibid., 43). Both issued coins with Jovian sym-
bolism on them (ibid., 454, illus. 7). A year earlier, it was reported in a
public speech given by a paid professional orator that Constantine himself, on his way back to the imperial palace at Trier in August of 310, had
stopped at a Temple of Apollo and received a vision of Apollo and the
goddess Victory, where he was told he would be the "savior of the world"
(ibid., 94). The emperor Maxentius portrayed himself as the "compan-
ion" of Mars, with Roma as the "protectress of her city" (ibid., 100). See
the extended note with other examples of emperors and heavenly signs
during battle in Alföldi, *The Conversion of Constantine and Pagan Rome,*
127. In other words, this quest for a new divine patron on Constantine's
part was not unusual: emperors were expected to procure whatever divine

assistance they could for looming battles, the founding of cities, public projects, and so on. Odahl (*Constantine and the Christian Empire*, 95ff.) provides a helpful description of the solar monotheism popular among recent Roman emperors, particularly Constantine's father, that seemed to function as a bridge for Constantine to pass over in his conversion to Christianity. This appears to have been a piety that Constantine never completely repudiated.

14. Eusebius *Vit. Const.* 1.27 (trans. E. C. Richardson; *NPNF*[2] vol. 1, 489.

15. Ibid., 1.28 (trans. Richardson, 1, 490). Eusebius admits in his account that this story would be hard to believe if it weren't for the fact that he heard it straight from the emperor himself "years later when I was privileged to be sharing his company." Who could doubt the word of the emperor? There is some disagreement as to the precise wording of the heavenly message, since Eusebius gives a Greek translation of the original Latin: αὐτοῖς ὀφθαλμοῖς ἰδεῖν ἔφη ἐν αὐτῷ οὐρανῷ ὑπερκείμενον τοῦ ἡλίου σταυροῦ τρόπαιον ἐκ φωτὸς συνιστάμενον, γραφήν τε αὐτῷ συνῆφθαι λέγουσαν· τούτῳ νίκα. For the original Latin version reportedly used by the Christian god (cited in the text), see Odahl, *Constantine and the Christian Empire*, 107, illus. 25, with convincing numismatic evidence at 318n11. If this story had been in the New Testament instead of a visible motto written in the sky, there would have been a "Voice from Heaven" (Hebrew: *Bath Qol*), such as we find mentioned in Matt 3:17 (Jesus' baptism), in John 12:28 (Jesus' crucifixion), and often in the Revelation of John.

16. Eusebius *Vit. Const.* 1.29 (trans. Cameron and Hall, 81).

17. Ibid., 1.31.2.

18. Ibid., 1.30.

19. The origin of this strange word is not certain. E. C. Richardson, translator of the *Life of Constantine* for *NPNF*[2] vol. 1, 490n1, suggests that it came from the dialect of Bretagne and meant "battle standard."

20. Odahl, *Constantine and the Christian Empire*, 107, illus. 26, shows a Roman coin from this period with Winged Victory marking a soldier's shield with the Chi-Rho insignia, evidence of how it looked at the time.

21. The best reconstruction of this battle is in Odahl, *Constantine and the Christian Empire*, 98–109; cf. Eusebius *Hist. eccl.* 9.9.1–13.

22. Johannes A. Straub, "Constantine as ΚΟΙΝΟΣ ΕΠΙΣΚΟΠΟΣ: Tradition and Innovation in the Representation of the First Christian Emperor's Majesty," in *DOP* 21 (1967): 41.

23. Eusebius *Vit. Const.* 1.39; cf. Alföldi, *The Conversion of Constantine and Pagan Rome*, 24; Odahl, *Constantine and the Christian Empire*, 110f.

24. Odahl, *Constantine and the Christian Empire*, 116.

25. I am quoting the translation of McGiffert, Eusebius *Hist. eccl.* 10.5.2–3 (*NPNF*[2] vol. 1, 379f.). The Latin was preserved by Lactantius *Mort.* 48; see the discussion of the text of this decree in Odahl, *Constantine and the Christian Empire*, 324n33.

26. On Constantine's early religious policy after 312 and its related strategy of "studied ambiguity," see Baynes, *Constantine the Great and the Christian Church*, Appendix, 95–103; Alföldi, *The Conversion of Constantine and Pagan Rome*, 26–35; and Barnes, *Constantine and Eusebius*, 44–61, et passim. Odahl paints a more single-minded policy of Constantine's desire to Christianize the empire: see *Constantine and the Christian Empire*, 110, 116f., 121, et passim. Drake, *Constantine and the Bishops*, focuses on a different question but subtly illustrates the many twists and turns of Constantine's struggle to control the bishops, and vice versa.

27. Examples of the specificity of Constantine's intentions can be seen from the following examples: the Edict of Milan offers freedom of religion to "the society of the Christians" (Latin: *corpori Cristianorum*; Greek: σώματι Χριστιανῶν), that is, to those who "belong to the *Catholic Church of the Christians*" (Greek: τῆς ἐκκλησίας τῆς καθολικῆς τῶν χριστιανῶν [*Hist. eccl.* 10.5.11, 16]). Constantine's letter to Caecilian and the Donatists concludes: "[I am summoning you to Rome for a hearing because] I have such reverence for the *legitimate Catholic Church* that I do not wish you to leave schism or division in any place" (Greek: τῆς ἐνθέσμως καθολικῆς [*Hist. eccl.* 10.5.20]). This exclusive approbation of the orthodox Catholic faction had been drilled into Constantine's receptive mind by Lactantius, Miltiades, and others in the group of his first Christian advisors in his immediate entourage. But Eusebius was precisely of the same opinion, as we can see from a quote where he summarizes the rising brilliance of the apostolic, orthodox church in the days of Hadrian, beset although it may have been with all kinds of evil, pernicious, and demon-inspired false teaching: "But the splendor of *the catholic and only true Church*, which is always the same, grew in magnitude and power . . . piety, simplicity, and freedom" (Greek: ἡ τῆς καθόλου καὶ μόνης ἀληθοῦς ἐκκλησίας [*Hist. eccl.* 4.7.13]). Eusebius and the orthodox bishops' use of *catholic* as a synonym for *orthodox* can also be seen in the accounts of excommunication and separation of heretical teachers "from the catholic church" (e.g., *Hist. eccl.* 6.43.3; 7.10.6; 7.29.1). For further examples of the

use of the word *catholic* in Eusebius *Hist. eccl.*, see the index to Greek terms in Schwartz and Mommsen, *Eusebius Werke*, n.F. 6, 3, p. 182.

28. Eusebius *Vit. Const.* 2.20.

29. Ibid., 2.30.

30. Ibid., 1.42; see Odahl, *Constantine and the Christian Empire*, 114.

31. Odahl, *Constantine and the Christian Empire*, 114.

32. Eusebius *Hist. eccl.* 10.7; cf. a similar letter in ibid., 10.6. (trans. McGiffert, *NPNF*[2] 1: 383). According to Odahl (*Constantine and the Christian Empire*, 323n26), the Latin original of this edict is preserved in the Codex Theod. XVI 2.2.

33. Odahl, *Constantine and the Christian Empire*, 113; Alföldi, *The Conversion of Constantine and Pagan Rome*, 51.

34. Odahl, *Constantine and the Christian Empire*, 115f.; Alföldi, *The Conversion of Constantine and Pagan Rome*, 51f.

35. Odahl, *Constantine and the Christian Empire*, 129–40, gives a particularly detailed account of Constantine's role in this dispute. See also Barnes, *Constantine and Eusebius*, 56–60, Drake, *Constantine and the Bishops*, 212–21; Frend, *The Rise of Christianity*, 488–92, 523, 653ff.

36. Quote taken from Odahl, *Constantine and the Christian Empire*, 135f. Odahl points out that the similar letter in Eusebius *Hist. eccl.* 10.5.21–24 is the *episcopal letter* sent to Chrestus, bishop of Syracuse. The excerpt quoted above is the *secular letter* sent to Aelafius, the Roman vicar of Africa, and is much more revealing (see Odahl, *Constantine and the Christian Empire*, 134, 331n29). The Latin original of the italicized phrases is found in ibid., 331n30:

> commovi possit Summa Divinitas... in me ipsum, cujus curae nutu suo caelesti terrena omnia moderanda commisit.... Tunc enim revera et plenissime potero esse securus et semper de promptissima benevolentia Potentissimi Dei prosperrima et optima quaeque sperare, cum universos sensero debito *cultu Catholicae religionis* Sanctimissimum Deum concordi observantiae fraternitate venerari.

37. Odahl, *Constantine and the Christian Empire*, 172.

38. Ibid., 170.

39. Eusebius *Hist. eccl.* 10.8; Eusebius *Vit. Const.* 1.49–56; Odahl, *Constantine and the Christian Empire*, 174.

40. Odahl, *Constantine and the Christian Empire*, 180.

41. Ibid.

42. Ibid., 181.

43. Ibid., 344n32, discusses the authenticity of this letter.

44. Eusebius *Vit. Const.* 2:24–42; cf. the discussion in Odahl, *Constantine and the Christian Empire*, 182–85.

45. Eusebius *Vit. Const.* 2:30–31.

46. Ibid., 2:32.

47. Ibid., 2:33.

48. Ibid., 2:35–39.

49. Ibid., 2:42.

50. For a superbly nuanced account of the early stage of the Arian/Athanasian Controversy, see Barnes, *Constantine and Eusebius*, 202–7; further, Drake, *Constantine and the Bishops*, 237–41; Frend, *The Rise of Christianity*, 492–98; Odahl, *Constantine and the Christian Empire*, 189–201.

51. Eusebius *Vit. Const.* 2.65, 68, 71 (trans. Richardson, *NPNF²* vol. 1, 516f.). Discussed by Barnes, *Constantine and Eusebius*, 208–10.

52. Thus Odahl, *Constantine and the Christian Empire*, 194: "As the ecclesiastical historian Socrates later commented, 'When the Emperor thus beheld the Church agitated on account of . . . these causes, he convoked a General Council, summoning all the bishops by letter to meet him at Nicaea in Bithynia.'"

53. On the Council of Nicaea, see Eusebius *Vit. Const.* 3.6–14, and the superb analysis by Drake, *Constantine and the Bishops*, 250–57; see further Barnes, *Constantine and Eusebius*, 212–19; Frend, *The Rise of Christianity*, 498–500.

54. Eusebius *Vit. Const.* 3.13 (trans. Richardson; *NPNF²* vol. 1, 523).

55. After the Council, Eusebius sent an embarrassed letter back to his home church attempting to explain his action; Athanasius received a copy of it and published it later. Needless to say, Eusebius did not include the episode in his account of the Council of Nicaea in his *Life of Constantine*. See the nuanced analysis in Drake, *Constantine and the Bishops*, 254–57; for a characteristically upbeat account of the Council, see Odahl, *Constantine and the Christian Empire*, 196–201.

56. Odahl, *Constantine and the Christian Empire*, 198f.

57. Ibid., 197–200.

58. Eusebius *Vit. Const.* 3.18 (trans. Richardson; *NPNF²* vol. 1, 524). Where did Constantine get this negative view of Judaism? Which of his Christian mentors taught it to him? We have no direct answer for this, but

Eusebius does proudly refer to a thank-you letter he got from the emperor, expressing his appreciation for a tract Eusebius sent him on the mysteries and origins of Easter (*Vit. Const.* 4.35). The fact that Eusebius singled out these statements to preserve in his *Life of Constantine*, without correction or reproof, makes it clear that he was at least sympathetic to them. And since they appear in a eulogistic biography of Constantine intended to be read by his sons and by the Christian court and by his fellow Christian bishops, it would seem that there probably existed a widespread anti-Jewish sentiment among orthodox Catholics, which had been around for two centuries at least (as in the writings of Melito and Justin Martyr).

59. Eusebius *Vit. Const.* 1.44 (trans. Cameron and Hall; *Eusebius, Life of Constantine*, 87; cf. trans. Richardson; *NPNF*² vol. 1, 494f.). For a discussion of this striking phrase, see Straub, "Constantine as ΚΟΙΝΟΣ ΕΠΙΣΚΟΠΟΣ," 37–55.

60. Eusebius *Vit. Const.* 4.18 (trans. Richardson; *NPNF*² vol. 1, 544).

61. Discussed in Odahl, *Constantine and the Christian Empire*, 172.

62. See Eusebius *Vit. Const.* 2.45 for legislation "commanding the heightening of oratories, enlargement in length and breadth of the churches of God, as though it were expected that, now the madness of polytheism was wholly removed, nearly all mankind would henceforth attach themselves to the service of God."

63. See the map of Rome with the locations of eight Constantinian-era basilicas, in Odahl, *Constantine and the Christian Empire*, 147.

64. For a description of the churches in the Holy Land, see Eusebius *Vit. Const.* 3.25–45; see also Odahl, *Constantine and the Christian Empire*, 211–20.

65. These activities are described by Eusebius (*Vit. Const.* 3.48–49, 4.58–60). For an extended description of these churches and Constantine's rebuilding and refortifying of the old city of Byzantium, see Odahl, *Constantine and the Christian Empire*, 232–44; for a line drawing showing the location of the churches, see ibid., 233; for the oldest extant map of "new Rome," see ibid., 244. A similar map can be found in Pohlsander, *The Emperor Constantine*, 63. See also Barnes, *Constantine and Eusebius*, 212; Frend, *The Rise of Christianity*, 501f.

66. Eusebius *Vit. Const.* 4.20 (trans. Richardson; *NPNF*² vol. 1, 545) (discussed in Odahl, *Constantine and the Christian Empire*, 172). Greek text of the prayer: σὲ μόνον οἴδαμεν θεόν, σὲ βασιλέα γνωρίζομεν, σὲ βοηθὸν ἀνακαλούμεθα, παρὰ σοῦ τὰς νίκας ἠράμεθα, διὰ σοῦ κρείττους τῶν

ἐχθρῶν κατέστημεν, σοὶ τὴν τῶν προυπαρξάντων ἀγαθῶν χάριν γνωρίζομεν, σὲ καὶ τῶν μελλόντων δοτῆρα ἐλπίζομεν, σοῦ πάντες ἱκέται γιγνόμεθα, τὸν ἡμέτερον βασιλέα Κωνσταντίνον παῖδάς τε αὐτοῦ θεοφιλεῖς ἐπὶ μήκιστον ἡμῖν βίου σῶον καὶ νικητὴν φυλάττεσθαι ποτνιώμεθα.

67. Eusebius *Vit. Const.* 4.23.

68. Ibid., 3.54–58.

69. Ibid., 4.5–8; the text of Constantine's letter to King Shahpur of Persia is given in 4.8–13 (discussed in Odahl, *Constantine and the Christian Empire*, 271f.).

70. Eusebius *Vit. Const.* 3.63 (trans. Richardson; *NPNF*[2] vol. 1, 539).

71. Ibid., 3.64.

72. Ibid. 3.65. Greek: εἰς τὴν καθολικὴν ἐκκλησίαν ἔλθετε καὶ τῇ ταύτῃ ἁγιότητι κοινωνεῖτε, κτλ.

73. Ibid., 3.66 (trans. Richardson; *NPNF*[2] vol. 1, 540).

74. Ibid., 4.24. I am using the translation of Cameron and Hall (*Eusebius: Life of Constantine,* 161), since it brings out Eusebius's shock more clearly than the other translations. Here is Richardson's translation (*NPNF*[2] vol. 1, 546): "Hence it was not without reason that once, on the occasion of his entertaining a company of bishops, he let fall the expression, that he himself too was a bishop, addressing them in my hearing in the following words: 'You are bishops whose jurisdiction is within the Church: I also am a bishop, ordained by God to overlook whatever is external to the Church.'" Greek: ἔνθεν εἰκότω αὐτὸς ἐν ἑστιάσει ποτὲ δεξιούμενος ἐπισκόπους λόγον ἀφῆκεν, ὡς ἄρα καὶ αὐτὸς εἴη ἐπίσκοπος, ὧδέ πη αὐτοῖς εἰπὼν ῥήμασιν ἐφ' ἡμετέραις ἀκοαῖς· ἀλλ' ὑμεῖς μὲν τῶν εἴσω τῆς ἐκκλησίας, ἐγὼ δὲ τῶν ἐκτὸς ὑπὸ θεοῦ καθεσταμένος ἐπίσκοπος ἂν εἴην. On the significance of this statement, see especially Straub, "Constantine as ΚΟΙΝΟΣ ΕΠΙΣΚΟΠΟΣ," 39–55.

75. Eusebius *Vit. Const.* 4.58–60; see a description in Odahl, *Constantine and the Christian Empire*, 269–74.

76. Odahl, *Constantine and the Christian Empire*, 271. Pohlsander (*The Emperor Constantine*) notes that "no one raised an objection at the time to this extraordinary arrangement" (76).

77. Eusebius *Vit. Const.* 1.41 (trans. Richardson; *NPNF*[2] vol. 1, 494).

78. Frend, *The Rise of Christianity,* 635ff., describes the rise of "state Catholicism" under the emperor Theodosius I (379–395) as "the first step toward enforcing a universal Catholic faith over the whole empire."

79. See chapter 5, notes 18 and 24.

80. See the discussions in Barnes, *Constantine and Eusebius,* 211, 233; cf. Drake, *Constantine and the Bishops,* 347f.

81. Eusebius, *Vit. Const.* 4.36.

82. Odahl, *Constantine and the Christian Empire,* 281. Barnes (*Constantine and Eusebius,* 124) speculates that Eusebius may have inserted chapter divisions and chapter headings into the text of the Gospels. He does not mention that Eusebius's Gospel Canons and Sections would have provided a good basis for both uniform pericope (not chapter) titles and that the chapter numbers were needed for his Gospel harmony (discussed above in chapter 5).

83. Metzger's discussion of the period of Constantine (*Canon of the New Testament,* Appendix IV, 311–15) shows two things: the paucity of discussions regarding which scriptures to use in church and the prevalence of the new term *canon*. Many scholars have noted that it was not until the mid- to late fourth century that the use of the term *canon* first appears in conjunction with lists of New Testament writings. Metzger, in ibid., 292f., lists the examples from the fourth century. The list provided by G. M. Hahnemann ("The Muratorian Fragment and the Origins of the New Testament Canon," in *The Canon Debate* [ed. L. M. McDonald and J. A. Sanders; Peabody, Mass.: Hendrickson, 2002], 413) must be used with caution.

84. Metzger (*Canon of the New Testament,* 293) takes up the question of whether "canonical" meant "legal rule" or just "approved list" and concludes that from the middle of the fourth century onward, it meant both.

85. Barnes, *Constantine and Eusebius,* 225.

86. Ibid.

87. Ramsay MacMullen, *Christianizing the Roman Empire* (A.D. 100–400) (New Haven: Yale University Press, 1984), 94.

88. The topic of the Christian Church's acceptance of force and coercion is the central theme of Drake's *Constantine and the Bishops.* See also MacMullen, *Christianizing the Roman Empire,* 86–101, particularly the discussion of the poisonous influence of governmental involvement in theological disputes (93).

89. On the great change within Eusebius's own outlook and attitude, see especially Glenn Chesnut, *The First Christian Histories: Eusebius, Socrates, Sozomen, Theodoret, and Evagrius* (2nd ed.; Macon, Ga.: Mercer University Press, 1986), 128f.

90. Quoted from Henry Chadwick, trans. and ed., *Origen: Contra Celsum* (Cambridge: Cambridge University Press, 1965), 3.12–13, 135f.

91. Drake (*Constantine and the Bishops*, 396) relates two telling anecdotes: "The fourth-century [pagan military officer and] historian Ammianus Marcellinus, after observing the bishop of Rome's lifestyle, decided that men who won that office 'will be secure for the future, being enriched by offerings from matrons, riding in carriages, dressing splendidly, and even feasting luxuriously, so that their entertainments surpass even royal banquets.' Indeed, the great pagan aristocrat Praetextatus is supposed to have jokingly told Pope Damasus at midcentury that, if he could be bishop of Rome, he would become Christian on the spot" (350).

Chapter 7. Epilogue

1. See Glenn Chesnut, *The First Christian Histories: Eusebius, Socrates, Sozomen, Theodoret, and Evagrius* (2nd ed.; Macon, Ga.: Mercer University Press, 1986).

2. The most important fourth-century synods dealing with issues of scripture were the Synod of Laodicea (ca. 363); the Synod of Hippo (ca. 390); the First Synod of Carthage; and the Third Synod of Carthage (397). Fourth-century theologians and bishops who commented on issues of scripture selection were Cyril of Jerusalem in *Catechetical Lectures* 4.36 (ca. 350); Athanasius in his *39th Festal Letter* (367); Gregory of Nazianzus (ca. 380); and Amphilochius of Iconium (ca. 400). For the texts of these synods and bishops' comments, see B. M. Metzger, *The Canon of the New Testament* (Oxford: Clarendon, 1989), 311–14. A small collection of "canons" dealing with the scriptures should also be mentioned, although they are of uncertain provenance and date: the "Apostolic Canons," ca. 380, found at the end of the *Apostolic Constitutions* (ca. 390); for the text of the Apostolic Canon, see ibid., 313. Also fitting into this picture is the much-disputed Muratorian Canon, which, according to the most recent scholarship, is a fourth-century writing. For a recent discussion of the issues and secondary literature, see G. M. Hahneman, "The Muratorian Fragment and the Origins of the New Testament Canon," in *The Canon Debate* (ed. Lee Martin McDonald and James A. Sanders; Peabody, Mass.: Hendrickson, 2002), 405–15, esp. 411.

3. Metzger, *Canon of the New Testament*, 315.

4. For an account of Pope Damasus commissioning Jerome to bring out an authoritative Latin version, see B. M. Metzger, *The Early Versions of the New Testament: Their Origin, Transmission, and Limitations* (Oxford: Clarendon, 1977), 330–34.

5. See the discussion of the Hexapla in Chapter 4.

6. He did have a few questions, but they seem to be speculations based on the data in Eusebius and not based on independent research; see examples of Jerome's few questions regarding the "disputed" writings in Metzger, *Canon of the New Testament,* 234–36 (the quotation is on 236).

7. See Chapter One.

8. Othman, or 'Uthman ibn' Affan, was the third and last of the elected caliphs, or successors of Muhammad. The word *caliph* comes from *khalifat rasul-Allah* ("successor of the Messenger of God"). When Omar, the second father-in-law of Muhammad and the second caliph, was assassinated in Medina in 644, the ruling council passed over Muhammad's son-in-law, Ali, to select the Prophet's other son-in-law, 'Uthman, an early convert from the aristocratic clan of the Omyyads, as the next caliph. See Matthew S. Gordon, *The Rise of Islam* (Wesport, Ct.: Greenwood, 2005), 30f.

9. See Geo Widengren, "Holy Book and Holy Tradition in Islam," in *Holy Book and Holy Tradition* (ed. F. F. Bruce and E. G. Rupp; Manchester: Manchester University Press, 1968), 210–36. See also Frederick M. Denny, "Qur'an and Hadith," in *The Holy Book in Comparative Perspective* (ed. Frederick M. Denny and Rodney L. Taylor; Columbia: University of South Carolina Press, 1985), 91–93.

10. See the most recent article of Jack P. Lewis, "Questioning the Consensus," in *The Canon Debate* (ed. McDonald and Sanders), 148–62; cf. his original article, "What Do We Mean by Jabneh?" *JBR* (1964): 125–32.

11. See Sid Z. Leiman, ed., *The Canon and the Masorah of the Hebrew Bible* (New York: Ktav, 1974); Sid Z. Leiman, ed., *The Canonization of the Hebrew Scripture: The Talmudic and Midrashic Evidence* (Hamden, Ct.: Archon Books, 1976); and Sid Z. Leiman, "Inspiration and Canonicity: Reflections on the Formation of the Biblical Canon," in *Jewish and Christian Self-Definition* (vol. 2 of *Aspects of Judaism in the Graeco-Roman World*; ed. E. Sanders; Philadelphia: Fortress, 1981), 56–63.

12. For a particularly insightful essay on the peculiarities of the canonization process with respect to the Hebrew scriptures, see J. A. Sanders, "The Issue of Closure in the Canonical Process," in *The Canon Debate* (ed. McDonald and Sanders), 252–63 (this quote is from 253).

13. See J. C. VanderKam, "Questions of Canon Viewed through the Dead Sea Scrolls," in ibid., 91.

14. See C. A. Evans, "The Scriptures of Jesus and His Earliest Followers," in ibid., 185.

15. This is one place where the discussion of Herbert Oppel, *KANΩN: Zur Bedeutungsgeschichte des Wortes und seiner lateinischen Entsprechungen*

(regula-norma), in *Philologus* suppl., Bd. 30, Heft 4 (Leipzig: Dieterichssche Verlagsbuchhandlung, 1933), is seriously deficient, except for the discussion of Philo (see 57–60).

16. The famous story of the life and death struggle between Eliezar ben Horkonos and the rest of the sages at Yavneh, led by Rabban Gamliel II, which resulted in the excommunication of Eliezar, turns on this very point; see *Baba Mezia* 59b; also reprinted in D. Cartlidge and D. Dungan, *Documents for the Study of the Gospels* (2nd ed.; Philadelphia: Fortress, 1994), 159–61.

17. See J. N. Lightstone, "The Rabbis' Bible: The Canon of the Hebrew Bible and the Early Rabbinic Guild," in *The Canon Debate* (ed. McDonald and Sanders), 163–84.

18. Ibid., 184.

19. *Yadayim* 3:5b, quoted and discussed in ibid., 176f.

20. Quoted in ibid., 178f. Note the curious order in which the biblical books are mentioned.

21. Josephus *Against Apion* 1:37–42. Notable Greek phrases are as follows:

> It therefore naturally, or rather necessarily, follows—seeing that with us it is not open to everybody to write the records, and that there is no discrepancy (μήτε τινὸς διαφωνίας) in what is written; seeing that, on the contrary, the prophets alone had this privilege, obtaining their knowledge of the most remote and ancient history through the inspiration which they owed to God (κατὰ τὴν ἐπίνοιαν τὴν ἀπὸ τοῦ θεοῦ μαθόντων), and committing to writing a clear account (σαφῶς συγγραφόντων) of the events of their own time just as they occurred (ὡς ἐγένετο)—it follows, I say, that we do not possess myriads of inconsistent books, conflicting with each other (μυριάδες βιβλίων ... ἀσυμφώνων καὶ μαχομένων). Our books, those which are justly accredited (τὰ βιβλία ... δικαίως πεπιστευμένα), are but two and twenty, and contain the record of all time (τοῦ παντὸς ἔχοντα χρόνου). . . . [Thus] we have given practical proof of our reverence for our own Scriptures. For, although such long ages have now passed, no one has ventured either to add, or to remove, or to alter a syllable (οὐδὲν μεταθεῖναι)."

22. For a detailed discussion of this passage and the problems it raises, see most recently Steve Mason, "Josephus and His Twenty-two Book Canon," in *The Canon Debate* (ed. McDonald and Sanders), 110–27. It is

also discussed in the same volume by Joseph Blenkinsopp, "The Formation of the Hebrew Bible Canon," 53f.

23. It is intriguing to observe that, in this otherwise model paragraph, the word κανών does not occur. I suggest that the word *canon* was not used by Josephus for the same reason it was not used by Irenaeus, Clement of Alexandria, Origen, and Eusebius (who invented a word to signify the same idea: ἐνδιάθηκος): it was somehow not appropriate to use with the term *scripture*.

24. Mason and other scholars have concluded that little in this passage is true or factually accurate. He explains that Josephus was "an incurable liar" ("Josephus and His Twenty-two Book Canon," in *The Canon Debate* [ed. McDonald and Sanders], 120). I suggest that something else is going on, having nothing to do with a desire for factual accuracy: honor. It is curious to see the same reaction among scholars looking for historical facts in Eusebius's *Life of Constantine*, with its over-the-top praise of Constantine. I suggest that Glenn Chesnut (*The First Christian Histories*, 123) is much closer to the truth when he explains that "by the early 330s, Eusebius had become one of the four or five most influential and powerful bishops in the entire Mediterranean world. . . . He was a key spokesman for a large and essentially still defenseless Christian community that had little direct power, but he was no more the servile tool of a Roman emperor than was Athanasius or Ambrose. His goal was always to control Licinius, Constantine, and the latter's sons, as much as possible in matters affecting the Christian community, and to avoid being controlled by them. When he flattered an emperor in public, Eusebius had either just obtained something he wanted for the Christians or was moving strategically toward some deliberate future goal." The same kind of observation may be applied to Josephus.

25. Lightstone, "The Rabbis' Bible," in *The Canon Debate* (ed. McDonald and Sanders), 181; on 182 he quotes Avot de Rabbi Nathan (version A, chap. 8), to illustrate "this four-fold curriculum of sacred teachings."

26. Ibid., 182.

27. It is sometimes alleged that there were two early Buddhist "councils" that "canonized" the "words of the Buddha." If so, this would form an important exception to the thesis being advanced in this chapter: that canons of scripture were found only where religious traditions had been influenced by Greek philosophy and *polis* ideology. However, the evidence for these alleged councils is tenuous at best. Etienne Lamotte's opinion reflects

recent scholarship: "Pour ne pas avancer trop imprudemment, nous dirons que dans le premier siècle après le Nirvana [du Buddha] un ou des groupes des spécialistes, réunis ou non en concile, ont tenté de codifier la parole du Buddha tant dans la domaine de la doctrine que dans celui de la discipline et qu'ils sont parvenus à élaborer un dharma et un pratimoksa cohérents, acceptés dans leur ensemble par la communauté primitive, et que consti-tuérent l'heritage commun des sectes bouddhiques" (Etienne Lamotte, Histoire du bouddhisme indien [Louvain: Bibliotheque du Muséon #43, 1958; rpr. 1967], 154). For a careful assessment of the evidence for these early, semi-legendary Buddhist councils, see ibid., 136–54; see also Miriam Levering, ed., *Rethinking Scripture: Essays from a Comparative Perspective* (Albany: State University of New York Press, 1989), 93n4, for additional bibliography. All Lamotte can point to is some form of minimal agree-ment about the oral tradition of Buddha's words (*buddha-pravachana*). But even this heritage splintered as Buddhist belief and practice rapidly broke up into numerous geographically defined sects, each with its own sacred traditions and exemplary texts. In other words, the so-called "Pali canon" never existed. As Vallée Poussin observes in "Councils-Buddhist" (*Hastings Encyclopedia of Religion and Ethics* IV:181), "the 'Pali canon' with its polygeneous loci communes, its repetitions, its parallel stories with interchangeable heroes, and its contradictions" is not a canon. "It would not be impossible," he writes, "to extract from 'the Pali Canon' two or three canons all complete, all like one another, all conflicting."

28. As near as I can determine, Augustine neither discussed the can-didates for inclusion in the New Testament in any detail, nor assessed the criteria for acceptance or rejection, nor introduced any new evidence. His remarks are speculations based entirely on Jerome's Latin translation of Eusebius's *Ecclesiastical History.*

29. Augustine *Doctr. chr.* 2.8.12.

30. The quotation goes on to explain how to deal with the disputed cases plainly listed by Eusebius: "Among the canonical Scriptures he will judge according to the following standard: to prefer those that are received by all the catholic churches to those which some do not receive. Among those, again, which are not received by all, he will prefer such as have the sanction of the greater number and those of greater authority, to such as are held by the smaller number and those of less authority. If, however, he shall find that some books are held by the greater number of churches, and others by the churches of greater authority (though this is not a very likely thing to happen), I think that in such a case the authority on the two

sides is to be looked upon as equal." Metzger (*Canon of the New Testament*, 237n16) aptly notes: "Although Augustine's criteria seem at first sight to be clear-cut and straightforward, the practical difficulties of applying them to any given case are formidable."

31. Augustine *Doctr. chr.* 1.39.43: *Homo itaque fede et spe et caritate subnixus eaque inconcusse retinens non indiget scripturis nisi ad alios instruendos. Itaque multi per haec tria etiam in solitudine sine codicibus vivunt.* See the discussion in Roland J. Teske, "Criteria for Figurative Interpretation in St. Augustine," in *De doctrina christiana: A Classic of Western Culture* (ed. D. W. H. Arnold and P. Bright; Notre Dame: University of Notre Dame Press, 1995), 118.

32. For a recent discussion of Augustine's *Cons.*, with pertinent secondary literature, see "Augustine Refutes the Manichaean Critique of the Gospels," in D. L. Dungan, *A History of the Synoptic Problem* (New York: Doubleday, 1999), 112–41.

33. For a typically scintillating presentation of this idea, with bibliography, see Robert W. Funk, "The Once and Future New Testament," in McDonald and Sanders, *The Canon Debate*, 541–57.

SELECT BIBLIOGRAPHY

Critical Text of Eusebius, *Ecclesiastical History*

Schwartz, Eduard, and Theodor Mommsen. *Eusebius Werke: Die Kirchengeschichte*. Zweite unveränderte Auflage von Friedhelm Winkelmann. Die Griechischen christlichen Schriftsteller der ersten Jahrhunderte, neue Folge: Band 6, 3. 3 vols. Berlin: Akademie Verlag, 1999.

English translations of Eusebius, *Ecclesiastical History, Life of Constantine*

Cameron, Averil, and Stuart G. Hall, *Eusebius. Life of Constantine. Introduction, Translation and Commentary*. Oxford: Clarendon Press, 1999.

Cruse, C. F. *Eusebius Ecclesiastical History*. Peabody, MA: Hendrickson Publishers, 1998.

Lake, Kirsopp. *Eusebius, the Ecclesiastical History*. Loeb Classical Library, vol. 1. Cambridge MA: Harvard University Press, 1959.

McGiffert, Arthur Cushman. *The Church History of Eusebius*. Nicene and Post-Nicene Fathers of the Christian Church. 2nd Series. Vol. 1. Grand Rapids: Eerdmans Publishing Company, 1971.

Oulton, J. E. L., and H. J. Lawlor. *Eusebius, the Ecclesiastical History.* Loeb Classical Library, vol. 2. Cambridge MA: Harvard University Press, 1957.

Richardson, Ernest Cushing. *The Life of Constantine by Eusebius.* Nicene and Post-Nicene Fathers of the Christian Church. 2nd Series. Vol. 1. Grand Rapids: Eerdmans Publishing Company, 1971.

Williamson, G. A. *Eusebius, The History of the Church from Christ to Constantine.* Harmondsworth, Middlesex: Penguin Books, Dorset Press, 1983.

Studies of Christian Scripture Selection (canonization)

Baum, Armin D. "Der neutestamentliche Kanon bei Eusebius." *Ephemerides Theologicae Lovaniensis* 73 (1997) 306–48.

Campenhausen, Hans von. *The Formation of the Christian Bible.* Trans. J. A. Baker. Philadelphia: Fortress Press, 1972.

Gamble, Harry Y. *The New Testament Canon. Its Making and Meaning.* Philadelphia: Fortress Press, 1985.

McDonald, Lee M., *The Formation of the Christian Biblical Canon.* Peabody, MA: Hendrickson Publishers, 1995.

McDonald, Lee Martin and James A. Sanders, eds. *The Canon Debate.* Peabody, MA: Hendrickson Publishers, 2002.

Metzger, Bruce M. *The Canon of the New Testament. Its Origin, Development, and Significance.* Oxford: Clarendon Press, 1989.

Studies of Constantine and Christianity

Alföldi, Andrew. *The Conversion of Constantine and Pagan Rome.* Translated by Harold Mattingly. Oxford: Clarendon Press, 1948.

Baynes, Norman H. *Constantine the Great and the Christian Church.* 2nd ed. Oxford: Proceedings of the British Academy, 1972.

MacMullen, Ramsay. *Christianizing the Roman Empire* (A.D. 100–400). New Haven: Yale University Press, 1984.

Odahl, Charles Matson. *Constantine and the Christian Empire.* London and New York: Routledge, 2004.

Pohlsander, Hans A. *The Emperor Constantine*. London: Routledge, 1996.

General Studies of Eusebius

Barnes, Timothy D. *Constantine and Eusebius*. Cambridge, MA: Harvard University Press, 1981.

Burgess, R. W. "The Dates and Editions of Eusebius's *Chronici canones and historia ecclesiastica*." *Journal of Theological Studies*, n. s. 48 (1997) 471–504.

Chesnut, Glenn. *The First Christian Histories. Eusebius, Socrates, Sozomen, Theodoret, and Evagrius*. 2nd ed. Macon, GA: Mercer University Press 1986.

Drake, Harold Allen. *Eusebius and the Bishops. The Politics of Intolerance*. Baltimore: John Hopkins Press, 2000.

Drake, Harold Allen. *In Praise of Constantine. A Historical Study and New Translation of Eusebius's Tricennial Orations*. Berkeley: University of California Press, 1976.

Diogenes Laertius and Greek Philosophical Schools

Baum, Armin D. "Literarische Echtheit als Kanonkriterium in der alten Kirche." *Zeitschrift für die Neutestamentliche Wissenschaft* 88 (1997) 97–110.

Mejer, Jørgen. *Diogenes Laertius and His Hellenistic Background*. Wiesbaden: Steiner Verlag, 1978.

History of Early Christianity and Church Fathers

Bauer, Walter. *Orthodoxy and Heresy in Earliest Christianity*. Trans. and ed. by Robert Kraft and Gerhard Krodel. Philadelphia: Fortress Press, 1971.

Frend, W. H. C. *The Rise of Christianity*. Philadelphia: Fortress Press 1984.

Hanson, R. P. C. *Origen's Doctrine of Tradition*. London: S.P.C.K., 1954.

Select Bibliography

Comparative Religions Study of "Scripture"

Denny, Frederick M., and Rodney L. Taylor eds., *The Holy Book in Comparative Perspective*. Columbia: University of South Carolina Press, 1985.

Levering, Miriam, ed., *Rethinking Scripture. Essays from a Comparative Perspective*. Albany: State University of New York Press, 1989.

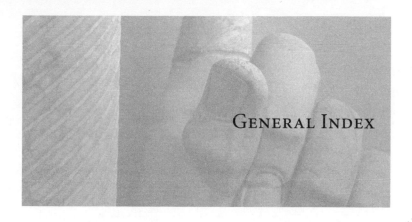

GENERAL INDEX

Index of Technical Terms discussed in the Text

1. English

2. Greek